"In the name of Allah,
the Most Beneficent, the Most Merciful"

Muslim Super Heroes

Volume 1

Compile by

Muhammad Mohee Uddin ibn Ahmad

Muslim Super Heroes

Volume 1

Muhammad Mohee Uddin

These are historical event, and I have tried to represent events as faithfully as possible. I am not a historian. This book and the content provided herein are simply for educational purposes. No liability is assumed for losses or damages due to the information provided. You are responsible for your own choices, actions, and results. Although this publication is designed to provide accurate information in regard to the subject matter covered, I assume no responsibility for errors, inaccuracies, omissions, or any other inconsistencies herein. This publication is meant as a source of valuable information for the reader, however it is not meant as a replacement for direct expert assistance. If such level of assistance is required, the services of a competent professional should be sought.

First paperback edition November 2020
ISBN: 9798554102127

For information about special discounts available for bulk purchases, sales promotions, fund-raising and educational needs, contact
mohee1990@outlook.com

Introduction

"My Lord! Enrich me with knowledge..."
(Quran, 20:114)

All praise belongs to Allah Tala, Lord of the worlds. May the peace and blessings be on our beloved Prophet (ﷺ), on his family, on all of his Companions and Muslim ummah.

These days, it seems that Muslims and Islam in general are almost always painted in a negative light by news channels around the world.

Yet the reality, though lesser known, is that much of the modern world we live in today was unquestionably shaped by the stellar achievements and inventions introduced by the Muslims.

From the dawn of Islam, Muslim scholars have made significant contributions to the world of learning. Indeed, from the 7th Century until the 15th Century, Muslims were the torchbearers of human civilisation. After the fall of the Roman Empire, Europe fell into the Dark Ages but Muslim scholars succeeded in preserving the classical wisdom of Ancient Greece and Rome. Due to their thirst for knowledge Muslims then went on to make spectacular advances in a wide spectrum of subjects, including mathematics, astronomy, geography, medicine, physics, chemistry, biology, botany, and veterinary science.

After nearly 900 years of intellectual leadership, however, internal bickering and complacency saw the influence of Muslims stagnate and then decline. It would, nevertheless, be true to say that advances made by Muslim scholars from such seats of learning as Baghdad, Muslim Spain and Cairo laid the foundations for Europe's 'Renaissance' [intellectual re-awakening] in the Middle Ages. This, in turn, fuelled the Industrial Revolution that has eventually given rise to the scientific and technical achievements of today.

Islamic history is replete with pioneering inventions and discoveries, many of which are ingrained in modern society, such as:

1. **Public Libraries:** During the early decades of Islam, mosques acted as hubs for intellectual discourse across the Muslim lands. They were not only places of worship, but also housed libraries full of books on religion, philosophy and science. These libraries were open to the masses and not just the ruling and intellectual elite, as was the common practice then.

2. **Surgical Tools:** The great 10th-century Muslim surgeon Qasim al Zahrawi, described as the father of surgery, invented many surgical tools still used in modern medicine, including the scalpel, the surgical needle and surgical scissors. He also discovered catgut as a reliable material to administer internal stitches as it can be absorbed by the body, preventing the need for a second surgery to remove them.

3. **Algebra:** The study of algebra flourished during the Islamic Golden Age under the scholarship of mathematician al-Khwarizmi. The word algebra is derived from 'al-jabr', an operation he used to solve quadratic equations.

4. **Optics:** In the 11th century, the scientist Ibn Haytham overturned ancient ideas of how our eyes see. While some said light rays came out of the eyes, others thought something entered the eyes to represent an object. Through systematic reason and experiment, Ibn Haytham discovered that light is

not emitted from the eye itself, but in fact is reflected off an object and enters the eye.

5. Coffee: Coffee beans were native to Ethiopia, but the Muslim Arabs developed the beverage we know as coffee in the 15th century in Yemen when they traded with the Ethiopians. They ground and roasted the beans, then boiled them in water. Religious men (Sufis) began to drink coffee to refrain from sleeping so that they could spend the night in prayer.

6. University: In 859 a young princess named Fatima al-Firhi founded the first degree-granting university in Fez, Morocco. Her sister Miriam founded an adjacent mosque and together the complex became the al-Qarawiyyin Mosque and University. Still operating almost 1,200 years later.

7. Flying machine: Abbas ibn Firnas was the first person to make a real attempt to construct a flying machine and fly. In the 9th century he designed a winged apparatus, roughly resembling a bird costume. In his most famous trial near Cordoba in Spain, Firnas flew upward for a few moments, before falling to the ground and partially breaking his back.

8. Clock: An ingenious man called al-Jazari from Diyarbakir in South-East Turkey was a pious Muslim and a highly skilled engineer who gave birth to the concept of automatic machines. By 1206, al-Jazari had made numerous clocks of all shapes and sizes. They knew it was important to know the time so it could be used for knowing when to pray at the right time each day and announce the call to prayer in mosques.

9. Toothbrush: The Prophet (peace be upon him) popularized the use of the first toothbrush in around 600. Using a twig from the Meswak tree, he cleaned his teeth and freshened his breath. Substances similar to Meswak are used in modern toothpast

Islam is simple and easy

The religion is easy, beautiful and simply perfect. Why make things hard? The Qur'an reads:

> "Allah intends for you ease and does not intend for you hardship." (Qur'an, 2:185)

This verse explains that Islam is easy to follow and rather encourages us to create ease in religion. Unfortunately some Muslims, including some reverts, are under the misconception that the more stringent they are in following religion, the more pious they become. This is totally in contradiction to what our religion teaches us. The misconception is a result of lack of understanding or knowledge of religion and at times drives some people away from religion, mainly because of the way it is presented to them.

It is known in fact that Prophet Muhammad (peace be upon him) always resisted any tendency toward religious excessiveness. He once said to his close companion Abdullah ibn Amr: "Have I heard right that you fast everyday and stand in prayer all night?" Abdullah replied: "Yes, O Messenger of God."

The Prophet (ﷺ) said: "Do not do that. Fast, as well as, eat and drink. Stand in prayer, as well as, sleep. This is because your body has a right upon you, your eyes have a right upon you, your wife has a right upon you, and your guest has a right upon you." (Al-Bukhari, 127)

Narrated Anas bin Malik: The Prophet (ﷺ) said, "Facilitate things to people (concerning religious matters), and do not make it hard for them and give them good tidings and do not make them run away (from Islam). (Al-Bukhari, 69)

Narrated Ibn Mas`ud: The Prophet (ﷺ) used to take care of us in preaching by selecting a suitable time, so that we might not get bored. (He abstained from pestering us with sermons and knowledge all the time). (Al-Bukhari, 68)

Narrated Abu Huraira: The Prophet (ﷺ) said, "Religion is very easy and whoever overburdens himself in his religion will not be able to continue in that way. So you should not be extremists, but try to be near to perfection and receive the good tidings that you will be rewarded; and gain strength by worshipping in the mornings, the afternoons, and during the last hours of the nights." (Al-Bukhari, 39)

Narrated Anas bin Malik (ra): A group of three men came to the houses of the wives of the Prophet (ﷺ) asking how the Prophet (ﷺ) worshipped (Allah), and when they were informed about that, they considered their worship insufficient and said, "Where are we from the Prophet (ﷺ) as his past and future sins have been forgiven." Then one of them said, "I will offer the prayer throughout the night forever." The other said, "I will fast throughout the year and will not break my fast." The third said, "I will keep away from the women and will not marry forever." Allah's Messenger (ﷺ) came to them and said, "Are you the same people who said so-and-so? By Allah, I am more submissive to Allah and more afraid of Him than you; yet I fast and break my fast, I do sleep and I also marry women. So he who does not follow my tradition in religion, is not from me (not one of my followers). (Al-Bukhari, 5063)

Narrated `Imran bin Husain: A man said, "O Allah's Messenger (ﷺ)! Can the people of Paradise be known (differentiated) from the people of the Fire; The Prophet (ﷺ) replied, "Yes." The man said, "Why do people (try to) do (good) deeds?" The Prophet said, "Everyone will do the deeds for which he has been created to do or he will do those deeds which will be made easy for him to do." (i.e. everybody will find easy to do such deeds as will lead him to his destined place for which he has been created). (Al-Bukhari, 6596)

Narrated `Abdullah (ra): I heard a man reciting a verse (of the Holy Qur'an) but I had heard the Prophet (ﷺ) reciting it differently. So, I caught hold of the man by the hand and took him to Allah's Messenger (ﷺ) who said, "Both of you are right." Shu`ba, the sub-narrator said, "I think he said to them, "Don't differ, for the nations before you differed and perished (because of their differences)." (Al-Bukhari, 2410)

Narrated Ibn `Abbas: A man said to the Prophet (ﷺ) "I performed the Tawaf-al-Ifada before the Rami (throwing pebbles at the Jamra)." The Prophet (ﷺ) replied, "There is no harm." The man said, "I had my head shaved before slaughtering." The Prophet (ﷺ) replied, "There is no harm." He said, "I have slaughtered the Hadi before the Rami." The Prophet (ﷺ) replied, "There is no harm." (Al-Bukhari, 1722)

Narrated Abu Huraira': Allah's Messenger (ﷺ) saw a man driving his Badana (sacrificial camel). He said, "Ride on it." The man said, "It is a Badana." The Prophet (ﷺ) said, "Ride on it." He (the man) said, "It is a Badana." The Prophet said, "Ride on it." And on the second or the third time he (the Prophet (ﷺ) added, "Woe to you." (Al-Bukhari, 1689)

Narrated Anas: The Prophet (ﷺ) saw an old man walking, supported by his two sons, and asked about him. The people informed him that he had vowed to go on foot (to the Ka`ba). He said, "Allah is not in need of this old man's torturing himself," and ordered him to ride. (Bukhari, 1865)

Narrated 'Aisha: A woman from the tribe of Bani Asad was sitting with me and Allah's Apostle (p.b.u.h) came to my house and said, "Who is this?" I said, "(She is) so and so. She does not sleep at night because she is engaged in prayer." The Prophet (ﷺ) said disapprovingly: Do (good) deeds which is within your capacity as Allah never gets tired of giving rewards till you get tired of doing good deeds." (1151)

Narrated Aisha (ra): Whenever Allah's Messenger (ﷺ) was given the choice of one of two matters, he would choose the easier of the two, as long as it was not sinful to do so, but if it was sinful to do so, he would not approach it. Allah's Messenger (ﷺ) never took revenge (over anybody) for his own sake but (he did) only when Allah's Legal Bindings were outraged in which case he would take revenge for Allah's Sake. (Al-Bukhari, 3560)

"Allah (SWT) does not burden a soul beyond that it can bear." [Surah Al-Baqarah (2:286)]

THE QURAN CALLS FOR CRITICAL THINKING AND REASONING

For many people, even Muslims, it would be surprising to find out what strong recommendations are made in Quran about research, thinking over and reasoning, and how the manner of the people who do not use their mind to analysis good and bad are criticised. Let us narrate directly from Quran,

"Positive fear of God (taqwa) can be attained only by those who have knowledge." (Quran 35:28)

"Say, [O Muhammad], "Travel through the land and observe how He began creation. Then Allah will produce the final creation. Indeed Allah, over all things, is competent." (Quran al-Ankaboot 29:20)

"Do they not see the birds controlled in the atmosphere of the sky? None holds them up except Allah. Indeed in that are signs for people who believe." (Quran an-Nahl 16:79)

"Indeed, in the creation of the heavens and the earth and the alternation of the night and the day are signs for those of understanding; Those who remember Allah while standing or sitting or [lying] on their sides and give thought to the creation of the heavens and the earth, [saying], "Our Lord, You did not create this without purpose …" (Quran Al-i-Imran 3:190-191)

"Indeed, the worst of living creatures in the sight of Allah are the deaf and dumb who do not use reason." (Quran al-Anfal 8:22)

"They will say: If only we had been listening or reasoning, we would not be among the companions of the Blaze." (67:10)

Say, "Is the blind equivalent to the seeing? Then will you not give a thought?" (Quran al-Ana'am 6:50)

"Indeed, the worst of living creatures in the sight of Allah are the deaf and dumb who do not use reason." (Quran al-Anfal 8:22)

"Read: In the name of your Lord Who creates – creates man from a clot. Read: And your Lord is the Most Bounteous, Who teaches by the use of the pen, teaches man that which he knew not." (Quran 96:105)

"And He has subjected to you, as from Him, all that is in the heavens and on earth: behold, in that are signs indeed for those who reflect." (45: 13)

"He [Allah] grants wisdom to whom He pleases; and he to whom wisdom is granted indeed receives a benefit overflowing. But none will grasp the Message except men of understanding." (2:269)

"Say: Travel through the earth and see how Allah originated creation; so will Allah produce the second creation (of the Afterlife): for Allah has power over all things." (29:20)

"Already have We urged unto hell many of the jinn and humankind, having hearts wherewith they understand not, and having eyes wherewith they see not, and having ears wherewith they hear not. These are as the cattle - nay, but they are worse! These are the neglectful." (7:179)

"Who hear advice and follow the best thereof. Such are those whom Allah guideth, and such are men of understanding. (39:18);

HOW OUR BRAIN WORKS

AND WHY IT IS IMPORTANT TO KNOW

The human brain is a network of approximately 100 billion neurons. Different experiences create different neural connections which bring about different emotions. Depending on which neurons get stimulated, certain connections become stronger and more efficient, while others may become weaker. This is what's called neuroplasticity. Someone who trains to be a mathematician will create stronger neural connections that link the two hemispheres of the brain in order to be mathematically creative. Rudiger Gamm, who was a 'self-admitted hopeless student,' used to fail at basic math and went on to train his abilities and became a famous 'human calculator,' capable of performing extremely complex mathematics. In the Quran Allah (SWT) says:

> "God changes not what is in a people, until they change what is in themselves ..." (13:11)

Rationality and emotional resilience worked the same way. These are neural connections that can be strengthened. Whatever you are doing at any time, you are physically modifying your brain to become better at it. Since this is such a foundational mechanism of the brain, being self-aware can greatly enrich our life experience. The Messenger of Allah (peace and blessing of Allah be upon him) said:

> "Be conscious of Allah wherever you are. Follow the bad deed with a good one to erase it, and engage others with beautiful character." Related by Tirmidhi.

"O you who believe! Take care of yourselves; he who errs cannot hurt you when you are on the right path." (5:105)

"Indeed he succeeds who purifies it (his soul)." [Qur'an – 91: 9]

Specific neurons and neurotransmitters, such as norepinephrine, trigger a defensive state when we feel that our thoughts have to be protected from the influence of others. If we are then confronted with differences in opinion, the chemicals are released in the brain are as same ones that try to ensure our survival in dangerous situations. In this defensive state, the more primitive part of the brain interferes with rational thinking and the limbic system can knock out most of our working memory, **physically causing 'narrow-mindedness.'** In the Quran Allah Subhanahu wa ta'ala says,

> "And We have put **a barrier** before them, and **a barrier** behind them, and We have covered them up, **so that they cannot see.**" (36:9)

We see this in the politics of fear or simply when someone is stubborn in a discussion. No matter how valuable an idea is, the brain has trouble processing it when it is in such a state. On a neural level, it reacts as if we're being threatened, even if this threat comes from harmless opinions or facts that we may otherwise find helpful and could rationally agree with. In the Quran Allah Subhanahu wa ta'ala says,

> "Then after him We sent (many) messengers to their peoples: they brought them Clear Signs, but they would not believe what they had already rejected beforehand. Thus do We **seal the hearts** of the transgressors." (10:74)

But when we express ourselves and our views are appreciated, these 'defense chemicals' decrease in the brain and dopamine neurotransmission activates the reward neurons, making us feel empowered and increasing our self-esteem. In the Quran Allah Subhanahu wa ta'ala says,

> "So woe unto those performers of Salat (prayers) (hypocrites), Who delay their Salat (prayer) from their stated fixed times, Those who do good deeds only to be seen (of men)." (107:4-6)

> "And when you look at them (hypocrites), their bodies please you; and when they speak, you listen to their words. They are as blocks of wood propped up. They think that every cry is against them. They are the enemies, so beware of them. May Allah curse them! How are they denying (or deviating from) the Right Path. (63:4)

Our beliefs have a profound impact on our body chemistry, this is why placebos can be so effective. Self esteem or self belief is closely linked to the neurotransmitter serotonin. In the Quran Allah Subhanahu wa ta'ala says,

> "It is the remembrance of ALLAH that hearts can find comfort." (13:28)

When the lack of it takes on severe proportions, it often leads to depression, soft-destructive behavior or even suicide. In the Quran Allah Subhanahu wa ta'ala says,

> "Then as to those who disbelieve, I will chastise them with severe chastisement in this world and the hereafter, and they shall have no helpers." (3:56)

Social validation increases the levels of dopamine and serotonin in the brain and allows us to let go of emotional fixations and become self-aware more easily. Social psychology often looks at the basic human need to fit in and calls this the normative social influence. When we grow up, our moral and ethical compass is almost entirely forged by our environment, so our actions are often a result of the validation we get from society.

> "And when it is said to them, follow what Allah has revealed, they say: Nay! We follow what we found our fathers upon. What! And though their fathers had no sense at all, nor did they follow the right way." (Al-Qur'an 2:170)

But new developments in neuroscience are giving us a better understanding of culture and identity. Recent neurological research has confirmed the existence of empathetic mirror neurons. When we experience an emotion or perform an action, specific neurons fire. But when we observe someone else performing this action or when we imagine it, many of the same neurons will fire again, as if we were performing the action ourselves. These empathy neurons connect us to other people, allowing us to feel what others feel. And since these neurons respond to our imagination, we can experience emotional feedback from them as if it came from someone else. This system is what allows us to self-reflect. In the Quran Allah Subhanahu wa ta'ala says,

> "Indeed there have been examples before you; therefore travel in the earth and see what was the end of the rejecters." (3:137)

> "And the inhabitants of Madyan. And Moses was denied, so I prolonged enjoyment for the disbelievers; then I seized them, and how [terrible] was My reproach.

> And how many a city did We destroy while it was

committing wrong - so it is [now] fallen into ruin - and [how many] an abandoned well and [how many] a lofty palace.

Have they not travelled through the land, and have they hearts wherewith to understand and ears wherewith to hear? Verily, it is not the eyes that grow blind, but it is the hearts which are in the breasts that grow blind." (22:44-46)

The mirror neuron does not know the difference between it and others and is the reason why we are so dependent of social validation and why we want to fit in. We are in a constant duality between how we see ourselves and how others see us. In the Quran Allah Subhanahu wa ta'ala says,

"To Him belongs all that is in the heavens and (all that is in) the earth and Ad-Din Wasiba is His [(i.e. perpetual sincere obedience to Allah is obligatory). None has the right to be worshipped but Allah)]. Will you then fear any other than Allah?" (16:52)

"And if you obey most of those in the earth, they will mislead you from the way of God. They follow but assumption/conjecture and they only guess/lie." (6:116.)

This can result in confusion in terms of identity and self-esteem. Brain scans show that we experience these negative emotions even before we are aware of them. But when we are self-aware, we can alter misplaced emotions because we control the thoughts that cause them. This is a neurochemical consequence of how memories become labeled and retrieved and how they are restored through protein synthesis.

Self-observing profoundly changes the way our brain works, it activates the self-regulating neo-cortical regions, which give us an incredible amount of control over our feelings. Every time we do this, our rationality and emotional resilience are strengthened. In the Quran Allah Subhanahu wa ta'ala says,

> Say, "Is the blind equivalent to the seeing? Then will you not give a thought?" (Quran al-Ana'am 6:50)

> "Positive fear of God (taqwa) can be attained only by those who have knowledge." (Al-Qur'an 35:28)

> O you who have attained to faith! If you remain conscious of God, **He will endow you with a standard by which to discern the true from the false,** and will clear evil from you, and will forgive you your mistakes: for God is limitless in the abundance of His blessing. [*Sürah al-Anfäl* 8:29]

When we are not in being self-aware, most of our thoughts and actions are impulsive. And the idea that we are randomly reacting and not making conscious choices is instinctively frustrating. The brain resolves this by creating explanations for our behavior and physically rewriting it into our memories through memory reconsolidation, making us believed that **we were in control of our actions.** This is also called <u>backward rationalization,</u> and it can be most of our negative emotions unresolved, and ready to be triggered at any time. They become a constant fuel to our confusion as our brain will keep trying to justify why we *behaved irrationally.* In the Quran Allah Subhanahu wa ta'ala says,

> "In their hearts is *sickness,* so Allah increased their *sickness,* and for them is a painful punishment on account of **how they used to lie.**" (2:10)

"For, when they (hypocrits) meet those who have attained to faith (Muslims), they say, 'We believe' - but when they find themselves alone with one another, they say (hypocrites say to each others), <u>Do you inform them of what God has disclosed to you, so that they might use it in argument against you, quoting the words of your Sustainer? Will you not. Then, use your reason?</u>'" (2:76)

All this complex and almost schizophrenic subconscious behavior is the result of a vastly parallel distributed system in our brain. There is a not known specific center of consciousness, the appearance of a unity is, in fact, each of these separate circuits being enabled and being expressed at one particular moment in time. Our experiences are constantly changing our neural connections, physically altering the parallel system that is our consciousness. Direct modifications to this can have some real consequences that bring into question what and where consciousness really is.

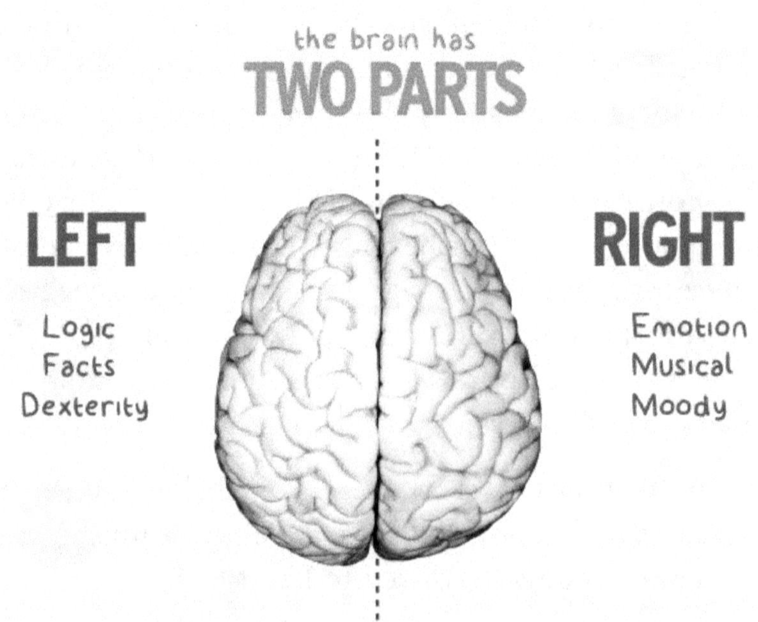

If your left cerebral hemisphere were to be disconnected from the right, as is the case in split brain patients, you would normally still be able to talk and think from the left hemisphere, while your right hemisphere would have very limited cognitive capacities. Your left brain will not miss the right part, even though this profoundly changes your perception. One consequence of this is that you can no longer describe the right half of someone's face. But you will never mention it, you will never see it as a problem or even realize that something has changed. Since this effects more than just your perception of the real world and also applies to your mental images, it is not just a sensory problem but a fundamental change in your consciousness.

> "In every town We have placed some sinful leaders who always make evil plans. These plans will only work against their own souls **but they do not realize this**." (Al-Qur'an 6:123)

Each neuron has a voltage which can change when ions flow in or out of the cell. Once the neurons voltage has reached a certain level, it will fire an electrical signal to other cells, which will repeat the process. When many neurons fire at the same time, we can measure these changes in the form of a wave. Brain waves underpin almost everything going on in our minds, including memory, attention and even intelligence. As they oscillate at different frequencies, they get classified in bands, such as alpha, theta and gamma. Each are associated with different tasks. Brain waves allow brain cells to tune into the frequency corresponding to their particular task, while ignoring irrelevant signals, similar to how a radio homes in on different waves to pick up radio stations. The transfer of information between neurons becomes optimal when their activity is synchronized. This is the same reason why we experience cognitive dissonance, the frustration caused by simultaneously holding two contradictory ideas. The Messenger of Allah, peace and blessings be upon him, said,

> "Leave what makes you doubt for what does not make you doubt. Verily, truth brings peace of mind and falsehood sows doubt." (Tirmidhī 2518)

Will (willpower) is merely the drive to reduce dissonance between each of our active neural circuits. When somone became self-aware and began to ponder its own existence, when a person faces the paradox of wanting purpose while thinking that human existence is meaningless, cognitive dissonance occurs. Throughout history, this has led many to each for spiritual and religious guidance, challenging science, as its failed to give answers to existential questions, such as, "Why or what am I?" In the Quran Allah (SWT) says,

> "We will show them Our signs in the horizons and within themselves until it becomes clear to them that it is the truth.1 But is it not sufficient concerning your Lord that He is, over all things, a Witness?" (Al Quran: 41:53)

The left cerebral hemisphere is largely responsible for creating a coherent belief system, in order to maintain a sense of continuity towards our lives. New experiences get folded into the pre-existing belief system. When they don't fit, they are simply denied. Counter-balancing this is the right cerebral hemisphere, which has the opposite tendency. Whereas the left hemisphere tries to preserve the model, the right hemisphere is constantly challenging the status quo. When the discrepant anomalies become too, large the right hemisphere forces a revision in our worldview. However, when our beliefs are too strong, the right hemisphere may not succeed in overriding our denial. This can create a profound confusion when mirroring others, when the neural connections that physically define our belief system are not **strongly developed** or <u>active</u>.

> "Verily, those who say: 'Our Lord is Allah,' and then they **stand firm**, on them the angels will descend (saying): 'Fear not, nor grieve! But receive the glad tidings of Paradise which you have been promised! *(Al-Qur'an 30-32)*
>
> "Our Lord! Let not our hearts deviate (from the truth) <u>after You have guided us</u>." (Al-Qur'an 3:8)
>
> "Our Lord! Pour out constancy [patience] on us and make our steps firm…" (2:250)

MY OTHER BOOKS ON AMAZON

Paperback

Name: Sahih al-Bukhari: (All Volumes in One Book) English Text Only

Copy this code and paste on Amazon search box and then click enter: B088LJJC2X

Customer review:

> *"Thank you for this work, it is a great blessing to scan through Hadith from time to time. I really hope the authors are from Ahlus Sunnah Wal Jama'at, and that the correct sources were used."*

Hardcover

Name: Sahih Al Bukhari: [Without Repetition] All Volumes in One Book

Copy this code and paste on Amazon search box and then click enter: B087SLGKRC

Customer review:

> *"This is very good in detail and easy to understand the translation, it is not repetitive, I have found it very helpful."*

Table of Content

MARYAM BINT IMRAN

Maryam bint 'Imran the greatest woman who has ever walked on the face of this Earth, that is Maryam (Mary), the daughter of Imran (Joachim), may Allah (SWT) be pleased with her. Allah (SWT) says,

يَا مَرْيَمُ

"Oh Maryam" (3:42)

إِنَّ اللَّهَ اصْطَفَاكِ وَطَهَّرَكِ وَاصْطَفَاكِ عَلَىٰ نِسَاءِ الْعَالَمِينَ

"Allah has chosen you, Allah has purified you, and Allah has chosen you over all of the women of the world." (3:42)

So Maryam is the greatest woman of all time. The Rasullah (peace be upon him) said she is the best woman of her time and Khadijah is the best woman of her time. What makes Maryam so special and Allah (SWT) says that she is

مَثَلًا لِّلَّذِينَ آمَنُوا

"An example for those who believe" (66:11)

وَمَرْيَمَ ابْنَتَ عِمْرَانَ

"Maryam, daughter of Imran" (66:12)

Notice that Allah (SWT) did not associate Maryam with Isa (Jesus) in every ayah of the Quran. In fact, as Allah (SWT) is mentioning her, just after mentioning that Aasiyah (the adoptive mother of Moses), as the wife of the Pharaoh, and the wives of Lut (Lot) and Nuh (Noah) as their wives, He doesn't say Maryam, the mother of Jesus (peace be upon him). He just says, "Maryam, daughter of Imran." What is the wisdom of that? Maryam's greatness is not necessarily tied to Isa (Jesus). She was great because of who she was and in fact, her name is even mentioned more than the name of Isa (Jesus) in the Quran because of how great she was.

She is not just a woman who is great because she happened to be the mother of a Prophet. She is recognized as a woman who perfected her faith as the Prophet (ﷺ) mentioned her amongst that group. She is a woman who demonstrates for all of us really how to have Tawakkul (faith) in Allah (SWT), to truly trust Allah (SWT) in the most difficult of times. She is an example of modesty for both men and women; because yes modesty exists for both men as well, so both men and women. She is an example of modesty. She is an example in her devotion, in her Ibadah, her worship. All of these things, Maryam excels in. So it is not just that she is the mother of Isa (Jesus).

Her story starts off in Ibadah (worship) and she was dedicated to Allah (SWT) even before she was born. Her mother is Hinna bintu Faaquut (Saint Anne) and her father of course is Imran (Joachim). Hinna bintu Faaquut and Imran, and Imran being the Imam (leader) of his people, they were unable to have children for many, many, many years. Very similar to the story of Zakariya (Zechariah) except he wasn't that old but he did reach an age where it wasn't expected that he would have children anymore or that she would have children. And then all of a sudden Allah (SWT) gives her the news that she is pregnant and she is not told what kind of child this is going to be, whether it is going to be a boy or a girl or whether it is going to be a Prophet or layman. She is not told anything about the type of child, the gender of the child, or anything of that sort. She just knows that she is pregnant and she praises Allah (SWT), Imran praises Allah (SWT), the people are celebrating, they are overjoyed because they love Imran and his wife and then all of a sudden, tragedy. Imran dies a sudden death. So now Hinna bintu Faaquut is left with this baby that is not even born yet that's going to already be born without a father and then as she delivers the child, expecting that it is going to be a boy, so that it can be a Prophet so he can do dawah and those types of things since she dedicated this child to Allah (SWT), Allah (SWT) gave her a girl. SubhanAllah! As Allah (SWT) is narrating this story to us in the Quran,

قَالَتْ رَبِّ إِنِّي وَضَعْتُهَا أُنثَىٰ

"When she gave birth, she said, "Oh Allah I gave birth to a girl." (3:36)

Allah (SWT) says,

وَاللَّهُ أَعْلَمُ بِمَا وَضَعَتْ

"Allah already knows what she gave birth to." (3:36)

And Allah is telling us that Allah knows what she gave birth to. It wasn't by accident. She gave birth to a girl for a reason.

وَلَيْسَ الذَّكَرُ كَالْأُنثَىٰ

"She says, "Oh Allah, A boy is not like a girl.""

She is complaining to Allah (SWT) in a way that I expected it to be a boy.

وَإِنِّي سَمَّيْتُهَا مَرْيَمَ

"I am naming her Maryam" (3:36) and

وَإِنِّي أُعِيذُهَا بِكَ وَذُرِّيَّتَهَا مِنَ الشَّيْطَانِ الرَّجِيمِ

"And I seek refuge in you O Allah for her and for her offspring from the cursed devil." (3:36)

Because of that Rasullah (ﷺ) said that when Maryam and her son were born, they were spared from the poking of Shaytan (Satan) which causes babies to cry when they are born. So they were born without crying because the Shaiytan did not appear to them and he could not affect them because of the dua (invocation) of Hinna bintu Faaquut (Saint Anne), the mother of Maryam.

Maryam now of course, now that she is born, and Hinna doesn't know what to do with her because in that society it wasn't practical or possible for a woman to be dedicated to the temple because there were only men in the temple at that time. It wasn't practical for a woman to go out and do dawah (religious invitation). SubhanAllah! She has this baby and she wanted to fulfill her promise to Allah (SWT). So Zakariyah (Zechariah) takes it upon himself and Rasullallah (ﷺ) says about Zakariyah that he was a carpenter and he used to eat from his daily earnings. So Zakariyah built a mehrab, not just an area in the masjid (temple) but rather he built a structure in the masjid (temple), a room in the masjid. Mehrab comes from the word Haaraba, to rage war, so she rages war on herself. When you are in this place of Ibaadah (worship), you rage war on yourself. What do I mean by raging war against yourself? It means to stand there and rage war against your desires, against yourself, against your laziness and stand there in devotion the way that Maryam did.

So he built this place for her where she could have her privacy, grow up in that temple, and worship Allah (SWT) just as a man would while at the same time not compromising her modesty.

So Zakariyah would go up and check on her every single day as she grew up and this young girl loved to worship Allah (SWT). I mean she craved it. And in fact, subhanAllah! This is actually the nature of when she would leave the masjid (temple) in the first place. She would leave to remember Allah (SWT) at the times she could not be in the masjid. She would still go out to the East and remember Allah (SWT), watch the sunrise and remember Allah (SWT). This woman ate, breath, and drank the dhikr of Allah (SWT), the remembrance of Allah (SWT), even as she was a young girl. So Zakariyah would come and find her in Ibaadah; find her worshipping Allah (SWT) all the time. And one day Zakariyah comes and Zakariyah is noticing that food is coming from somewhere and that food is out of season. So back then they did not have refrigerators. So it's not possible to store food that is out of season at that time. So Zakariyah is wondering, "What is going on here?" So one day he asks her. He says (mentioned in the Quran),

قَالَ يَا مَرْيَمُ أَنَّىٰ لَكِ هَٰذَا

"Where is this coming from? Who is giving this to you?" (3:37)

Maryam (A) responds and says,

قَالَتْ هُوَ مِنْ عِندِ اللَّهِ

"It is from Allah." (3:37)

إِنَّ اللَّهَ يَرْزُقُ مَن يَشَاءُ بِغَيْرِ حِسَابٍ

"Allah gives to whom He wills whenever He wills." (3:37)

Notice that Maryam and Zakariyah have an understanding of dua (invocation) here. Maryam does not claim to have a special relationship with Allah (SWT) where only she can ask Allah (SWT) and be given. She is saying to Zakariyah that Allah (SWT) gives to whomever He wants, whenever He wants, so you should call upon Allah (SWT) and ask Allah (SWT) for what you desire. That is something that is very, very beautiful because Zakariyah did not say, "make dua (supplication) for me."

Zakariyah understood the dawah of Maryam. He got the message, "You know what, I should ask Allah (SWT) even if it seems improbable, I should ask Allah (SWT) for that child." So Zakariyah goes and he makes his Qiyam ul Layl (night prayer) and make dua,

هُنَالِكَ دَعَا زَكَرِيَّا رَبَّهُ قَالَ رَبِّ هَبْ لِي مِن لَّدُنْكَ ذُرِّيَّةً طَيِّبَةً إِنَّكَ سَمِيعُ الدُّعَاء

"At that, Zakariyah called upon his Lord, saying, "My Lord, grant me from Yourself a good offspring. Indeed, You are the Hearer of supplication." (3:38)

Allah (SWT) grants him Yahya-John the Baptist. Maryam then leaves at the time she would leave the masjid and go to the East. As she is there by herself, remembering Allah (SWT), a beautiful man comes – a perfect symmetrical human being. Beauty scientifically is measured by symmetry.

Allah (SWT) describes Jibril (Archangel Gabriel) as a perfectly symmetrical human being. So she has already shown us, Maryam, what she is in terms of her Ibaadah (worshipping), look at her modesty. She sees this man that she doesn't know and she realizes she is all alone and this beautiful man comes. She doesn't flirt with him and says, "Hi. How are you? What are you doing? What's your name?" She sees him and before he can even speak, before he can even say, "Assalamu alaykum (peace be upon you)," she looks at him and says,

أَعُوذُ بِالرَّحْمَٰنِ مِنكَ إِن كُنتَ تَقِيًّا

She said, "Indeed, I seek refuge in the Most Merciful from you, [so leave me], if you should be fearing of Allah." (19:18)

Now sisters don't say that to people out in public just because you see them. Maryam was not used to being approached by a man. SubhanAllah! In one sentence, Maryam does so much, number one she shows, "I am not interested. I don't know what you are going to say but you need to know I am not interested in any way." Number two, she mentions the name of Allah (SWT), Ar-Rahman (The Merciful). "I am scaring you by mentioning Ar-Rahman (The Merciful)." Why didn't she mention Jabbaar or Azeez or a name of Allah (SWT) that denotes wrath, honor, dignity, or power? Why Rahman?

Maryam wants to let him know that you can make taubah (repent). You can go back and make Istigifirullah; seek forgiveness from Allah (SWT). He is merciful enough to forgive you if you have any form of Taqwa (faith, piety) inside of you.

At that point, as the Ulama (scholars) tell us, usually Allah (SWT) sends Jibreel (Archangel Gabriel-peace be upon him) as a human being first, as was the case of the Messenger (ﷺ); because it is less intimidating to see a human being than to see an angel in their actual form because the angels are huge. They fill up the entire sky with their wings. SubhanAllah! They are not what we think of them, they don't just have two white feathers as wings and fly around and have shiny hair, no. The angels are huge creations of Allah (SWT), and have thousands of wings. So it's less intimidating when you see a human being, but this person's modesty was at that level where even when a human being comes to her it is less intimidating than when Allah (SWT) sends an angel and his creation. So at that point, when she said those words, Jibreel went to his original form.

Jibreel gave her the news of Isa (Jesus), "He responded, "I am only a messenger from your Lord, ˹sent˺ to bless you with a pure son." She wondered, "How can I have a son when no man has ever touched me, nor am I unchaste?" He replied, "So will it be! Your Lord says, 'It is easy for Me. And so will We make him a sign for humanity and a mercy from Us.' It is a matter ˹already˺ decreed."

So she conceived him and withdrew with him to a remote place. Then the pains of labour drove her to the trunk of a palm tree. She cried, "Alas! I wish I had died before this, and was a thing long forgotten!" So a voice reassured her from below her, "Do not grieve! Your Lord has provided a stream at your feet. And shake the trunk of this palm tree towards you, it will drop fresh, ripe dates upon you. So eat and drink, and put your heart at ease.

But if you see any of the people, say, 'I have vowed silence to the Most Compassionate, so I am not talking to anyone today.'"

Then she returned to her people, carrying him. They said ʿin shockʾ, "O Mary! You have certainly done a horrible thing! O sister of Aaron! Your father was not an indecent man, nor was your mother unchaste." So she pointed to the baby. They exclaimed, "How can we talk to someone who is an infant in the cradle?"

Jesus declared, "I am truly a servant of Allah. He has destined me to be given the Scripture and to be a prophet. He has made me a blessing wherever I go, and bid me to establish prayer and give alms-tax as long as I live, and to be kind to my mother. He has not made me arrogant or defiant. Peace be upon me the day I was born, the day I die, and the day I will be raised back to life!" (Quran 19:19-33)

FOUR ADVICE FROM THE QURAN

✓ Men and Women have equal rewards for their deeds (3:195)

✓ Most noble of you is the most righteous (49:13)

✓ Do not even approach unlawful sexual intercourse (17:32)

✓ And establish prayer; surely prayer keeps one away from indecency and evil. (29:45)

Narrated Masruq: Abdullah bin 'Amr mentioned Allah's Messenger (ﷺ) said, 'The best among you are those who have the best manners and character.' (6029)

"Once you begin to see everything beautiful as only a reflection of God's beauty, you will learn to love in the right way." [Yasmin

Mogahed].

A thought-provoking questions you should ask yourself every day

Who am I, really?

Practical Ways to Improve Yourself

<u>Meditate</u>

Mindfulness meditation involves sitting silently and paying attention to thoughts, sounds, the sensations of breathing or parts of the body, bringing your attention back whenever the mind starts to wander.

Mindfulness meditation isn't just about letting your thoughts wander. But it isn't about trying to empty your mind, either. Instead, the practice involves paying close attention to the present moment — especially our own thoughts, emotions and sensations — whatever it is that's happening.

<u>Ponder</u>

Think intentionally, constructively, purposefully and positively.

Ask youself some Questins

What is the purpose of my life?

What am I doing? What would I do if today was my last day?

WHAT'S YOUR MINDSET? – WORKSHEET

TASK # 1: Under each category, write down the

type of mindset you believe you have

NOTE: Be honest to yourself. You can only become a better version of you by being completely honest to yourself.

A USEFUL TIP: If you start feeling a little uncomfortable inside while writing your answer, you might be writing the wrong one!

GROWTH 1. Growth or fixed?	
ENERGY 2. Optimistic or pessimistic?	
GRATITUDE 3. Grateful or ungrateful?	
PRODUCTIVITY 4. Productive or lazy / lethargic?	
EMOTIONS 5. Emotionally resilient or emotionally labile?	
GENEROSITY 6. Giver, taker or matcher?	
CONFIDENCE 7. Confident, arrogant or fearful?	

THOUGHT 8. Contemplating or wandering / superficial?	
PURPOSE 9. Purposeful or aimless/ Confused?	

9-WORD SUMMARY OF THE TYPE OF MINDSET YOU CURRENTLY POSSESS:

I have

Mindset.

ASIYA BINT MUZAHIM

Asiya bint Muzahim (Arabic: آسِيَا ٱبْنَت مُزَاحِم), was the Great Royal Wife of the ancient Egypt's Pharaoh of the Exodus and the adoptive mother of Islamic prophet Mūsā (Moses).

Despite being married to the worst human being who ever walked the face of the earth, Asiya (may Allah be pleased with her) still was a woman of perfect iman (believe). Allah (SWT) describes her in the Quran saying,

> "And Allah presents an example of those who believed: the wife of Pharaoh, when she said, "My Lord, build for me near You a house in Paradise and save me from Pharaoh and his deeds and save me from the wrongdoing people." (66:11)

And the reason why Allah (SWT) called her the wife of Firaoun (Pharaoh) is to show us that this woman, the wife of Firaoun, Asiya bint Muzahim, may Allah be pleased with her, despite being married to the absolute worst human being who has ever walked the face of the Earth, she still was a woman of perfect iman (faith). That's why in the previous ayah Allah (SWT) says,

> "Allah presents an example of those who disbelieved: the wife of Noah and the wife of Lot. They were under two of Our righteous servants but betrayed them, so those prophets did not avail them from Allah at all, and it was said, "Enter the Fire with those who enter." (66:10)

That these women despite being married to the Prophets, who obviously have perfect iman (believe), still managed to disbelieve. So Allah (SWT) was showing us that iman (believe) is an individual struggle and it is attained by the individual. And your associations and your affiliations and your families will not be able to save you on the Day of Judgment.

Nevertheless, when we are talking about Asiya, it is absolutely phenomenal, extraordinary who this woman managed to become despite being married to Firaoun. When we look at her biography, we don't find much about her even when we look at Biblical sources, we don't find much about her. We find that her life is very similar initially to the wife of a king or a prince that you would see in the Middle East today. A very secretive life, not much is known about her. You don't know where she came from, you don't know much about her family and even until today, usually you don't even know the names of the wives of the kings.

And so in this situation with Asiya, the only thing that we know about her is that she was a very beautiful woman, obviously, that came from a very rich family. So her father was obviously an important man as well. She was in an arranged marriage with Firaoun as was their tradition. At the same time, she was only known for her generosity. So when we look at Firaoun obviously we see the opposite of generosity. We see Asiya was a very generous woman.

This woman, her story starts, at least from an Islamic perspective, or when things get interesting, is when one day she is at the Nile River with her maids and as she is sitting there with her maids at the Nile, she sees this small crate come and her maids think; when they see this box that it must be some form of treasure that is inside of it. Instead, when they open this box they find a baby. And that baby was Musa (peace be upon him), look at the precision of Allah (SWT)'s divine decree. Not only did Allah (SWT) tell Musa (Moses)'s mother to place him in the

Nile, and don't worry he'll be taken care of, he will be safe, and let your heart be at ease, but Allah (SWT) on top of just taking care of Musa, planned it in a way that Asiya would be outside at that moment and would see this box come by and then take Musa, open that box and she fell in love with the baby.

She was absolutely in love with the baby. And subhanAllah! When we say 'in love', this is something that was from her fitra (original disposition), from her nature because the Prophet (ﷺ) said, "the souls are like constricted soldiers.' They're like troops. In the realm of souls, those souls that loved one another and that came close to each other in that realm, come close to each other in this realm of dunya (earth). They have a natural affinity towards each other in this dunya (earth). Which is why sometimes you love people for the sake of Allah even though you barely know them. And those that do not get along, don't get along in this world as well.

So when Asiya saw Musa, she instantly fell in love with him and this baby that fell into her hands was even more special because Asiya was unable to have children. The 'ulama (scholars) say the wisdom of that is obviously that Musa would be taken in as if he was her child.

So, Asiya brings this baby, she falls in love with this baby, and she says to Firaoun, let us keep this baby, "He will be the coolness of my eyes and the coolness of your eyes." Musa is raised in this palace of Firaoun and Asiya. And Asiya dedicates herself to Musa as if she is indeed his mother. She raises him, she continues to love him, and SubhanAllah! Eventually, as we know the story goes, she brings in the mother of Musa, not knowing that she is the mother of Musa to be a wet nurse for Musa. Musa's mother was reunited with him and on top of that Asiya had the pleasure and the honor of raising this child Musa in her own palace.

As times goes on and Musa comes out and Musa shows that he is a Prophet and calls to Tawheed (monotheism), and Firaoun is infuriated. Firaoun is in this battle now with Musa. Asiya immediately believed in the message that was given to Musa. She immediately believed in Tawheed (oneness of God) and she started to practice the religion of Musa on a personal level without Firaoun recognizing that she was amongst the monotheists and she was amongst those that were following the message of Musa. Why? Because if Firaoun mutilates children and has women raped the way that he does for believing in Allah, then what would he do to his wife? What sense of betrayal would he feel if he saw his own wife accept that message of Musa.

As time goes on, however, there is an incident that would lead to Asiya coming out and exposing her Islam. And that was the incident that is known as the incident of the hairdresser of the daughter of Firaoun. And the hairdresser of the daughter of Firaoun, one day she was doing her hair and she dropped a comb. And when she dropped the comb, she said "BismAllah" (in the name of Allah). And Firaoun's daughter, obviously from another wife, or a concubine other than Asiya, she said to the hairdresser, "أبي الله؟" [abee Allah?] – My father? The hairdresser responded and said no. The Lord of your father and the Lord of me and the Lord of you, Allah (SWT).

So the daughter goes back to Firaoun and says to Firaoun, and narrates this incident to Firaoun. Firaoun doesn't think twice, he doesn't have an ounce, or an atom's worth of mercy in his heart. Firaoun orders for a pit to be dug and copper to burn in that pit so that that woman and all her children could be thrown into that pit in front of everyone.

Firaoun wanted to make an example out of everyone who believed. And SubhanAllah! Allah (SWT) made an example out of him for all time. To even where his corpse has been preserved so that we can see the humiliation that he was put through. But he wanted to make an example out of this woman. So Firaoun calls the town and Asiya is obviously witnessing this incident. This woman has all of her children and she is a poor woman. And Firaoun says that I am going to throw each and every single one of your children into this pit. And the woman says, 'I have a request from you oh Firaoun." He says, "What is that request? " She says, "The request is that whenever you finish burning us is that you gather our bones in one cloth." SubhanAllah! Look at how much this mother loves her children which makes the test even greater. And Firaoun says, "لكِ ذلك" [laki dhaalik] - you have that request honored.

So one by one Firaoun started to throw her children into that boiling oil and they were parishing right in front of her until it came down to just her and the baby that was in her arms that she was suckling. And she became hesitant because she didn't want to throw this baby into the fire. And the baby spoke, and Rasul Allah (ﷺ) said that this is one of the babies that Allah (SWT) caused to speak amongst three babies. You can try to figure out who the other two babies were. This baby spoke and said to the mother, "Go ahead and jump. Throw me in. Because torture and punishmed in this world is much lighter than the torture and he punishment in the hereafter." And so she takes this baby and she jumps with her baby into this pit and she parishes.

And SubhanAllah! when Rasul Allah (ﷺ) on the night of Al-Israa and Al-Miraaj in Sahih Muslim, the Prophet (ﷺ) as he was going through the heavens, he smelled the beautiful scent and he said, "Oh Jibreel (Gabriel), what is this beautiful smell that I'm smelling?" And Jibreel (peace be upon him) says, 'that is the scent of the hairdresser of the daughter of Firaoun. That is her scent in Jannah." SubhanAllah!

It was at that moment when Asiya saw the cruelty of Firaoun and the bravery of that woman, and by the way, history repeats itself. Whenever a tyrant oppresses believers and other believers see that, and the tyrant tries to make an example out of those believers, instead he increases the iman (believe) of those who have iman; as Allah (SWT) says in the Quran that even when the believers were told, "That everyone is gathering against you. They're going to torture you, and do this to you and that to you, Allah (SWT) says, – it increases their faith.

So, Asiya sees that and Asiya says you know what if Firaoun is like that and this woman had the guts to stand up to him and that courage, then I'm also going to go up to him and stand up to him. So she walks up to Firaoun that night as Abu Al-'Aliyah says, "She says, 'Oh Firaoun I have disbelieved in you. I don't care what you're going to do. And I believe in the Lord of Musa and the Lord of Harun, the Lord of all of the worlds.'" Firaoun was shocked! He said, 'Do you know what I'm going to do to you?' She said, "I know and I don't care." SubhanAllah! "I have disbelieved in you, I have rejected you and I don't care." This was a woman of perfect iman and she saw a woman of lesser iman stand up to Firaoun. 'I don't care. Do what you want.'

So Firaoun drags this woman, Asiya bint Muzahim. Asiya bint Muzahim grew up her entire life as a Queen. She has never encountered any adversity. She has never had any inconvenience and she has never had to lift a finger. Anything she wanted in life she just tells her maids to do it. And Firaoun drags her to the desert, ties her down, tortures her, deprives her of water, deprives her of food, deprives of her dignity and honor. And the daughters of Firaoun from the concubines and from the other wives are laughing at her. She has no support.

And while that is going on, she looks up to the heavens and she says, "Oh Allah build for me with You a palace in Jannah." You know what's so beautiful is that the scholars say here that before she asked for the palace in Jannah she asked for Allah's company. And that shows us something very significant. She didn't ask for another husband, she asked for Allah (SWT)'s company. Her goal was the akhirah (hereafter). Just as the child said to the mother, "that the punishment of this world, this lust, and the punishment of the hereafter." She was only thinking akhirah. So instead of Firaoun, "Oh Allah! I want to be with you." "عِنْدَكَ" ['Indaka]- I want to be with you. Replace the company of Firaoun with the company of Allah (SWT) and replace this palace that I've sacrificed for your sake with a palace in Jannah.

So Allah opened up the skies and she was able to see her palace in Jannah. Therefore when the people lashed her over and over again, the angels shaded her. The angels shaded her the same way they shade the people of al-sham as the Prophet (ﷺ) said, "The same way the angels shade the people of al-sham. That when they are tortured their iman (belife) rises." So, as she was being tortured she looked up, she saw what she saw, and she was shaded and she laughed. And Firaoun said to the guards, "look how crazy this woman is." And she laughed and she laughed and she laughed until Firaoun got frustrated and he said, "You know what? This woman is not coming back to her senses." He said, "Go to the highest cliff and tie her under there. And push off a boulder that would smash her body to pieces." So they go up to that cliff and they push this boulder to fall on the body of Asiya but Allah (SWT) did not give Firaoun that pleasure. Abu Al-'Aliyah said, "Allah took her soul when she said, 'Save me from Firaoun and his evil.'" Allah took her soul before the boulder landed on her body. So although to the people of this world her body was shattered to pieces, Allah (SWT) had taken her for Himself. And Allah (SWT) had given her a palace in Jannah as she requested.

What an amazing woman! And what an amazing example. And what a test of faith and SubhanAllah! We ask Allah (SWT) to gather us with her and those that have perfected their faith from the Saliheen, the Siddiqeen, and the 'Anbiyaa and the Prophet (ﷺ) the highest of levels jannat-ul-firdous. Allahumma ameen.

FOUR ADVICE FROM THE QURAN

✓ Do not follow anyone blindly (2:170)

✓ Place your trust in Allah. Surely, Allah loves those who place their trust in Him. (3:159)

✓ Then when you have taken a decision, put your trust in Allah (SWT) (3:159)

✓ If Allah helps you, there is none to overcome you. And if He abandons you, then, who is there to help you after that? In Allah the believers should place their trust. (3:160)

Narrated Mujahid (ra): `Abdullah bin `Umar said, "Allah's Messenger (ﷺ) took hold of my shoulder and said, 'Be in this world as if you were a stranger or a traveler." The sub-narrator added: Ibn `Umar used to say, "If you survive till the evening, do not expect to be alive in the morning, and if you survive till the morning, do not expect to be alive in the evening, and take from your health for your sickness, and (take) from your life for your death." (Al-Bukhari, 6416)

"Your fate has been written with the ink of His love and sealed with His mercy so fear not, place your trust in Him and have hope in His decree." (Gems of Jannah)

"And worship your Lord until there comes unto you the certainty (death). (15:99)

A thought-provoking questions you should ask yourself every day

How shall I live, knowing I will die?

Practical Ways to Improve Yourself

Get out of your comfort zone

Real growth comes with hard work and sweat. Being too comfortable doesn't help us grow, it makes us stagnate.

Have the will to change

Allah won't change you unless you decide to change. That's why you need to be willing to change and actually put some thought and effort into the idea because when there's a will there's a way in'sha'Allah.

SELF-ACCEPTANCE WORKSHEET

LIST # 1: MY GOOD QUALITIES + GOOD HABITS

ALHAMDULILAH

1.
2.
3.
4.
5.

LIST # 2: MY ACHIEVEMENTS IN LIFE

ALHAMDULILAH

1.
2.
3.
4.
5.

LIST # 3: MY SHORTCOMINGS + INSECURITIES

√ THINGS I CAN CHANGE ABOUT MYSELF	⊘ THINGS I CAN NOT CHANGE ABOUT MYSELF
INSHA'ALLAH	After writing the things you can't change about yourself, gently cross them out. This way, everytime you see the list of your insecurities crossed off, you will gradually train your mind to cross them out of your life.
1.	
2.	
3.	
4.	
5.	

KHADIJA BINT KHUWAYLID

The Prophet (ﷺ) said that there is no doubt that Khadija (May Allah be pleased with her) was the best woman of her time. And she, along with her daughter, is amongst the four women that perfected their faith. SubhanAllah!

This woman Khadija before the revelation of salah (prayer), before the revelation of fast, before the revelation of zakat (charity) or hajj, before the revelation of most of the rules and legislation, Khadija managed to perfect her iman (belife). And you might wonder how that is even possible?

It's possible because the Prophet (ﷺ) is the one who told us that, "The most perfect of the believers in their faith are the ones who have the best character."

And Khadija even before Islam, was known as "الطاهرة" [altaahirah] – the pure woman, subhanAllah!

She is the daughter of two royal people, Khuwaylid and Fatima, and she was a rich woman, a very wealthy business woman. She had been married before to some of the leaders of Quraish but she became a widow both times and subhanAllah! She wants to marry the Prophet (ﷺ) who is 15 years younger than her. Why? Because she started to ask around about his character. She asked Maysadar, she asked Nafisah. She wanted to know what the Prophet's (peace be upon him) character was like because she had seen so much honesty and truthfulness from him. And that was her reason for pursuing him following the command that would come later on, "إذا أتاكم من ترضون دينه وخلقه فزوجوه" ['itha 'ataakom man tardawn deenaho wa khuluqaho fazawwijooh] – if someone comes to you with good religion and good character then you marry that person. Do not reject that person.

And subhanAllah! At that time you didn't have the revelation yet. You just had good character.

And that's why the Prophet (peace be upon him) was pursued by her and that's why RasoolAllah (ﷺ) accepted this woman for marriage who was 15 years older than him and was a widow two times and had a son, Handab ibn Abi Hala and all that baggage that would keep people away from a divorcee or a widowed woman today. But subhanAllah! They came together for character and that is why there is not a single narrated fight or argument between the Prophet (ﷺ) and Khadija. But rather their marriage was praised by all of the people of Mecca.

Now, when RasulAllah (ﷺ) had bestowed upon him the love for isolation and seclusion and the Prophet (ﷺ) started to go to mount Hira and started to contemplate. SubhanAllah! For anyone who has been to Mecca you can see that Hira is an hour's climb at least and that is with all the stairs and things of that sort nowadays. But imagine what it was like for the Prophet (ﷺ) at that time to climb up there. And Khadija, she didn't say to the Prophet (ﷺ), "Why are you staying away from home? Why are you spending weeks up there? And sometimes over a month?" In fact, she supported the Prophet (ﷺ) in trying to find guidance and trying to find those answers.

By the time the Prophet (ﷺ) is 40, she is 55 now. She is climbing up that mountain to take food to the Prophet (ﷺ) and to comfort the Prophet (ﷺ). And then when the Prophet (ﷺ) comes down from Hira and he comes to Khadija with the famous words of "زملوني دثروني" [zammilooni dathirooni]- embrace me, cover me up, seeking comfort in Khadija, she didn't say to the Prophet (ﷺ), "maybe you shouldn't be going out there so long. Maybe you should stay home more often. Maybe you shouldn't have been out there in the first place." Or, "you know I think you're getting a little crazy on us." She didn't say, "I think that it must be some demons or something like that." Rather, she would reassure the Prophet (ﷺ). She supported him emotionally and religiously here. Think about this. She says to the Prophet (ﷺ),

"والله لا يخزيك الله أبدا" [wallahi la yukhzeek Allah 'abada] -Allah (SWT) will never disgrace you. Why did she say that Allah will never disgrace you? And she started to mention, "because you uphold the ties of kinship, you're good to your neighbors and generous to them, you treat the orphans well, you take up the cause of the one who has been wronged."

In essence, what is she saying to the Prophet (ﷺ)? She is saying Allah (SWT) loves you for the same reasons that I love you and the same reasons that I pursued you for marriage. Again, good nature is good iman (faith). Good character is good iman.

She recognized those things in the Prophet (ﷺ) and looked at the way that this wife speaks about her husband. How beautiful that a spouse will speak about her spouse or a spouse would speak about his spouse in that beautiful manner. "This is how I see you."

And not only did she support him emotionally here, but she also said to the Prophet (ﷺ), "Let's go to Waraqah ibn Nawfal, let's go to my cousin who is a Biblical scholar and let's see what he has to say." She's the one reassuring him and taking him over to Waraqah who would reveal to the Prophet (ﷺ) that this was his first encounter with Jibreel (Gabriel). Think about this.

And then 'Ali (peace be upon him) who was raised in that household, he recalls the nights where Rasulullah (ﷺ) would wake up and pray. And Khadija would wake up and stand right next to the Prophet (ﷺ) and also pray. I mean that's incredible. She didn't say to the Prophet (ﷺ) I don't know what this journey is that you're going on right now, but I'm not going to stand up and pray but I'll let you stand up and pray. She stood up and prayed with him. So she gave him emotional support. She gave him religious support.

When the Prophet (ﷺ) called to his people and the people rejected him she didn't say, "We were doing well in society, we had high status, and now our reputation is being tarnished," because she is the "pure woman" and he is the "most trustworthy." She stood by his side and reassured him and told him that Allah (SWT) will bring victory to you and honor you. And then she even went to the length of financially supporting the Prophet's (ﷺ) call and mission and purpose.

And this woman who lived her life like a queen would support the Prophet (ﷺ) with everything that she had. And subhanAllah! Even when times got so tough in the boycott on Bani Hashim and Bani Muttalib (these were two tribes in Mecca) and this woman who lived her whole life in luxury is now not even able to eat. And she's in her 60's. And the only one who is delivering food is Hakeem ibn Hizaam (RA), the nephew of Khadija. He would sneak food to her and some nourishment to her and the Prophet (ﷺ). Abu Jahal caught him and even stopped that route. And this woman never says to the Prophet (ﷺ), "Look at where we are? Look at what's happened to us?" But rather she stands by him with all loyalty and she says to the Prophet (ﷺ) that she's by his side all the time.

And that's why when the Prophet (ﷺ) lost her as a result of not being able to eat and drink properly. And the Prophet (ﷺ) loses her, some sources say three days, some say three weeks, and in a matter of weeks after he loses his uncle Abu Talib.

When the Prophet (ﷺ) loses her, he was devastated. She was 65 years old whenever she died. And the Prophet (ﷺ) was still a very youthful 50-year-old man. But the Prophet (ﷺ) always remembered the loyalty that she had towards him and the Prophet (ﷺ) only showed her the greatest loyalty. And that's why Aisha (RA) says, "I never was jealous of any of the wives of the Prophet (ﷺ) except for Khadija." But because the Prophet (ﷺ) was obviously so moved every time any mention of her was made. If the Prophet (ﷺ) heard the voice of her sister calling upon him, he would say, "Allahumma Hala!" (Oh Allah, it's Hala!) And he would run because he remembered the voice of Khadija. She says, "The Prophet (ﷺ) never slaughtered a goat or a sheep except that he sent some of it to Khadija's friends. And anytime she was mentioned it would be visible on the Prophet's (ﷺ) face that he was moved. And he would send gifts to her friends out of his loyalty to her (ﷺ). And she says, "One time I got jealous and I said to the Prophet (ﷺ), 'should you have gotten now this old woman of Quraish with that Allah (SWT) has replaced with something better?'" The Prophet (ﷺ) became so angry, He says, "I swear by Allah, Allah did not give me something better than her." And he started to mention all forms of loyalty- "آمنت بي إذ كفر بي الناس" ['aamanat bi 'ith kafar bi alnaas] – she believed in me when no one else believed in me. "وصدقتني إذ كذبني الناس" [wasaddaqatnee 'ith kathabanee alnaas] – and she trusted me and considered me truthful when other people belied me and denied me. "وأنفقت بي إذ حرمني الناس" [w 'anfaqat bi 'ith haramani al naas] – and she spent on me when no one else would spend on me. "ورزقني الله ولدها" [warazaqani Allahu waladaha] – and Allah (SWT) gave me children from her. "إذ حرمني أولاد النساء" ['ith haramani awlaad al nisaa'] – And Allah (SWT) did not give me children from anyone else.

And subhanAllah! In honor of Khadija is that it was only the children that were given to the Prophet (ﷺ) through her that the lineage of the Prophet (ﷺ) would survive. SubhanAllah!

When the Prophet (ﷺ) saw even in the battle of Badr, when al-'Aas, who was married to the Prophet (ﷺ) and Khadija's daughter, Zaynab (may peace be upon her), al-'Aas was married to her before jahiliyyah (before Islam) and here you had the Prophet (ﷺ) capturing his son-in-law who came to kill him and who came to fight against him. Zaynab sends her necklace, the necklace that was given to her by her mother Khadija on her wedding night as ransom for al-'Aas; her husband.

The Prophet (ﷺ) sees that necklace and it moves him so much that the Prophet (ﷺ) says to the sahaba (Companions), "If you will, send her back her prisoner and send her back this necklace." Why did he say, "If you will?" Because it wouldn't be fair to the sahaba who had to observe all of these rules and if the Prophet (ﷺ) exercised that exception just for himself. So he said to the sahaba, "if you all will…send back her prisoner, her husband and send back that necklace."

Because of her loyalty to the Prophet (ﷺ), Jibreel (Gabriel), the one who was sent with the revelation of the Qur'an is sent by Allah (SWT) to the Prophet (ﷺ) to give salam; salam (greeting) not to the Prophet (ﷺ) per se. but to Khadija.

He says to the Prophet (ﷺ) that your wife Khadija is coming to you right now and Allah (SWT) sends his salam (greeting). And Jibreel (Gabriel) too sends his salam to her. And gives her the glad tidings of a house in paradise with no noise and no distress.

SubhanAllah! Because of what she provided to the Prophet (ﷺ) in this life of silence and tranquility and contentment and also provided the Prophet (ﷺ) not with stress, but rather she was a source of stress relief and it was when the Prophet (ﷺ) lost Khadija that the scholars say, "that's when Allah (SWT) gave the Prophet (ﷺ) salah (prayer)." That's when Allah gave the Prophet (ﷺ) those five daily prayers. He lost his emotional support in Khadija and RasulAllah tasted the bitterness of this dunya (earth) and that's when Allah (SWT) gave him salah (prayer). SubhanAllah! To replace that emotional loss, that emotion devastation of the Prophet (ﷺ). And when Rasulullah (ﷺ) went back to Mecca, the only one he remembered whenever they told the Prophet (ﷺ), "Where would you like us to place your tent? Where would you like us to have your residence? Would you like to stay in this person's house or that person's house?" The Prophet (ﷺ) said no, I want to stay in Hijoon, which is where Khadija was buried. And just as she believed in him, emotionally supported him and financially supported the Prophet (ﷺ) responded to each one of those supports with dua and with love and with loyalty. And we take from that woman the beautiful character of loyalty and good manners.

We ask Allah to make us like the Prophet (ﷺ) and Khadija in all of our affairs but specifically our marriages. We ask Allah (SWT) to grant us the concept of loyalty and that great character. And we ask Allah (SWT) to better our iman as a result. Allahumma Ameen.

Four advice from the Quran

✓ Spend wealth in charity (57:7)

✓ Cooperate in righteousness (5:2)

✓ I only complain of my suffering and my grief to Allah (12:86)

✓ Help one another in acts of piety and righteousness. And do not assist each other in acts of sinfulness and transgression. And be aware of Allah. Verily, Allah is severe in punishment. (5:2)

Narrated Salim's father: The Prophet (ﷺ) said, "If the wife of anyone of you asks permission to go to the mosque, he should not forbid her." (Al-Bukhari, 5238)

"Indeed, the Muslim men and Muslim women, the believing men and believing women, the obedient men and obedient women, the truthful men and truthful women, the patient men and patient women, the humble men and humble women, the charitable men and charitable women, the fasting men and fasting women, the men who guard their private parts and the women who do so, and the men who remember Allah often and the women who do so – for them Allah has prepared forgiveness and a great reward." (Quran, 33:35)

"When you forget that you need Allah (God), He puts you in a situation that causes you to call upon Him. And that's for your own good." Omar Suleiman

A thought-provoking questions you should ask yourself every day

Am I holding onto something I need to let go of?

Practical Ways to Improve Yourself

<u>**Acknowledge your flaws**</u>

Everyone has flaws. What's most important is to understand them, acknowledge them, and address them.

<u>**Stop making excuses**</u>

You can't expect to change if you keep making excuses for anything that goes wrong with you, because you won't see anything that needs to be changed with you that way. You should take accountability for your actions and take responsibility for your decisions. You shouldn't blame anyone or anything for your mistakes. Instead, try to learn from your mistakes, which in turn will help you be a better person.

♡ GIVE YOURSELF SOME LOVE ♡

♡ 3 Physical features I love about my body:

ALHAMDULILAH
1.
2.
3.

♡ 5 Qualities I love about my personality

ALHAMDULILAH
1.
2.
3.
4.
5.

♡ 3 Things I am good at (or enjoy doing):

ALHAMDULILAH
1.
2.
3.

AISHA BINT ABI BAKR

She was truthful, daughter of the truthful, wife of the most truthful. The Prophet of Allah (peace be upon him) passed away in her lap.

Our Mother, Our Teacher, Aisha bint Abu-Bakr (may Allah be pleased with her).

You know, the Prophet salAllahu alayhi wa sallam, he treated every single one of the companions so well that they all thought they were the most beloved to him. So, Amr bin al-'As decides one day that he's going to ask the Prophet (ﷺ), in front of everyone else, "who is the most beloved person to you?" So he says, "One day we're sitting together, all the sahaba (companions) are there." So, he says, I said to the Prophet (ﷺ), "Oh Messenger of Allah, who's the most beloved person in the world to you? RasulAllah (ﷺ) says, "Aisha."

That was something that was very different because obviously in those times, they didn't treat their women very well, they were embarrassed about their relationship with their wives. The Prophet (ﷺ) said, I love my wife more than anyone else, particularly he mentioned Aisha (RA). He said, "No, no, I mean from the men." RasulAllah (ﷺ) said, "أبوها" (abooha), her father. He didn't say Abu Bakr (RA), he said her father. Still connecting Abu Bakr to her. Then Amr bin al-'As (RA) said, then who? He said, "Umar." Then Amr bin al-'As said, "I just stopped asking because I was afraid the Prophet (ﷺ) would never say my name."

So Aisha was that woman that was the most beloved to the Prophet (ﷺ). RasulAllah (ﷺ) said that comparing Aisha to all the other women in the world is like comparing the dish of thareed to all other dishes, and thareed was his favorite dish. It was a very good dish that the Arabs had, it was a delicacy. So the Prophet (ﷺ) said she's that special.

When we look at the life of Aisha, we truly do see a special woman, and this woman excelled in so many ways. There was a reason why she was so beloved to the Prophet (ﷺ).

Allah subhanahu wa ta'ala of course, revealed to the Prophet (ﷺ) in the form of a dream to marry Aisha, as the Prophet (ﷺ) saw Jibreel (Gabriel), and Jibreel (AS) directed him to Aisha, so the Prophet (ﷺ) married Aisha. Her name is as-Siddiqa Bint as-Siddiq; she's the truthful one, the daughter of the truthful one being Abu-Bakr.

Now Aisha, because she grew up primarily in Medina, at least her adult life was in Medina, she had the characteristics and the traits of the women of Ansar. She was a very assertive woman, she was a very intelligent woman, as the women of the Ansar were. And subhanAllah! We find so many incidents between her and the Prophet (ﷺ), and we learn so much from just their marital life. And subhanAllah! She gives us access to the life of the Prophet (ﷺ) that no one else could give us because she lived a very long life after the Messenger (ﷺ), she died 58 years after Hijra. So, she lived for many years after the Prophet (ﷺ).

She was very intelligent, she was a scholar, and many of the hadith come from Aisha. How the Prophet (ﷺ) slept, when the Prophet (ﷺ) would take a bath, and when the Prophet (ﷺ) would do his tasks behind closed doors, how else would we have known that was it not for Aisha. So we all owe her a great deal of love and respect because it's through her that we gained that access to the life of the Prophet (ﷺ). His qiyam, his sleeping, everything. The intimacy of the Prophet (ﷺ), the romance of the Prophet (ﷺ). It truly allows us to have that whole picture of the Messenger (ﷺ).

The argument of the Prophet (ﷺ) with his wives, and which you know, subhanAllah! We find that sometimes Aisha narrates arguments that she had with the Prophet (ﷺ), and she was wrong, and she narrates those things about herself because she wants the ummah (Muslim nation) to be educated about that, I mean who would do that? Who would actually say, I made a mistake and the Prophet (ﷺ) reprimanded me? We had this argument and I was wrong. She did that so that the ummah could learn, and that was her passion, she was a scholar. So, she taught the ummah (Muslim nation), even through her personal life, through her encounters with the Prophet (ﷺ). It only endears the Prophet (ﷺ) more by giving us that access to his life.

So, we see that the Prophet (ﷺ) used to love to joke with her. The Prophet (ﷺ), as Aisha says, "Once we were traveling with a group of companions, and the Prophet (ﷺ) told the companions, you guys go ahead, you go forward. Aisha didn't know what was going on, as they moved forward RasulAllah (ﷺ) looked at Aisha and he said, let's race. So they started to race, the Prophet (ﷺ) and Aisha." And Aisha says, "The first time I beat the Prophet (ﷺ), and she said I put on some weight, and the second time the Prophet (ﷺ) beat me, and the Prophet (ﷺ) would make fun of me for that. He would say, see? One for one." SubhanAllah! There was that level of playfulness in their relationships. Such a level of romance, a strong connection between the Prophet (ﷺ) and Aisha (RA).

She would drink from a glass and the Prophet (ﷺ) would say to Aisha, which part of the glass did you drink from? He would drink from that exact same spot.

He would take Aisha to see the Abyssinians (Ethiopian) that were doing their war dances and war games inside the mosque, and watched that until she was satisfied. The Prophet (ﷺ) loved her, and he loved to be playful with her. Even in his time of death, he joked with her. So the Prophet (ﷺ) would joke with her.

In his last few days, the Prophet (ﷺ) walks in and Aisha complains that she has a headache, she says, "My head hurts." The Prophet (ﷺ) says, "Oh Aisha, what would be better for you than dying before me, and the Prophet of Allah would wash your body, and he would do your ghusl (bath), and he would pray janaza (funeral) on you." So, the Prophet (ﷺ) was joking with Aisha in those last moments of his life; and she joked back with him. Through that, we have a fiqh ruling about the husband washing the wife at the time of death, just from that joke between the Prophet (ﷺ) and Aisha. So there was a deep love, a deep connection.

Obviously, during her lifetime Allah subhanahu wa ta'ala mentions the hadith al-ifk; the slander that was made towards Aisha, and obviously that was made by the chief of the hypocrites; Abdullah bin Ubayy bin Sulul, who accused her of adultery to hurt the Prophet (ﷺ) because everyone knew how much the Prophet (ﷺ) loved Aisha. So, Abdullah bin Ubayy bin Sulul made an accusation. He slandered her, and subhanAllah! Those were very difficult moments in the life of the Messenger (ﷺ). But, we learn something very, very precious there. It shows us the status of Aisha. You know, when Mariam/Mary was accused of what she was accused of, Allah subhanahu wa ta'ala allowed a baby to be born to her, being Isa/Jesus, and Allah subhanahu wa ta'ala allowed that baby to speak and defend her. When Yusuf; the prophet of Allah Joseph was accused of what he was accused of, Allah subhanahu wa tabula "وإذا شهد شاهد من أهلها

" (wa itha shahid shaahidun min ahliha) allowed a young man from the family of the wife of al-Aziz to bear witness to what had actually happened, and to defend Yusuf (may peace be upon him). But, Allah subhanahu wa ta'ala, with Aisha, Allah Himself took it upon Himself to reveal ten ayat (verses) to declare the innocence of Aisha, in Surah Nur, verses 10-20. That's incredible. Allah subhanahu wa ta'ala saw the honor of this woman and defended her Himself, so that shows us her status.

Now, how did the Prophet (ﷺ) pass away? RasulAllah (ﷺ) passed away in her lap. The Prophet (ﷺ) was in her lap, and his head was on her chest. The Prophet (ﷺ) looked at the siwak and Aisha said, "Do you want the siwak?" He said, "Yes." She said, "I softened it with my own teeth, and I gave it to the Prophet (ﷺ)." That's when the Prophet (ﷺ) used the siwak, then Jibreel entered upon him and gave him the choice, and the Prophet (ﷺ) choose "الرفيق الأعلى" (alrafeeq Al a'la) the high companionship, the companionship of Allah subhanahu wa ta'ala. He died, in her lap. And she said, "What an honor, subhanAllah (Glory to God)! This love that my saliva mixed with the saliva of the Prophet (ﷺ) in his last moments." SubhanAllah! So that connection cannot be taken away.

We're just talking about her status just regarding the Prophet (ﷺ). Aisha once had a dream that three moons fell into her lap. So she asked her father, Abu Bakr (RA), she said, what does this dream mean? Abu Bakr was a skilled dream interpreter. So Abu Bakr, he said to her that there is going to be good news that's going to come to you. And when RasulAllah (ﷺ) passed away, RasulAllah (ﷺ) was buried in that same area, where he passed away in her room. The Prophet (ﷺ) was buried, Abu Bakr came to Aisha and said, the first of those moons have fallen, and he is better than the other two moons. And subhanAllah, the prophecy of that dream was that in the room of Aisha, the Prophet (ﷺ) would be buried, then Abu Bakr, then Umar. Of course, Aisha wanted the spot that Umar would be buried in for herself, but when Umar made that request, she recognized how significant it would be for Umar to be buried next to the Prophet

(ﷺ) and Abu Bakr as Siddiq.

So she had a very special status. Obviously, all of the wives of the Prophet do, Allah subhanahu wa ta'ala called them the Mothers of the Believers. But just in her personality, you know, she was the knowledgeable of all the women "أعلم نساء الأرض" (a'lam nisaa al ard) she was the most knowledgeable of all of the women.

By the way, this counters a lot of the claims that are made against Aisha, and against the Prophet (ﷺ) for marrying her while she was young. She's the opposite of everything that you would expect from a young girl that was supposedly forced into a marriage at a young age. She was confident, assertive, knowledgeable, eloquent. She loved her husband; she loved the Prophet (ﷺ), she was jealous of the Prophet (ﷺ)'s other wives. But, her knowledge, Imam az-Zuhri says that she was the most knowledgeable of all of the wives of the Prophet (ﷺ), he said in fact if you took all of the knowledge of all of the wives of the Prophet (ﷺ), and compared it to the knowledge of Aisha, her knowledge was more.

Urwah ibn Zubair; who was her nephew; there are beautiful narrations of Urwah, for example, walking in one day and seeing Aisha reading for an entire day and night, one ayah (verse) from the Quran, standing up, crying and making dua. The ayah from Surah at-Tur, فَمَنَّ اللَّهُ عَلَيْنَا وَوَقَانَا عَذَابَ السَّمُومِ, (famanna Allahu AAalayna wawaqanaAAathaba assamoom), "Allah was kind to us and protected us from the punishment, from the grievous punishment." Urwah is the one who got to see that because Urwah was her nephew. So Urwah gives us some of her personal virtues, and he also narrates many of the hadith and seerah from Aisha. Urwah, he says, I have heard the speeches of Abu Bakr, and the speeches of Umar, and the speeches of Uthman, and the speeches of Ali, and he says that there is no person, none of them was as eloquent as Aisha. She was a better speaker, she was more eloquent than all of them, even khulafa ar-rashideen (four khalifa). He said she was the most knowledgeable in fiqh, she was the most knowledgeable in hadith, he said she even excelled everyone else, she passed everyone else in her knowledge of poetry, and her knowledge of medicine. SubhanAllah! She became knowledgeable, a faqhi, a scholar in all of those different regards. So Aisha surpasses everyone in those regards.

Abu Musa al-Ashari said, whenever we, the companions, couldn't figure something out, we just went to Aisha, and she always had clarity on the issue. Even on issues of inheritance, which are the hardest. She always was able to figure it out. Her fiqh was that great. She was that knowledgeable, she was such a genius. Again, eloquent, assertive, she was the shaykha (scholar), she was the teacher of all of the other sahaba (companions). Urwah said, there was not a scholar from among the companions, except that I saw him seeking knowledge from Aisha, so she is the shaykha of all of the other companions.

Through her, we have 2,210 hadith. Can you imagine? 2,210 hadith that give us access to the life of the Prophet (ﷺ) that otherwise we simply would not have.

Again, she lived for many, many, many years and taught the ummah, and educated the ummah. And she lays the ground. She shows us that a woman can have a role in society, can be a scholar, can be a speaker, and maintain her modesty at the same time. Aisha (RA) did not need to do anything immodest to hold that position. She maintained her modesty, and at the same time excelled in every single way. May Allah subhanahu wa ta'ala have mercy upon her, and allow us to meet with our mother Aisha (RA) in Jannat ul-Firdous. Allah humma.

FOUR ADVICE FROM THE QURAN

✓ "Allah will exalt those who believe among you, and those who have been granted knowledge to high ranks." (Qur'an 58:11)

✓ "…they could devote themselves to studies in religion, and admonish the people when they return to them, – that thus they (may learn) to guard themselves (against evil)" (9:122)

✓ And those who strive in Our (cause), – We will certainly guide them to our Paths: For verily Allah is with those who do right (29:69)

✓ So when the Quran is recited, then listen to it and pay attention that you may receive mercy. (7:204)

"He grants wisdom to whom He pleases, and whoever is granted wisdom, he indeed is given a great good and none but men of understanding mind." (2:269)

رَبِّ زِدْنِي عِلْمًا "O my Lord! Increase me in knowledge" (20:114)

It was narrated that Anas bin Malik said: "The Messenger of Allah said: 'Allah has His own people among mankind.' They said: 'O Messenger of Allah, who are they?' He said: 'The people of the Qur'an, the people of Allah and those who are closest to Him." (Sunan Ibn e Majah, Book of Sunnah, Hadith no 214, Classified as Sahih By Allama Albani)

It was narrated that Abu Hurairah said: "The Messenger of Allah said: 'Allah wills good for a person, He causes him to understand the religion.'" (Sunan Ibn e Majah, Book of Sunnah, Hadith no 220, Classified as Sahih By Allama Albani)

"Sell this life for the next and you win both of them. Sell the next life for this and you lose both of them." (Hasan al-Basri)

A thought-provoking questions you should ask yourself every day

What do I want most in life?

Practical Ways to Improve Yourself

Read every day

When you're reading every day, you will feed your brain with more and more knowledge.

Be more self-aware

In order to become a better person, you should learn to notice yourself and know how you behave in different situations. Then you'll know when to improve yourself if you do something improperly, and continue to do what you're doing right. This point is very important because you can't be a better person if you don't know what you should improve of yourself in the first place.

☠ TOXIC TRIGGERS ☠

Write the things that make you feel low about yourself. Now identify whether you can change them or not. If you can, keep them on your self-improvement to-do list. If you can't, then forget about them and focus on the self-love section contents (things you've been blessed with).

THINGS THAT HURT YOUR SELF-ESTEEM:	CAN YOU CHANGE THEM?
Example 1: Hearing that I'm dark-skinned.	No, that's how Allah has made me.
Example 2: The fact that I'm overweight	Yes, I just need to lose 10 pounds.
1.	
2.	
3.	
4.	
5.	

KHALID IBN AL-WALID

"On the day of the Battle of Mu'tah, nine swords were broken in my hand, and nothing was left in my hand except a Yemenite sword of mine."

In my never-ending search for inspiration from history, let me introduce you all to Khalid ibn al-Walid, known as the Sword of Allah. Whatever you think of the era of Arab conquests, it would be intellectual dishonesty not to pay homage to this the fiercest and the most successful Arab warlord of all time.

Khalid was a companion of the Prophet (peace be upon him) and the commander of his army. It was under his military leadership that Arabia, for the first time, was united under a single political entity, the Caliphate. He then helped expand the Rashidun Caliphate during the early Muslim conquests, defeating armies of the Sasanian Persian Empire and Byzantine Roman Empire.

Khalid commanded the army of the Caliph in fifty major pitched battles, and over 150 skirmishes (unpremeditated fighting) and sieges -over 200 military engagements all told. He was never defeated even once -a record that is almost absurdly flawless, and unmatched in world history by almost any metric you want to measure it. He defeated the superpower of not one but two superpowers of the age, all while being massively outnumbered and out-equipped in virtually every encounter.

Strategically brilliant Khalid was especially adept at lighting marches, dictating the flow of events with an astonishing speed of his army and a superb understanding of terrain. Tactically he was almost flawless: his favorite tactic was to pin his opponent with a frontal assault and then using his light Arab cavalry to outflank and encircle his enemies.

To put the quality of his generalship in context, it is worth mentioning that in the dozens of battles and skirmishes against the Sassanid Empire (perhaps the greatest military power of its day famed for its invincible cataphract heavy cavalry) al-Walid was heavily outnumbered in each battle and yet every encounter he fought ended in a decisive Rashidun victory. It was Khalid who conquered Firaz, the capital of the Sassanid Persia, Damascus and even Jerusalem itself.

Khalid is also the only general to hold a distinction of inflicting a major defeat on the Prophet (peace be upon him) himself in a pitched battle, before Khalid's conversion to Islam.

> "The son of Al-Walid has come! Is there anyone here who will duel me!?"

Perhaps the most unique aspect of Ibn Walid was his habit of challenging the enemy generals and champions to single combat before the battle. In pre-Islamic Arab, Byzantine and Sassanian warfare, battles usually began with duels between the champion warriors of the opposing armies -there were specialized units for this purpose known as the Mubarizun (Arabic: مبارزون, "duelists", or "champions"), but Al-Walid refused to gain victory by gazing at the backs of his men. Despite the enormous risk to his forces in losing their commander before the battle even started, a win would ruin the morale of the opponents -a chance Khalid was willing to take in every single battle he fought. The best military minds of two great empires couldn't produce a commander or even a soldier to beat this genius. Dozens of the greatest warriors of the age lost their lives dueling the Sword of Allah, including Hazar Mard (known as 'the hundred men'), Arab Christian chief Abdul-Aswad, Thomas the Byzantine and many, many others.

> "When I am on the battlefield, I love it more than my wedding night with the most beautiful

of women."

To learn something of the character of the man behind the myth, we can turn to his correspondence. The Byzantine emperor Heraclitus sent the following message to Khalid after the Arab general had defeated Emperor's son-in-law Thomas in a duel and broken his army:

"I have come to know what you have done to my army. You have killed my son-in-law and captured my daughter. You have won and got away safely. I now ask you for my daughter. Either return her to me on payment of ransom or give her to me as a gift, for honor is a strong element in your character'."

Khalid sent this simple message back: "Take her as a gift, there shall be no ransom."

No enemy could bring him down, but eventually, the new Caliph Umar relieved A-Walid of his command. Khalid, who enjoyed an immense prestige amongst the army and the people could have easily challenged the new ruler and claimed the throne for himself, but instead, he accepted the authority of the new ruler and honored his vow by saying:

"If you were to appoint a small child over me, I would obey him."

Within less than four years of his dismissal, Khalid died and was buried in 642 in Emesa, where he lived since his retirement from military services. His last words were:

"I've fought in so many battles seeking martyrdom that there is no spot in my body left without a scar or a wound made by a spear or sword. And yet here I am, dying on my bed like an old camel. May the eyes of the cowards never rest."

His prestige was such that the strict religious rule forbidding women weeping in funerals was lifted by the Caliph the only time in history.

Khalid is buried along with his son in a corner of this mosque in Homs which has now been partially destroyed in the ongoing war in Syria.

When we remember the great generals of the past, we rightfully recall Alexander the Great, Hannibal and Caesar, as well as Napoleon and Frederick the Great, but we should also pay respects to commander such as Khalid Ibn al-Walid, the Sword of Allah.

BATTLE OF YARMOUK

On a warm August day in 636 CE, the Arab army under Khalid ibn al-Walid challenged the supremacy of the mighty Byzantine Empire. The two armies stared each other down across the grassy field of the Yarmouk plateau, while the vultures circled above. One Arab warrior stepped forward, crying out: "I am the killer of Romans, I am the scourgesent upon you!" The battle that would change the course of history is about the take place…

After the Prophet's (ﷺ) death in 632, the First Caliph Abu Bakr coordinated military campaigns, over vast territories of Arabia, turning the peninsula into a stronghold of Islam. This expansion was spearheaded by battle-hardened and experienced commanders, most notably Khalid ibn al-Walid. The most dependable commander for the Prophet (peace be upon him) and his successors.

The Caliph's goal to bring all Arab tribal groups under Rashidun rule, including those in the steppes and cities of Iraq and Syria, led to the first direct clashes with the Byzantines and Sassanians. The two empires had been at war with each other for decades and the prolonged conflict exhausted the two super-powers. The

Byzantines formally restored control over their territories, but decades of war brought political and economic strife across their territory in the Levant, and the Imperial authority wasn't yet fully re-established beyond the Dead Sea in the south-east. Foreign policy changed as well. The Empire stopped subsidizing many tribal groups that fought on their side, deeming this financial expenditure was no longer needed now that the war against the Sassanians was won. Instead, they began building defensive coalitions with nomadic groups of northern Hejaz to guard Syria against the southeast, extending their political control into Arabia, thereby directly threatening the Muslims who sought to unite Arab tribes under the banner of Islam. Hence Abu Bakr needed to assert Rashidun influence in the direction of Syria before the Byzantines could make headway in pulling this area into their sphere of influence.

In early 633, four Arab armies entered Byzantine territory, commanded by Amr ibn al-As, Shurahbil ibn Hasana, Yazid ibn Abi Sufyan, and Abu Ubayda. They were ordered not to attack, besiege or raze any major cities. The objective of this initial phase of the campaign was to occupy the countryside inhabited predominantly by the Arabic-speaking population, many of whom would join the Islamic cause, thus swelling Rashidun ranks and providing valuable logistical support. These early operations laid the groundwork for the upcoming invasion and, ironically, Abu Bakr's focus on the countryside would fool the Byzantines into perceiving the Muslims as mere raiders, and therefore no significant Imperial forces were assembled to combat the threat in early 633.

Meanwhile, in the east, Caliph's orders were the same – bring the Arab tribes of Iraq into the fold. From the south, Abu Bakr dispatched Khalid, his most trusted commander, in early spring. As the army assembled, the core of Khalid's force of loyal volunteers was augmented by troops from several tribes across

Arabia. Some of these tribes fought against Medina in the Ridda Wars, but some sections remained loyal, and it was these troops that now reinforced the campaign against the Sassanians.

What followed was one of Khalid's greatest strategic achievement. The swift conquest of Sassanian lands west of the Euphrates in a series of battles would be a display of true tactical genius. With his versatile implementation of the Indirect Approach, Khalid would attack opposing armies from unexpected directions with multiple rapid flanking maneuvers.

Furthermore, he was one of only a few commanders in history who used Double Envelopment to encircle and destroy armies larger than his own, launching perfectly timed cavalry attacks on the opponent's flanks. This daring war of movement reflected his lightning-fast conquest of the territory west of the Euphrates. Then, as he laid the groundwork for Rashidun administration and planned the offensive into central Iraq and the Sassanian capital, a message arrived from the Caliph – Khalid was to urgently march to Syria to take command of the invasion of the Byzantine Empire.

In April 634, he departed Iraq with a small force of veterans whose loyalty to Islam was absolute, striking out across the desert towards Syria – a most perilous of journeys. The troops couldn't carry enough water to last until they reached Syria, so Khalid forced twenty of the camels to drink large quantities of water, then tied their mouths so they wouldn't spoil it by eating or chewing their cud. Camels would then be slaughtered daily and the preserved water in their stomachs would quench the thirst of the troops. The march through largely waterless country lasted for SIX days, becoming one of Khalid's most famous military feats.

Upon entering Syria he moved south-west to meet with the three Muslim armies near Damascus, capturing forts and towns along the way. Byzantine garrisons were caught completely by surprise, not expecting that Muslim troops could enter their territory from an inhospitable desert.

So far the Empire relied on a system of forts along the border that would relay information about enemy troop movements to the interior, giving the Imperial army time to mobilize and respond to the threat. The prevailing mindset was that any attack that penetrated the interior would eventually be repulsed, thus any loss of territory would only be temporary. But by now the Muslims gained full control over rural areas in the southeast and with Khalid's arrival; the Caliph turned his full attention to the conquest of important Syrian towns.

Bostra fell first, and the four Muslim armies marched towards Palestine to join Amr ibn al-As, who was facing a large concentration of Byzantine troops commanded by Emperor Heraclius' brother Theodore. The Byzantines reportedly recruited Bedouin-Christian spies and were able to anticipate the movement of the Muslim army, managing to position themselves for the upcoming attack.

The Battle of Ajnadayn, the first major engagement, was bitterly fought. Many prominent Muslims fell as martyrs on the field of battle, but under Khalid's leadership, the Arabs managed to wipe out the presence of the Byzantine field army in Syria and were now advancing north.

Theodore retreated to join the emperor at Emesa, while remnants of the Imperial army fled in disorder to nearby walled cities and forts, with many of the survivors converging on Pella, joining the garrison that was stationed there.

Alarmed by Khalid's rapid advance, Heraclius dispatched two contingents to fortify key roads south of Damascus, to give the city time to prepare for a siege that was soon coming, and then subsequently headed for Antioch to begin preparations to deal with the Arab threat.

But the Byzantines were not able to hold Khalid's advance for long, as the Muslim army outmaneuvered their entrenched positions and proceeded to surround Damascus two days later. The siege lasted for 20 days and, after a Byzantine relief force was defeated, the city capitulated.

But then came news from Medina that Caliph Abu Bakr died about a month earlier, making Umar ibn al-Khattab, Khalid's cousin, his successor. Aware of Khalid's popularity, the deeply religious Umar demoted him and placed Abu Ubayda in charge of the Muslim army, aiming to show that no matter who commands the troops, it is Allah alone who gives victory on the battlefield. Under the command of the more cautious Abu Ubayda, the Muslim advance continued at a slower pace over the coming months. He divided the army in two, advancing north with the majority of the troops, while sending two armies to capture Palestine, where several strong Byzantine garrisons remained in the rear during the initial rapid Muslim advance. Meanwhile, in Antioch, Heraclius wasn't sitting idle. He displayed the military might of the Byzantine Empire as five armies assembled and began their march back into Syria from multiple directions, under the overall command of Vahan, an Armenian general. Furthermore, Heraclius sent word to all major cities, reminding the people of the Byzantine superiority after recent victories against the Sassanians. The message was clear - that Syria belonged to the Empire was a fact of life after centuries of Byzantine rule and the current situation, while alarming, was a setback that will be dealt with. Heraclius' army was prepared to defeat the Arabs in a decisive battle or destroy their separate army's piece meal. Upon learning of the initial movement of enemy troops Khalid immediately recognized that the Muslim position in the north will be surrounded by the numerically superior Byzantine army.

He urged Abu Ubayda to abandon northern Syria and retreat south to a stronger position where the rest of their forces could join them. After some consideration, Abu Ubayda ordered the army to march south. Messengers were sent to the two commanders in Palestine to meet with the main army on the north-east of the vast plain of Lake Tiberias, which offered plenty of fodder for the horses and were conducive to cavalry maneuvers. And, just as Khalid had suspected, four Imperial armies marched on Emesa, which would've pinned the Arabs in the north, while another Byzantine army was to re-capture Damascus and cut off their line of retreat – the Muslim army withdrew just in time.

Meanwhile, Yazdegerd negotiated with Heraclius to mount an offensive from the east. However, the Sassanian army would not be ready in time for a simultaneous attack.

Back west, faced against a massive Byzantine army, Abu Ubayda sent word to Caliph Umar to send all available reinforcements to Syria. And, as the Muslim armies met, scouts reported that a strong Byzantine garrison gathered at Caesarea. This made encamping on the plains near Lake Tiberias a dangerous proposition, as the Arab army could now potentially be attacked on two sides.

Abu Ubayda again heeded Khalid's advice to move the army to a stronger position on the eastern end of the Yarmouk plateau. With the battle looming, Khalid was recognized as the ablest field commander and was given temporary control of the troops, while Abu Ubayda remained in overall strategic command.

And the Byzantine army followed close behind.

The Yarmouk plateau is predominantly an undulated flat plain, dotted with rocky outcrops. Rivers Yarmuk, Ruqqad, 'Allan and Harir slice deep into the level plateau, creating deep gorges with steep cliffs. The grassy plain offered enough fodder and several springs to supply both armies.

And the Byzantines were not in a rush. Vahan was instructed by the emperor to try and pay off the Muslims to go back to Arabia, or at the very least to stall negotiations until the Sassanians were ready to attack in Iraq. Jabalah and Gregory did much of the mediation, but as the talks dragged on for up to three months, reinforcements sent by Umar began arriving. Concerned that he might lose the numerical advantage, Vahan took matters into his own hands and asked to negotiate with Khalid in person.

By his own words, the Armenian general regarded the Arabs as nothing more than "impoverished, hungry, wretched Bedouins" and he offered Khalid food and gold to leave Byzantine lands. Unimpressed by Vahan's condescendence, Khalid responded: "It is not hunger that brought us here…" calling on the Christian general to embrace Islam in exchange for peace, adding: "If you refuse there can only be a war between us... and you will face men who love death as you love life." Enraged, Vahan fired a warning: "Better men tried to take our lands but were all defeated." Negotiations were over…

Vahan positioned the main Byzantine camp near al-Yaqusah from where one of the main Roman roads connecting Egypt and Syria could be defended. He anchored his battle line to the gorge in the south and arrayed his troops along the 'Allan river, stretching to the town of Jabiyah in the north. On his left flank, he placed the Slavic infantry, commanded by Qanatir, a Slavic prince. In the center, Jabalah commanded the Ghassanid contingent, while Dairjan led the Armenians. Gregory commanded the experienced Greek infantry on the right flank. It is said that the last Roman legion, the Macedonian 5th, was under his command. Archers were mixed with the infantry. Cavalry contingents were supporting each of the four divisions of infantry. Byzantine army numbered around 40,000.

Across the field, Khalid stretched his infantry to match the length of the Byzantine line, with the left flank anchored on the gorge in the south, while his right flank reached the vicinity of the town of Nawa. He placed Amr in charge of the right flank, Shurahbil and Abu Ubayda in the center, and Yazid on the left, with archers mixed in with the infantry. Cavalry contingents were positioned to prevent breakthroughs, while Khalid took command of the handpicked cavalry reserve. The Arab army was around 25,000 strong.

The long battle line, stretching around 10km across the plain, would test the leadership of commanders on both sides. Early on August 15th, the two armies stared each other down. One Arab warrior came forward, dropped his shield and removed his armor, crying out: "I am the death of the pale faces, I am the killer of Romans, I am the scourge sent upon you, I am Zarrar Ibn al-Azwar!" Several Byzantine officers challenged the Muslim champion. In a matter of minutes, Zarrar cut them down in single combat. More Muslim champions stepped forward, and as the dueling spectacle continued Byzantine troops witnessed the slaying of many of their officers.

Then, at noon, Vahan ordered the army to advance. Using his numerical advantage to extend the front, he forced Khalid to stretch his infantry thin, and he planned to probe the Muslim line for any weak spots that he could punch through.

As the Byzantine army closed the distance, Vahan ordered a third of his infantry to advance on the enemy. The fighting was not too intensive, as both sides tested each other's resolve. Nevertheless, Vahan was surprised by the determination of Arab troops. He observed that the deep gorge to the south would restrict cavalry maneuvers and offer some protection to the Muslim left flank, while the terrain to the north was open, leaving the Muslim right exposed. Khalid was also aware of this problem and he positioned himself slightly closer to the right-wing so that he could reinforce it quickly, if necessary.

As the day began drawing to a close, Vahan broke off the attack and ordered his troops back into position on the 'Allan river. During the night both commanders contemplated their next move. Khalid knew that a frontal assault against a better equipped and more numerous enemy would be dangerous, especially when supported by contingents of Byzantine heavy cavalry. Vahan, meanwhile, was ready to attack and break the Muslims.

Early the next morning, the Byzantine commander committed all of his troops forward. He intended to catch the Muslims unprepared during their morning prayers. But Khalid expected this. During the previous night, he ordered the construction of outposts in front of his line to prevent any surprise attacks.

Despite losing the element of surprise, Vahan remained confident in his drilled veterans. The Byzantine commander planned to apply steady pressure against the Muslim center in order to tie down as many of Khalid's troops as possible while focusing the main thrust of his attack on the flanks where he expected to overwhelm and drive the enemy from the field with his superior numbers.

As the two armies clashed, Khalid's men held their ground in the center against the stalled Byzantine advance. But for his troops on the flanks, the situation was different…

Qanatir attacked Khalid's right flank in force. The outnumbered Muslim infantry held fast but was pushed back. Amr ordered his cavalry to check the Byzantine advance in order to buy time for the infantry. The cavalry counterattack blunted the Byzantine charge, but Qanatir kept pushing the Muslims back toward their camp. Women from the camp rallied, and some joined the fighting. They hobbled the camels around the camp, thus providing additional protection. A desperate struggle ensued as the Byzantines could not dislodge the determined Muslim fighters. Qanatir's heavy cavalry bogged down as their horses balked at the smell of aggressive camels, refusing to respond to the commands of their riders. In close quarters, the legs and bellies of the partially armored Byzantine horses now became exposed and many of the heavily armored riders were pulled down from their saddles. Qanatir could not sustain the attack any longer…

With Vahan's attack against the Muslim right flank broken, Khalid seized the moment to exploit the gap that had opened up between

Qanatir and the Byzantine center. He ordered Amr to send his cavalry regiment and attack Qanatir's flank from the north. With incoming cavalry support, Amr ordered a general advance. The three-pronged attack forced Qanatir to abandon his advanced position and retreat towards the main Byzantine line. By timing his flanking maneuver to perfection Khalid managed to push the Byzantines back with fewer troops. Had it not been for the disciplined retreat of Qanatir's experienced Slavic infantry the Byzantine flank could've collapsed entirely. But the situation on the Muslim left was considerably more serious…

With much of Khalid's mounted units currently on the right flank, Yazid's position was being overrun. Byzantine cavalry broke through the ranks and pushed towards the Muslim camp. Gregory's infantry slowly ground their way forward as Yazid's outnumbered infantry could not stop them. As they fell back to the camp, Yazid's troops were met with a barrage of insults and rocks thrown at them by the ferocious Arab women who urged them to not let the enemy defeat them, with some of the women taking part in the defense of the camp. Yazid was finally able to stabilize his line near the camp, temporarily stemming from the Byzantine assault.

Just as Vahan's plan appeared to be succeeding on the Muslim left, Khalid again showed his ability to adapt quickly. With the right flank stabilized he dashed across the battlefield to aid the embattled Yazid. He detached a cavalry contingent under the command of Dharar ibn al-Azwar, ordering him to round the Byzantine center. This decision proved crucial, for when Dharar struck the flank of the Byzantine center, he fixed them in place, preventing reinforcements from reaching Gregory to support his push against the Muslim left. But most importantly this maneuver gave the impression to the Greeks that they were being outflanked, damaging their morale. Further on the left flank, Khalid came to Yazid's aid, Hatting Gregory's division. The Greeks gave ground under pressure, suffering particularly heavy casualties. During the fighting in the center, Dharar's troops killed the Byzantine commander Dairjan, who fought with his troops in the front. Finally, as dusk approached the two exhausted armies ceased hostilities for the day.

For Vahan, losing one of his key lieutenants was an enormous blow and the speed of Khalid's counterattacks exposed weaknesses in his plan, forcing him to change tack. The battle resumed with the Byzantines again advancing on the Muslim line.

This time, however, Vahan focused mainly on Khalid's right flank where the Byzantine heavy cavalry could do more damage. Bitter fighting ensued as the Byzantine heavy cavalry charge outmatched Arab light mounted units. Amr's division fell back, followed shortly by Shurahbil. As Jabalah's flank slowly became exposed, Khalid sprang into action at this critical moment, charging into the gap towards the Ghassanid flank. Finally, Amr managed to rally his forces and re-engage.

Shurahbil too reorganized after taking some losses and went on the offensive. The fighting developed into a bloodbath as the outflanked Ghassanids took a heavy beating and retreated in disarray. Seeing Jabalah disengaging, Qanatir too withdrew in good order. Khalid's well-timed flanking attack again stopped the Byzantines.

The next day, Vahan persisted with the same battle plan. Qanatir leads the Slavs against Amr's division. Jabalah's Ghassanid division, now reinforced by Vahan's Armenians, advanced on Shurahbil. As soon as they met the Byzantine charge, the Muslims were hard-pressed. Arab light cavalry was especially having trouble holding the push of the Imperial cataphracts. Meanwhile, Vahan ordered the Armenians and Greeks forward, at a slower pace. Khalid now feared a general Byzantine assault along the entire line. He understood that considering the losses on the previous day, he no longer had the numbers to repulse a general advance by Imperial troops, and his cavalry reserve would not be able to reinforce both flanks at the same time. To avert disaster, Khalid sent Abu Ubayda and Yazid forward, aiming to stall Vahan's advance and buy some time for his troops on the right. He then hastily rushed towards the gaps that opened between Shurahbil and Amr, as their lines started buckling under the weight of the Byzantine attack.

Meanwhile, the Muslim left held the initial Byzantine push, but Vahan reinforced the attack with horse archers, subjecting the Arabs to ceaseless barrages of arrows. The point-blank volleys caused such losses to Abu Ubayda's and Yazid's divisions that the incident became known as the "Day of Lost Eyes." Unable to withstand the storm of arrows, the Muslim left retreated to get out of range of Byzantine archers.

On the other side of the battlefield, Amr rallied his forces and halted Qanatir's advance, while Khalid shored up Shurahbil's ranks and pressed Jabalah's division. The Ghassanids fought stubbornly, but having taken heavy losses they slowly gave ground.

Now that he was committed to the right, Khalid's worst fear was realized - Gregory ordered the general advance of his division, sensing that the Arabs were shaken by the losses they took from Byzantine arrow volleys. Sure enough, Yazid's battered division gave way, with Abu Ubayda barely holding Vahan's Armenians. With the Rashidun left in dire straits, Arab women from the camp picked up weapons and joined the fighting. The desperate last stand of the women inspired the Muslims to hold their ground against all odds. Meanwhile, on the right, the Byzantines finally retreated after several hours of fighting, and the rest of Vahan's line soon followed.

The fourth day of the battle was devastating for the Arabs, particularly the left-wing. But incredibly they managed to hold back the Byzantines.

The next morning, Vahan unexpectedly sent an emissary, offering a truce. Arab commanders met for an impromptu war council. Some argued to accept the truce, seeing it as a victory after fighting a much larger army deep within enemy territory, while others noted that the men are tired, wounded and vastly outnumbered. The consensus was to leave and come back to fight another day.

Khalid listened to his comrades, then stood up saying: "The past four days tested our resolve." "Now is not the time to concede, now is the time to be decisive!" He argued that the strategy was to be on the defensive, wear out the enemy, then counter-attack. And now he sensed that the Byzantines lost heart and that Vahan was trying to buy time to raise the morale of his troops. The time to attack is now! There would be no truce...

During the night Khalid inspected the troops. Wounded soldiers leaned on each other, but even in the face of such overwhelming odds their spirit never wavered. Determined to go on the offensive, the Muslim commander sent Dharar with 500 riders on a wide flanking maneuver to capture a key bridge across the Raqqad gorge that served as the mainline of communication between the Byzantine army and their camp…

The fightback has begun. As the sun rose on the next day, from the Byzantine line a hulking figure trotted out on his warhorse into the no man's land. It was Gregory, the commander of the Byzantine right flank, reputed to be a formidable fighter. Abu Ubayda answered the challenge. As the overall strategic commander of Arab forces in Syria, before leaving he told Khalid: "If I don't return you shall resume command of the army after the battle until the Caliph decides otherwise."

And with that, the tall, slim figure of Abu Ubayda, a man in his 50's, rode out to meet Gregory. The two met in the middle, both excellent in single combat.

Circling each other they traded blows for several minutes, as both armies anxiously watched. Then Gregory ran back towards his line – a trick designed to fool Abu Ubayda into lowering his guard. As the Arab general caught up with him, in a split second Gregory turned to strike, Abu Ubayda ducked to evade the blow, striking the Greek general across the neck with his blade. Gregory dropped his sword and slumped from his horse. Moments later Khalid ordered the Muslim line forward!

Having spent most of the night reorganizing the troops, Khalid left a token force of cavalry behind the infantry divisions, spreading their formations to make it appear to the Byzantines like the disposition of the Arab army remained the same as it was during the previous days, and he took all of the remaining cavalries, hiding it in the shallow dips of the plateau. Some of the men in the Byzantine line could hardly believe that, despite such heavy losses, the Muslim army went on the offensive.

As the clash in the center erupted, the Arabs pressed hard. They were determined to drive the enemy back, but their substantial numerical disadvantage meant that they could not sustain this battle of attrition for long. Just as Vahan's troops managed to slow the momentum of the Muslim advance, Khalid sprung his trap. From the gentle dips in the terrain 8,000 riders galloped forward. By amassing most of his cavalry Khalid planned to surround the Byzantine left flank. Knowing that time was of the essence he urged his men to ride fast and without hesitation. Speed would decide the outcome of the battle.

Busy with commanding the troops in the center, Vahan glanced to the left and saw the ominous cloud of dust. He scrambled to send his cavalry to cover the flank, realizing that the Muslim commander has outwitted him. In full gallop, Khalid surged past Amr's division and began to envelop Qanatir's Slavs. The rest of the Arab riders followed their general as he guided them around Byzantine ranks. Over his left shoulder, Khalid could see the fierce fighting in the center as he pushed his steed to go faster. Qanatir's and Jabalah's line began folding, as they braced for the impact of the Arab cavalry.

As the Muslim riders smashed into Vahan's left, Khalid pierced an enemy soldier, breaking his lance in two. He drew his sword, striking anyone in a red tunic. The horses twisted and turned, wreaking havoc among the Byzantine infantry. Jabalah and the Ghassanids disengaged and started fleeing.

But to their horror, they realized that the bridge across the Ruqqad, their main escape route, was blocked. Jabalah's troops dispersed as each man tried to save himself. Qanatir fought on bravely, but the Slavic division was surrounded and stood no chance. The entire Byzantine line began collapsing.

Shocked by Khalid's rapid maneuver, the Imperial heavy cavalry tried in vain to stem the tide. The noose was tightening as Vahan's army was being pushed back towards the cliffs. The Armenian general barked orders, and while some Byzantine units kept their cohesion, others were in total disarray. Unable to cope with the rapid movement of the Arab light cavalry, Byzantine cataphracts were attacked on all sides. Seeing that the situation was hopeless they fled, abandoning the infantry to their fate. Khalid steadied his steed, closed his eyes and whispered a prayer of gratitude. Though it was not immediately apparent, he knew that the battle was won. Vahan's army was cornered against the steep cliffs of the Raqqad and Yarmouk gorges, and over the next several hours Byzantine troops were systematically killed. Such was their desperation that hundreds, if not thousands of Imperial soldiers jumped to their deaths from the cliffs to escape the wrath of Khalid's troops. On that day the Rashidun army achieved a victory that would change the course of history forever…

The Battle of Yarmouk was certainly the battle of the century and one of the most pivotal battles in world history. The juggernaut that was the Byzantine army was made up of disciplined warriors, who probably thought they can easily outmatch the Arabic desert army.

Unfortunately for them, in Khalid ibn al-Walid they faced possibly the greatest military mind of the age. In just a few short years he restructured the rag-tag Arab forces into an army that would conquer half of the known world.

On August 20th 636, at Yarmouk, after six grueling days, only one side was left standing. Islam stepped onto the world stage...

FOUR ADVICE FROM THE QURAN

✓ Order righteousness to people only after practicing it yourself (2:44)

✓ The good deed and the bad deed are not the same. Return evil with good (41:34)

✓ Treat non-Muslims in a kind and fair manner (60:8)

✓ But (remember that an attempt at) requiting evil may, too, become an evil: Hence whoever pardons (his foe) and makes peace, his reward rests with God - for, verily, He does not love evildoers. (42:40)

"... whoso kills a soul, unless it be for murder or for wreaking corruption in the land, it shall be as if he had killed all mankind; and he who saves a life, it shall be as if he had given life to all mankind." (Quran, 5:53A

Narrated Ibn `Abbas: The Prophet (ﷺ) said, "Whoever disapproves of something done by his ruler then he should be patient, for whoever disobeys the ruler even a little (little = a span) will die as those who died in the Pre-lslamic Period of Ignorance. (i.e. as rebellious Sinners). (Al-Bukhari, 7053)

"When your private (conduct) is the same as your public, then that is good character, when your privacy is better than your public appearance, then that is virtue, and when your public appearance is better than your private, then transgression." Sufyān b. ʿUyaynah

Thought-provoking questions you should ask yourself every day

Is there someone who has hurt or angered me that I need to forgive?

Practical Ways to Improve Yourself

Set goals for yourself

Every person should have a certain aim in life. After all, we were brought into this life for a reason; build this world and work for the hereafter. For that reason, you should set goals and objectives for yourself to conquer. Write them down in a note on your phone or on a journal you keep at hand. Every time you accomplish a goal, you'll objectively learn more about yourself and figure out ways of improvement in'sha'Allah.

Slow growth is gold, fast is overrated

We are so impatient with life that when we set out to do something, we want it to be perfect right off the bat.

However, All good things in life grow slow. All great relationships, babies, trees bearing fruits, successful businesses, even the muscles on your body take their time after months of regular strength training before becoming visible!

☠ TOXIC TRIGGERS CONT... ☠

Write the names of four people with whom you spend the most time. Then identify whether their presence has a negative/ positive influence on your self-esteem. If being in their company is toxic for you (COLUMN B), spend less time with them. If you feel great being in their company, spend more time with them (COLUMN A).

PERSON 1: ....

1A) POSITIVE ATTITUDE	1B) NEGATIVE ATTITUDE
2A) CHEERFUL (MOST OF THE TIME)	2B) UNHAPPY (MOST OF THE TIME)
3A) GIVES THANKS TO ALLAH	3B) COMPLAINER

PERSON 2: ....

1A) POSITIVE ATTITUDE	1B) NEGATIVE ATTITUDE
2A) CHEERFUL (MOST OF THE TIME)	2B) UNHAPPY (MOST OF THE TIME)
3A) GIVES THANKS TO ALLAH	3B) COMPLAINER

PERSON 3: ....

1A) POSITIVE ATTITUDE	1B) NEGATIVE ATTITUDE
2A) CHEERFUL (MOST OF THE TIME)	2B) UNHAPPY (MOST OF THE TIME)
3A) GIVES THANKS TO ALLAH	3B) COMPLAINER

DEATH OF

UTHMAN IBN AFFAN

Uthman (RA) was very close to the first two caliphs, Abu Bakr and Umar ibn al Khattab, and advised both after the Propet's (peace be upon him) death. Umar ordered his fellow Muslims to form a council to elect his successor instead of nominating one. The famous "Council of Six," including Uthman and Ali, finally elected Uthman as the third caliph, which lasted 12 years until his assassination in 656.

Uthman, a merchant, made some quick economic reforms that helped trade in the Islamic lands flourish. As a result, Muslims enjoyed an economically prosperous life during his reign.

Uthman also transformed the Muslim lands into a great empire. His armies conquered Iran, Afghanistan, Armenia, Northern Africa and some Byzantine territories.

Uthman continued his predecessors' work on the Quran and commissioned a committee to produce a standard version of the text. Six copies of the standard text were produced and five of these were sent to major Muslim cities, while Uthman kept the last for himself in Medina.

Though having a pious, shy and humble character and having made Muslims richer, there was severe opposition to Uthman's rule. Some historians believe he was not strong enough to handle the opposition, while some others think he made several mistakes that angered the public, an argument that lacks proof.

Whatever the reason was, an armed opposition was formed against Uthman, and finally, the rebels laid siege to his home. Uthman refused to use force against the rebels despite his cousin and governor of Damascus Muawiyya's aid offers. He also refused to leave Medina, the place he called "Prophet's (ﷺ) city."

Summarizing the events at the end of Uthman's reign, Justice Abu Bakr ibn Al-Arabi says: "After he had properly exercised power, he was unjustly killed so that God would accomplish His purpose. He neither set out to fight, nor raised an army, nor stirred strife. He did not call upon the Muslim community to pledge their loyalty to him. Indeed, none of his peers fought against him or sought to replace him. It is unanimously agreed that no one may do that against a much lesser ruler than Uthman, let alone stand against Uthman, the Prophet's companion (may God be pleased with him).

"Reports mention the names of those who rose against Uthman. When we examine the list we find that it includes only people who had their wicked purposes foiled. They were reprimanded time and again. They stayed for a while (in Hums) where Abd Al-Rahman ibn Khalid ibn Al-Waleed warned them of severe punishment. As a result, they declared their repentance, whereupon he sent them to Uthman where again they declared that they were no longer hostile to him.

Uthman offered them a choice and they chose to travel to different provinces. When each group of them went to the land of their choice, they began to instigate rebellion against him and came back in force. He was in his garden when he spoke to them, reminding them that they should fear God and refrain from shedding his blood. Talha ibn Ubaydellah came out with tears in his eyes warning people against committing a very grave crime. Ali sent his two sons (to keep guard at the Caliph's place). The rebels said to them: 'You have sent to us to come here to support you against the one who has changed course (Islam). When we came in response to your call, this man (meaning Ali) sits in his home, while you come out with your eyes swelling with tears. By God, we will not return until we have shed his blood.'

"This was certainly an attitude of grave injustice, fabricating lies against the Prophet's companions and stating these lies to their faces. Had Uthman wished, he would have asked the Prophet's (ﷺ) companions for support and they would have immediately come to his aid. Those rebels adopted an attitude of one seeking the removal of injustice, but Uthman warned them, and they were furious. The Prophet's (ﷺ) companions wanted to stop them by force, but Uthman made it clear to them that none should fight on his account. He thus gave himself up, and the Prophet's companions let him have his choice.

This is an important question of Fiqh: Is it open to a man to give himself up, or must he defend himself? If he gives himself up and forbids others to defend him by shedding blood, is it permissible for such others to defend him against his wish? Scholars have different views on this. In short, Uthman committed no offence at any time in his reign. Nor did the Prophet's (ﷺ) companions. People should ignore any false report they may hear on these events."

This is a very concise report of the serious events leading to the assassination of Uthman, the third Caliph who was dearly loved by the Prophet (ﷺ) and the overwhelming majority of his companions. As usual, Muhibb Al-Deen Al-Khateeb adds extensive footnotes to explain what Ibn Al-Arabi had written several centuries earlier. As we have seen, Ibn Al-Arabi begins his account by saying that Uthman was unjustly killed. Al-Khateeb quotes here a Hadith related by Ahmad on the authority of Abdullah ibn Umar: "The Prophet (peace be upon him) mentioned some future trouble, and as he spoke a man passed by. The Prophet (ﷺ) added: 'This hooded man will be wrongfully killed then.' I looked up and saw the man to be

Uthman ibn Affan." This Hadith has been verified by the scholar Ahmad Shakir to be certainly authentic.

Explaining Ibn Al-Arabi's words, Al-Khateeb clarifies that Uthman never contemplated a fight against fellow Muslims. As for fighting unbelievers to ensure the spread of Islam, his reign witnessed greatly successful activities on several fronts. He never sought power for himself. In fact, he was chosen by the Muslim community without ever aspiring to be in the position of Caliph.

Al-Khateeb also endorses the statement that "none of (Uthman's) peers fought against him or sought to replace him." He explains that his peers were those nominated by Umar as candidates to succeed him. Sufficient to say here that the jihad movement that started in Abu Bakr's time came to a very long halt as a result. Imam Ibn Taimiyah says: "None of the good Muslims shared in any way in Uthman's killing, by word or deed. Those who took part in his murder were some of the worst people. Indeed, Ali ibn Abi Talib used to pray: 'My Lord! Let Your curse overwhelm Uthman's killers in land and sea, in the plains and on mountains'."

Al-Khateeb also mentions that those people were repeatedly warned against rising in rebellion. They were first warned by a number of scholars in their own provinces, like Kufah, Basrah and Egypt. They were also strongly warned by Muawiyah, the governor of Syria, after Uthman had sent them there. Abd Al-Rahman ibn Khalid, who was the governor of Hums and surrounding areas, arrested them and warned them severely, and they pretended to him that they had taken heed. He then gave them the choice of traveling to see the Caliph, and one of their leaders, Al-Ashtar Al-Nukha'ie, took up that offer. But when they arrived in Madina they took a hostile attitude. Hence, the Caliph warned them that they would put themselves in very serious trouble if they were to kill him.

Yet those rebels found in Madina a situation totally unlike what they expected. They found the great figures among the Prophet's (ﷺ) companions supporting Uthman. Ali sent his two sons to guard him in his home, and Talhah spoke to them passionately, with tears in his eyes. They expressed their surprise telling Talhah that they had received from him and others letters calling on them to come over and stop the Caliph who had adopted a course different from that of the Prophet (peace be upon him). Yet Talhah and other companions of the Prophet never wrote such letters, but apparently, letters of the sort were forged **to persuade ordinary people that by joining the rebellion, they would be putting the Muslim state back on the course followed by the Prophet (ﷺ) and his first two successors.**

Indeed, many of the Prophet's (ﷺ) companions tried to persuade Uthman to stand up to those rebels. Muawiyah suggested to him to move his capital to Syria, or that he should send him a powerful army to defend Madina against any rebellion. Uthman, however, refused all these offers, holding the rebels to their claims that they came up with complaints. He felt that if the complaint was genuine, then he should explain his case. But they did not listen to him. On the contrary, they were determined to kill him. Therefore, he felt that he would spare the Muslim community further bloodshed by sacrificing his own life. He ordered all those who came to guard his home to leave and stay in their own homes so that no more trouble should develop. He thought that by sacrificing his own life, he would let the trouble subside.

The rebels increased their pressure, and reaching the door of the house of Uthman set it on fire. Some rebels led by Muhammad ibn Abu Bakr climbed the houses of the neighbours and then jumped into the house of Uthman. It was the seventeenth day of July in the year 856 C.E. Uthman was keeping the fast that day.

The previous night he had seen Prophet (ﷺ) in a dream.

The Prophet had said, "If you wish help can be sent to you and if you want you can break your fast with us this evening. We will welcome you." Uthman opted for the second. That made Uthman know that it was his last day of life.

He prepared himself for death. He sat reading the Holy Quran, and his wife Naila sat by his side. Some rebels entered the room of Uthman, but they could not dare murder the Caliph. Then Muhammad ibn Abu Bakr entered the room and held the beard of Uthman. Uthman said, "O son of my brother (Abu Bakr), this is not your place. Had your father been here; he would never approve of this." That made Muhammad ibn Abu Bakr waver in his resolve, and he walked out of the room. Seeing this some of the rebels entered the room and struck blows at the head of Uthman. Naila threw herself on the body of Uthman to protect him. She was pushed aside, and further blows were struck on Uthman till he was dead. "From Allah, he had come and to Allah, he returned."

He died while keeping the fast, and true to his dream he broke the fast in the company of the Holy Prophet (ﷺ) that evening. He was assassinated while reciting the Quran, The ayat of Surah Baqarah-137. "So if they believe in the like of that which you believe, then they are rightly guided, but if they turn away, then they are only in opposition. So Allah will suffice you against them. And He is the All-Hearer, the All-Knower." The blood-stained Quran he was reciting from is still preserved in a museum in Tashkent today.

ACCUSATIONS AGAINST UTHMAN (رضي الله عنه)

Those who took part in killing of Uthman, later on, joined the extremist Khawrij group. One of Tabieen said, "I saw the people who killed Uthman, most of them were the people of Khawrij, most of them became Khawrij." These are the people who thought they know the Quran better. They are only people on rightly guided. It is their duty to guide other people even if necessary with force and violence.

The opponents of Uthman who took part in the rebellion that led to his wrongful assassination had a long list of false accusations against him. These include:

1. He burned The Quran.
2. He made certain land a protectorate;
3. He stopped the Sunnah of shortening prayers during travel;
4. He gave Marwan one-fifth of Ifriqiya;
5. While Umar used his whip, Uthman used a stick to beat people;
6. He mounted a step up on the pulpit to be at the level used by the Prophet while Abu Bakr and Umar moved a step down;
7. He did not take part in the Battle of Badr, and fled during the Battle of Uhud, and was absent on the day when the Prophet's companions made the pledge under the tree, known as Bay'at Al-Ridwan;

Uthman (RA) said: "These people have mentioned certain things which you are aware of as well. However, their plan is to debate with me on these issues so that they can return and say, 'We engaged in a debate with Uthman regarding these matters and he has been defeated.' These people allege that whilst on journey, I offered the prayer in full but the Holy Prophet (ﷺ) used to perform qasr (short) whilst on journey. However, it was only in Mina where I offered the prayer in full and even that was due to two reasons: firstly, because I owned property there and I had married there; secondly, because I came to know that in those days people had converged for the hajj and the uneducated from among them would begin to say that the Khalifah only offers two rak'at so there must only be two rak'at in the prayer. Is this not true?"

The companions replied, "Yes this is correct."

Then Uthman said: "The second allegation that they raise is that I have introduced the innovation of establishing public pastures, although this is a false accusation. Pastures were established before me. They were introduced by Umar and I have only made them more spacious due to the growing number of camels that are given in alms. Then, the land designated for public pastures is not the wealth of anyone. I have no benefit in this; I have only two camels, whereas at the time when I became Khalifah I was more wealthy then all the Arabs. Now I only have two camels which I have kept for hajj. Is this not true?"

The noble companions affirmed, "Indeed, it is."

Then Uthman said: "They say that I appoint comparatively young men as governors, even though I only appoint such individuals as governors who posses virtuous attributes and manners. Holy men before me appointed even younger people as governors than those appointed by me. Far more objections were raised against the Holy Prophet (ﷺ) for appointing Usamah bin Zaid as the General of an army than are now being raised against me. Is this not true?" The companions responded, "It is true."

If the Noble Quran is recited in a different dialect than the Quraishi one, and if one tries to write down what he is reciting, he could and would end up with different words in spelling and in some cases in meaning as well than the original copy of the Noble Quran.

When Uthman got hold of all of the Qurans that were written in different dialects, and in some cases were altered to sound exactly like the other dialects, he ordered for them to get burnt.

Many people during the time of Uthman had their own explanatory notes in their personal copies of the Quran. Others had written down portions of the Quran themselves. In order to prevent any future issues of explanatory notes being considered as part of the Quran or arguments due to a mistake on the part of the writer – claiming that he has something of the Qur'an which others do not have – these old copies were burnt.

What all this is concerned with is the fact that in Islamic law, one fifth of the spoils of war goes to the Muslim state, and the ruler should give it to those who are descendants of the Prophet (peace be upon him), the needy, orphans and travelers in need. Ibn Al-Arabi makes clear that Imam Malik considers that the ruler has sole and free discretion on how to use it. Other scholars have different views. However, the whole accusation is false. Uthman did not give this one-fifth to any one person.

Al-Khateeb adds the following details: "What is true is that he gave one-fifth of the share of the state, i.e. 20 percent of 20 percent of the spoils of war to Abdullah ibn Abi Sarh, the commander of the army which liberated the region, but he took it back later. Al-Tabari mentions that Uthman ordered Abdullah to launch a campaign from Egypt up to Tunisia, and said to him: 'If tomorrow God gives you victory and you have Ifriqiya, you will get from the spoils the Muslims gain one fifth of the one fifth of the state as your free share.' He started his campaign, moving deep into Ifriqiya, securing its plains and mountains. Abdullah divided the spoils of war among the soldiers in line with the Islamic rule, and took for himself his promised share of 20 percent of the one-fifth due to the state, and sent the rest to Uthman. The people who carried it to

Madina complained to Uthman about Abdullah's share. Uthman said to them: 'I have given him this share, but if you are displeased, then I will claim it back.' They said that they were displeased. Therefore, Uthman wrote to Abdullah to give it back, and he did."

People claim that Uthman used to favour his relatives with gifts. He certainly did and this is one of his virtues. Ali praised Uthman for being the kindest of all the Prophet's companions to his relatives. Uthman himself explained his attitude to his relatives saying: "They claim that I love my family and give them gifts. My love of them has never caused me to be unjust to others on their account. Indeed, I make them shoulder more responsibility when dealing with others. What I give them comes out of my own property. I have never considered the property of the Muslim community to be lawful for me to take or to give to anyone else. I used to give generously from my own property during the Prophet's (ﷺ) lifetime and during the reigns of Abu Bakr and Umar, when I was still keen to retain my wealth. Now that I have attained to old age and my life is coming to an end, people would claim this about me!"

What Uthman did was to distribute his own wealth among his relatives, treating his cousins in the same way as his own children. This is indeed the action of one who was preparing to depart this life. Since he felt it unlawful to take any money from the public treasury for himself, he was less likely to take it for his relatives, or indeed anyone else. The allegations of those who rebelled against him this fall.

The rebels made further allegations against him, some of which are ridiculous indeed. They said, for example: "While Umar used his whip, Uthman used a stick to beat people." Ibn Al-Arabi says in reply to this allegation: "As for him using a stick to beat people, the truth is that I never heard this from anyone, pious or not. It is all false, and its falsehood would be readily apparent to anyone who investigates it a little." But who would Uthman beat with his stick? Certainly not grown up men. And if beating by a ruler was appropriate, considering what they say about Umar, why would using a whip be preferable to using a stick. The whole accusation stinks.

They made a further allegation saying that "Uthman mounted a step up on the pulpit to be at the level used by the Prophet while Abu Bakr and Umar moved a step down." What this is concerned with is the position where the Caliph stood when addressing the people, either before Friday prayer or indeed at any time he wanted to convey something to them. The fact is that Abu Bakr and Umar each lowered his position a step, but it is not to be expected that every successive ruler will take a further step down. Otherwise, with the passage of time, rulers and speech makers would go down below the floor level.

Imam al-Bukhari relates: "A man from Egypt was on his way to perform the pilgrimage when he saw a group of people sitting together. He inquired about them and he was told that they belonged to the tribe of Quraysh. He asked: 'Who is the learned man among them.' He was told: 'Abdullah ibn Umar.' He addressed him saying: 'I want to ask you about something and please speak to me about it.'

Do you know that Uthman fled during the Battle of Uhud?' Ibn Umar answered in the affirmative. The man asked him: 'Do you know that he was absent from the Battle of Badr?' Again the answer was in the affirmative. The man put his third question: 'Do you know that he was not present either at the time of the pledge known as Bay'at Al-Ridwan?' Ibn Umar said: 'Yes.' Elated, the man said: 'God is great.'

Ibn Umar said to him: 'Come forward and I will explain things to you. As for his flight on the Day of Uhud, I declare that God has forgiven him. And as for his absence on the Day of Badr, he was married to the Prophet's daughter and she was ill. The Prophet told him to stay back to look after her. He later said to him: 'You will have the same reward and share of the booty as anyone who took part in the Battle of Badr.' And as for Bay'at Al-Ridwan, had there been among the Prophet's companions anyone with better standing in Mecca than Uthman, the Prophet would have sent him in his stead. However, the Prophet sent Uthman (as his ambassador to the people of Mecca) and the Bay'at Al-Ridwan took place after Uthman had gone there. The Prophet raised his right hand and said: 'This is Uthman's hand' and held his two hands together saying: 'And this on Uthman's behalf.' Ibn Umar then said to the man: 'Take with you what I have just said.'"

QUOTES BY UTHMAN (RA)

"Worrying about the dunya is a darkness in the heart, while worrying about akhirah is a light in the heart."

"Acquire wisdom from the story of those who have already passed."

"Enjoin what is good and forbid what is evil before the worst amongst you are given authority over you and then when even the best of you make dua against them, their dua will not be accepted."

"It is sufficient for you that the one who envies you is distressed at the time of your joy."

"Had our hearts been pure, we would never tire with the Dhikr of Allaah."

"If anyone stumbles then he must repent. If anyone errs then he must repent. And no one must insist on (the path of) destruction. If anyone insists on tyranny then he is far away from the path."

"Three worldly things have made dear to me: feeding the hungry, clothing the naked and reading the Qur'an."

FOUR ADVICE FROM THE QURAN

✓ You prefer the life of this world, while the hereafter is better and more lasting. (87:16)

✓And hold firmly to the rope of Allah all together and do not become divided. (3:103)

✓ O ye who believe! Avoid suspicion as much (as possible): for suspicion in some cases is a sin: And spy not on each other behind their backs (49:12)

✓ Oh you who believe! Persevere in patience and constancy. Vie in such perseverance, strengthen each other, and be pious, that you may prosper. (3:200)

"No one will be granted such goodness except those who exercise patience and self-restraint, none but persons of the greatest good fortune." (41:35)

"And whoever fears Allah – He will make for him a way out and will provide for him from where he does not expect. And whoever relies upon Allah – then He is sufficient for him…" (65: 2-3)

Narrated Abu Huraira: Allah's Messenger (ﷺ) said, "Beware of suspicion, for suspicion is the worst of false tales. And do not look for the others' faults, and do not do spying on one another, and do not practice Najsh (fake bidder/ ghost bidder/ phantom bidder), and do not be jealous of one another and do not hate one another, and do not desert (stop talking to) one another. And O, Allah's worshipers! Be brothers!" (AL-Bukhari, 6066)

"Before going to sleep every night, forgive everyone and sleep with a clean heart." Anonymous

A thought-provoking questions you should ask yourself every day

Am I on the right path?

Practical Ways to Improve Yourself

<u>Control your anger and jealousy</u>

Anger and jealousy are very common human traits. But they are unpleasing and self-destructing if they get out of control. Again, you'll be hurting yourself before others when you get angry at or jealous of someone, hence, being unhappy and dissatisfied. Try not to compare yourself to others and think they are better than you.

Instead remember that there are so many people who are unfortunate and that you have better circumstances than them Alhamdulillah. That would help a lot.

Also, try not to get easily angered by anything, but if you do, try to forgive who ever angered you. This doesn't mean that you're weak and that it'll be like nothing bad happened, on the contrary, what happened still happened but you're strong enough to relieve yourself from the heavy weight that was keeping you down, now letting you heal.

🔦 LIGHTING UP THE THOUGHT TUNNEL 🔦
(Scripting positive beliefs within ourselves)

Identify the toxic trigger that starts a negative self-talk in your mind. Write down the negative thought and the associated emotion that you feel when you say the thought out loud. Now replace it with a positive alternative version of the thought. Then write the emotion you feel when thinking about the positive thought. Practice this every time you catch yourself in a negative self-talk. This way you'll completely transform your negative self-talk (a major cause of low self-esteem and unhappiness) into positive self-talk.

Toxic trigger	Negative thought	Associated emotion	Positive thought	Associated emotion

IMAM ABU HANIFA

Imam Abu Hanifa was endued with intelligence beyond measure. One time the Roman, who were at war in the time of Umar (RA). The Muslims had conquered Rome and they had reached as far as China and Spain. So, thoughts of philosophy and argumentation began to come into the lands of the Muslims. And so, there were disagreements about things. People started to use their opinions and became quarrelsome. So, these scholars came to set straight these people's thoughts once again.

The Roman sent an envoy to put doubt in Muslim about Islam. So, The man came along and he said to the people, "I have come with three questions."

He stood up and he said, "My first question is, who was there before God?" and the second question is, "Right now Allah Tala is facing in which direction?" and the third question is, "What is Allah Tala doing right now?"

Abu Hanifa was only about ten or twelve years old at the time. No one could answer. So, Abu Hanifa said, "Let me answer father." Abu Hanifa came up and he said to the man; "As for who is before God, count from ten to backward?" and the man counted until he reached zero. Abu Hanifa asked, "What's before one?" The man said, "Zero, zero is the end." Abu Hanifa asked again, "What's before one?" The man said, "Nothing."

Then Abu Hanifa said, "The Lord of the worlds, the Glorious Creator; how can He not be the beginning of everything? When in actual common sense and logic, you count backward and you end up with one and there's nothing before that."

Then the man asked Abu Hanifa the second question; "What

about God, where is He facing? In which direction is He facing now?" Abu Hanifa said, "If you light up a candle, what do you see?" The man said, "Light." Abu Hanifa said, "In which direction is the candle light facing?" The man said, "It's not facing any particular direction. Light is facing everywhere." Abu Hanifa said, "Then what do you say about Allah Tala, Who is the light of lights? Nurun Ala Nur; how can I say in which direction He's facing?"

As for the third question, Abu Hanifa said to him, "To answer your third question you have to come down here and I go up there. Because the people want to hear the answer and if you want to, only fair because you made your question in front of people; let me answer in front of people." The man thought that's common sense; so, the man came down and said, "What is Allah Tala doing right now?" Abu Haifa said, "Right now, He's making the one who is on falsehood, come down off the pulpit and the one full of success to climb up the pulpit to answer and prove you wrong." He said, "This is what Allah Tala is doing right now. Every action that happens in life, this is what Allah Tala is doing. Right now, Allah Tala is doing this, if it wasn't for God, we will all be non-existent, dead, gone. Because we don't keep ourselves alive, Allah Tala keeps us alive, Allah Tala keeps everything in motion."

Al-Qadi Abu Yusuf describes his teacher Abu Hanifa in the following,

"Imam Abu Hanifa was extremely pious, he avoided forbidden things. He remained silent and absorbed in his thoughts most of the time. He answered questions only if he knew the answer to them. He was very generous and self-respected. He never asked a favor from anybody in his life. He shunned the company of the worldly-minded people and he didn't like having a position of status. He avoided gossip and slander. He only spoke well or he was silent. Abu Hanifa, even his enemies who imprisoned him and whipped him, he had nothing to say, only good or he was silent. Generous with his knowledge, as well as his wealth. This was Abu Hanifa."

Allah Tala bears witness of greatness; to Himself that there is no God worthy of worship but Him. And He bears witness to the greatness of His creation of the angels. And He bears witness to the importance and greatness of those endued with knowledge.

The first of them is the great Imam Abu Hanifa. His real name is Al Numan Ibn Thabit Ibn Zuta Ibn Marzuban. Marzuban is a Persian name. So, Imam Abu Hanifa was of Persian origin. He was a non-Arab but he was born among the Arabs, lived among the Arabs and learned the Arabic language. Abu Hanifa was also nicknamed "Imam al-Muslimeen;" the leader of the Muslims. He was also nicknamed "Al-Imam al-azam;" the ever so great imam, the great scholar. He was nicknamed this even by the scholars who came after him. And even by the contemporary scholars, scholars that lived in his time.

Imam Abu Hanifa was what we call one of the generations of At Tabieen. At Tabieen is anyone who met a companion of the Prophet (ﷺ), believed in the message of the Prophet (ﷺ) and died on that message. The majority of the scholars and historians said that Imam Abu Hanifa was a Tabiee. The reason why they say he was a Tabiee was that he lived and met some of the companions of the Prophet (ﷺ). And one of them was Anas Ibn Al-Malik (RA). Abu Hanifa was only about thirteen years old when he sat in one of the classes of the companion Anas Ibn Al-Malik. And when Abu Hanifa was at the age of thirteen, Anas Ibn Malik (RA) died.

Abu Hanifa was born in Iraq, in a city called Kufa. He was born in 699 AD (80 Hijri). Abu Hanifa was tall, wide, very handsome looking, with long black hair of Persian origin, beautiful big eyes.

Imam Abu Hanifa operated a business in textiles; silk and materials. His grandfather, Zuta, came to Kufa and started a business of garments and excelled in it. This business eventually was bequeathed to Imam Abu Hanifa. He too possessed a great deal of expertise in this trade as he would partake in it along with his father, Thabit, from a very young age. Later, when this burden was placed on his shoulders, not only did he take care of the business, considering it his duty, but also gave it new heights.

A famous type of garment at the time was khaz and this was very popular with customers. Khaz was made by combining silk and cotton. He installed weaving looms that could make this cloth and began trade with this cloth as a partnership. He established agencies in various cities, where he would send the product and earned profit. Due to his professionalism, other people would also invest in his business.

Once, he sent 170,000 dirhams to a young man and said, "This was given to me by your father, which he was not able to take back before his death."

When he passed away, he had about 50,000 investments from different people, which were returned after his demise. Nonetheless, Imam Abu Hanifa was very affluent and never experienced any financial problems.

Abu Hanifa was passing by one day; he was about nineteen or twenty-one years old (some say 15 years old) and a great Imam Sha'bi in Kufa saw him. Imam Sha'bi had something called Farasah; this means that if he looks at someone, he can tell a lot about that person.

He looked at this young boy and mistakenly thought that he was a student of his. So he asked him, "Where are you going?" Imam Abu Hanifa said, "I'm going on a business errand." He said,

"That's not what I'm asking you, why aren't you in class?" He thought that Abu Hanifa was his student. Abu Hanifa said, "I'm not a student of knowledge." Imam Sha'bi looked at him with a sad face and said, "No, you look like an intelligent young man and I can see it in your face. How about I advise you to take on knowledge of this deen, I think a lot's going to come out of you."

Imam Abu Hanifa that day, he thought about it, and truly this inspired him to become a student of Imam Sha'bi. And so, he began his journey of knowledge. Imam Abu Hanifa took some lessons under Imam Sha'bi but there was one problem. As I said before there was philosophy and argumentation, signs of argumentation in the land. So, Abu Hanifa used to sit in some of the circles, and the students and people began, they loved to talk about issues and arguments. And he started to get sucked into the philosophy and argumentation. But then he found that this philosophy was not based on real proof, and all it did was hardened the hearts. So, he said, "I don't like it." After Imam Sha'bi passed away, he went to his renowned Sheikh Hammad Ibn Suleiman. Sheikh Hammad Ibn Suleiman came to be his teacher for the rest of the eighteen years of Abu Hanifa's life. Imam Hammad, he studied of companions like Abdullah Ibn Masud, Anas Ibn Al-Malik; great companions of the prophet (ﷺ).

On the first day, Imam Hammad placed Abu Hanifa in the back row. On the first day, he noticed Abu Hanifa was very bright. So, from the next day onwards, Abu Hanifa always sat on the right side of his Imam until his death.

There was no scholar that Imam Abu Hanifa did not sit within Kufa or Busra or even Mecca and Madina. He sat with them all. Once, when he went to Madina, and he sat in one of the circles of Imam Malik. At the time, Imam Malik was thirteen years younger than Imam Abu Hanifa. And when he left, Imam Malik met with another contemporary scholar who was sitting there. He said, "Do you know who this man is?" Imam Malik said, "No." He said, "He is Abu Hanifa. He is the man that if you were to tell me that this pillar, which is made of brick, is made of water, he can convince me because he was so intelligent in his words." So Imam Abu Hanifa learned of Imam Hammad over in Kufa. And then in Busra, he learned of Imam Hasan Al Basri. And he continued his knowledge from these great eminent scholars.

When Imam Abu Hanifa was about thirty years old and one day his teacher said, "I have a funeral to attend, a family member of mine died, can you take my place?" For two months Imam Abu Hanifa had to be the teacher to the students. He goes, "In those two months, sixty issues were presented to me and I answered them all. And I wrote them all down to check them with my Imam. When my Imam came back, I gave my sixty matters to him to check and the Imam found that forty of my answers were correct and twenty were incorrect." Imam Abu Hanifa said, "I said, W Allahi! I will never take a class until my Imam dies." And truly that's what happened. As soon as someone learns a hadith or two, you want to give fatwas left, right. You become an Imam and a Sheikh. And you like people calling you a Sheikh?

When his Imam Hammad died, he took over his school. When he took over his school, he had one thousand students. In one year, every single school in the Kufa had closed down and they all joined the school of Abu Hanifa. More than fifty thousand students at one go, they were with them every single day in hardship and in ease.

Imam Abu Hanifa refused to ever accept any money or wealth or reward for teaching his knowledge. What he did was, from his business, the profit that he made was to sustain himself and to sustain his students. He had over a thousand students in one time and he used to pay them. He gave them his knowledge and he gave them wealth to sustain themselves. So, he did not have to obey the government's injustice, he did not want anything from them, he didn't need anything from them.

Imam Abu Yusuf's father was an extremely destitute and impoverished laborer. He once said to his son, "Instead of attending Abu Hanifa's classes, you should work so that we can have some money to run the house." Therefore, upon his father's persistence, he withdrew himself from the lessons and began work as a tailor.

When Imam Abu Hanifa came to learn of this, he called Abu Yusuf and enquired from him about his circumstances. He then assigned a reasonable allowance for him and from then on, always looked after him.

Imam Abu Hanifa developed something that no other imam before him had it. He developed something called a code of principles in how to directly look at the Quran and Hadith and make a ruling out of it. And be able to study that verse and study that hadith to bring out more than ten, twenty, or even a hundred different principles and rules. No one knew how to do that.

Now, remember, why did he have to do that? Because the Muslims had dispersed throughout the world. They had gone to places like Spain and Greece and so on. And the societies were different there and the Muslims needed more information, more things to be able to settle their affairs in life. For example, today we have cigarettes and smoking. How do we know cigarettes and smoking is haram or halal? In the Quran, it doesn't say cigarettes are forbidden so don't smoke cigarettes, or ecstasy pills are forbidden, so don't take ecstasy.

But Imam Abu Hanifa; he helped us. He said "In order to derive new things that come up in your society, and to know whether they're halal or haram, when you can't find direct information in the Quran or the words of the Prophet (peace be upon him) or his actions, then I will teach you how to use the same sources to understand everything in your life. Whether it's good or bad, permissible or not permissible." He was the first to create that system, no one before him could do that. And the later scholars that came after him also used Qiyas and the same principles after him. In fact, they elaborated on it, they improved it even more.

So, don't anyone say Imam Abu Hanifa innovated something! No, he did not innovate anything and none of the scholars that came after him ever said so. What he did was, he made the understanding of our religion easier. And that's why the majority of people of the world follow the school of thought of Imam Abu Hanifa.

Imam Abu Hanifa taught us to use evidence and always not to take something blindly. He also said, my words and the words of others can be rejected at any time. We say something today and tomorrow we may change our mind. All except what goes back to the Quran and to the Prophet (peace be upon him) that cannot be rejected. And if what you see and what your scholars discover that is more closer to the truth of the Quran and the Sunnah, is better than mine, then throw my saying across the wall and take that as my saying. For this is all my goal and this is the goal of all the scholars anyway.

Imam Abu Hanifa would adopt a beautiful approach when addressing contentious matters. He would try his utmost to clear the matter, without hurting anyone's sentiments.

He once presented a beautiful example regarding this. He said:

"If four people dispute about a white-colored sheet – one saying that it is red, the other saying that it is black, another calling it is green and the last one, who knows that the actual color is white – and remain adamant on their stance, then the person who knows the true color should not say to the others, 'You are wrong', but rather should say, 'As far as I am aware, the color is white.'"

Imam Abu Hanifa was very clean. He would wear clean, presentable clothes and would desire the same for others.

Once, some scholars arrived to meet him, of whom one wore old, dirty, torn and tattered clothes. After their meeting, when they got up to leave, Imam Abu Hanifa asked the gentleman with torn clothes to stay behind. When the others had left, he gave 1,000 dirhams to the gentleman to purchase new, decent clothes. The man replied, "I am a wealthy person. I do not need such financial help." Abu Hanifa replied, "When God has given you wealth and has made you affluent, then you should be thankful to Him for this blessing upon you. There should be a practical display of this blessing upon you. It is thanklessness to wear such torn and tattered and unclean clothes. It goes against the verse: 'And as for the bounty of your Lord, do relate it (to others)' (Surah al-Duha, Ch.93: V.12). It goes against the hadith that says that there should be a practical display of God's beneficence."

Imam Abu Hanifa was a steadfast and intelligent person who would resolve conflicts. He would respond to harsh words in such a way that would leave the other feeling ashamed, yet wanting to correct their way.

Once, Imam Abu Hanifa was sitting in a mosque when a person following an opposing scholar came and started hurling abuse at him. Imam Abu Hanifa remained quiet throughout his abuse, but that person increased in his verbal abuse. When Abu Hanifa got up to leave, that person started to follow him and continued his verbal assault.

When he eventually reached his home, he turned to the man and said, "This is my home. I must go inside. If anything remains, please express it now. Otherwise, do not say later on that you still have a desire to continue." Upon hearing this reply, the man felt ashamed and repented for his actions.

There is a story, there was a man by the name of Imam Bakeer. Imam Bakeer was from the family line of the Prophet (peace be upon him); great-great-grandson of the Prophet (ﷺ). One day he came up to Abu Hanifa and he said to him, "So you're the one who contradicts my grandfather, by using logical reasoning?"

Abu Hanifa looked at him and said, "How dare I? Let me prove it to you." He goes, "How?" He said, "Let me ask you a question. Who is weaker; the man or the woman?" He said, "The woman is weaker physically." He said, "Well then it only makes sense that the inheritance; the girl should get more than the son. But I didn't say that. I said what the Prophet (peace be upon him) said or what Allah Tala said, for the boy, double of what the girl gets."

Then Abu Hanifa asked him another question, "Which is more important; praying or fasting?" He said, "Praying." Abu Hanifa said, "Then by logical reasoning, the woman during her menses doesn't fast or pray. But by logic, she should make up her prayers and not make up her fasting or at least both together. But instead, I said the opposite; I said what the Prophet (peace be upon him) said that you make up your fasting but you don't make up your prayer."

He used one more example that if you wear your Khuff (sock) and you want to make wudu, logical reasoning says that you should wipe underneath, underneath that Khuff rather than over on the top, but Islam says wipe over the top.

So, Imam Abu Hanifa for those who think that he was a man that just uses logic and reasoning, you are far from the truth and you are far away from understanding who he really was. When he said that, Imam Bakeer who is the great-great-grandson of the Prophet (peace be upon him), a tear came from his eye and he grabbed Abu Hanifa's forehead and kissed it. And he said, "Thank you." He loved him after that.

Once as we said, he was a businessman, right? So, once he had to go to teach somewhere and he got one of his pupils, his name was Hafs and he said to him, "Can you take this silk to sell in the market for me?" So, the man said, "Of course." He said, "But wait before you take this silk, there are defects in it, there are problems in this silk and before you sell it to the people, you have to tell them about the defects in this product." He said, "Sure."

So, Hafs was so happy that he's selling the product of Imam Abu Hanifa. He was so excited that he forgot to tell people about the defects, and he started advertising, "Silk, silk, silk." Everybody came and bought it. That day he made so much profit; he made thirty thousand dinars, so that was a large amount of money.

He came back and gave it to Abu Hanifa. Abu Hanifa looked and he goes, "Oh you sold all of the material?" He said, "Yes and I made thirty thousand dinars." Abu Hanifa got happy and said, "Now I can spend it on the students and on the poor and the needy." Then he remembered, he goes, "What happened to the people when they heard about the defects? And you still made that profit?"

He said "Oh! No, I forgot to tell them." Imam Abu Hanifa said, "Then this money is not lawful for us, we took it unlawfully; we cannot keep it." He said, "Give it to charity." And he gave it all to charity. He didn't take any of it, nothing.

Once a man owed Abu Hanifa ten thousand dinars and this man tried to avoid him. So Abu Hanifa went up to him and stopped him. Took him aside and said, "Why are you avoiding me?" And the man said to him, "WAllahi! Abu Hanifa, I'm embarrassed. I'm too shy because I owe you the money and I can't pay it off." Abu Hanifa looked at him and said, "But you don't need to avoid me, I rather you would be my friend. If you can't pay, then don't." He let him off ten thousand dinars.

There was once a neighbor of his. He was an alcoholic and he likes singing a lot. And by the way, the Madhab of Abu Hanifa is the strictest and harshest against musical instruments. And he had a neighbor who used to love singing music. He was an alcoholic. So, let's see how Abu Hanifa dealt with him.

Every night Abu Hanifa would sit back to write and study, and his neighbor would be singing and drinking. He would say the following words, "Nobody cares about me, everybody shuns me. I'm nobody, I wish I was dead."

One night the man didn't sing. So Abu Hanifa asked about him, and he found that at night, the area's chief of police was walking past. He heard the disturbance from the man's house. When he approached the house to enquire about the disturbance, he ended up arresting him and putting him in jail.

So Abu Hanifa went to the governor and he was a good friend of his. The governor said to him, "Abu Hanifa has come to my house? You don't have to do that. Ask me and I'll go to your house." That's how much he was respected. He said, "Why have you come for?" Abu Hanifa said, "I've come for my neighbor." The governor said, "What would you like us to do?" He said, "I'd like you to release him. I want to intercede for him. Buy him out." He said, "There's no need." So, they bought him and he was excited; Abu Hanifa looked at his neighbor and he said, "Have I done well by you my neighbor?" He said, "You have done so well. As for me, WAllahi! I will never drink again." And guess what? He became one of the close students of Abu Hanifa and one of the renowned scholars (I couldn't find his name).

Yazid Ibn Kumayt says, "I once prayed behind Abu Hanifa in prayer, and Abu Hanifa recited the following verses; when the Earth is shaken to its final quake; and the verse goes on by saying in the end; and there isn't an atom worth of good on that day except that it shall be revealed." He says, "We finished the salah (prayer) and everybody left, I looked and I found Imam Abu Hanifa still in the masjid exactly where he was sitting. And he was weeping and weeping tremendously." He said, "We left after Isha and I came back at Fajr to pray in the masjid and Abu Hanifa was still sitting in the same position he was still weeping and grabbing his beard like this, it was soaked and I heard him say the following words "Allah Tala rewards the smallest of virtues and punishes for the smallest of sin. Oh Allah Tala, save Numan (Abu Hanifa) from the hellfire." And such were the scholars of Islam really.

Once a man came to Abu Hanifa and said to him in distress, "I lost my money, I lost my money." Abu Hanifa looked at him and he said, "This is not a Fiqh question. You know I don't really deal with these matters." But because of his spirituality, he said, "Go home and pray to Allah Tala." Meaning I don't have an answer for you. I can't find your money for you.

So, he went, he started praying and praying and praying. Then the man remembered and he found his money. Immediately, he raced back to Abu Hanifa and said, "Imam, Imam it worked! You're the greatest, I thank you. I prayed until I found it." Abu Hanifa looked at him and he said, "Of course you're going to find it. That was the shaytan who made you forget. But when you stand at praying. He thought that this is not a good deed. He didn't want you to keep praying so he reminded you where it was and you found it. Rather than coming and thanking me; you should have spent more time praying to thank Allah Tala."

Whenever Abu Hanifa would see his students, he'd look at them first before he started his lessons and you could see his eyes full of compassion. And sometimes with tears and he'd smile and say to them, "You are the joy of my heart and the removal of my sorrow." Removal of which sorrow? The sorrow of hereafter because they will testify for him. And the joy of his heart; they are his legacy.

He had over nine hundred dedicated students. We're talking about nine hundred of the most specialized in every area. Whenever Abu Hanifa was about to give a matter, he would give his students and they would study it, study it, study it and he would not confirm the verdict until everyone had agreed that it was right. And every time they agreed, he would prostrate to Allah Tala and pray two rakats and say, "Alhamdulillah! Who has not urged me off the path." That's how he used to reach his rulings.

Today we live in the twenty-first century, there is new ideologies such as atheism, Scientology; well in those days, there was something called Mu'tazila* and the Khawarij.**

The problem with the Khawarij, they were terrible men. They had beards longer than yours and mine, they prayed more than you and me in the nights, they memorized the Quran and read it better than anyone of us, they had so many goods; you'd think that they are saints, these were angels sent from the sky. But their character opposed them tremendously, these people were barbaric and violent and they went to extremes. They were so extreme that they said, they made a person a kafir just when they did a major sin like drinking or zina (adultery); "You've become a kafir, have become a disbeliever." They also said that anyone who doesn't agree with our view is also put to the sword.

Abu Hanifa didn't agree with the Khawarij. So, one day, they entered upon him with the sword. That's what they were doing.

They were going around to people and they were questioning them, "Do you believe or do you not believe?" Abu Hanifa was a very smart man and he said something that started the trend which saved the lives of many more people. They entered upon him one day while he was studying; they had bashed the door down and they said to him, "Repent." He said, "For what? What do I have to repent from?" They said, "Repent from your views that are against us." When he saw that he had to either agree with them or get himself out of it someway otherwise they're going to kill him; he recited a verse from the Quran, "And if anyone of the polytheists, idol worshippers seeks you refuge, then give him refuge." Like, don't touch him until he hears the words of Allah Tala.

They considered Abu Hanifa a polytheist, a kafir. So, he used the verse about the kafir. What can he do? He didn't say, "I'm a Kafir." So, he just went their way. And if you can't beat them, you go along their way. And that's a very smart, wise thing to do. By that, he saved his life. So, he said "If polytheists seek refuge, give him refuge" and the Khawarij, they looked at each other and they said, "Leave him alone, he has used the words of God against us. He is a polytheist; we can't touch him." So he became a thorn in the hearts of the Khawarij.

Once, a group of Khariji came to visit Imam Abu Hanifa with swords in their hands. They were of the belief that a person who had committed atrocious sins would be summoned to the hellfire for eternity. Therefore, they said to Imam Abu Hanifa, "We have two questions only. Answer them, otherwise, we shall kill you." He responded, "What are the questions?"

They said, "The first question is that if a person consumes a lot of alcohol and dies whilst drunk, or if a woman commits adultery and gets pregnant as a result and dies whilst pregnant with that child, tell us, will they both be considered Muslims?"

Imam Abu Hanifa replied, "Were they Jewish?" They replied in the negative. "Were they Christians?" They replied negatively. "Were they Zoroastrian?" They again replied in the negative. He then asked, "Then what religion did they belong to?" They replied, "They were Muslims." Imam Abu Hanifa immediately replied, "You have yourself answered the question." This shows that he considered anyone a Muslim who called themselves a Muslim. Feeling somewhat embarrassed, they said, "Alright, then tell us, are they hell-bound, or can they enter paradise?" Imam Abu Hanifa replied, "My answer is that which Abraham and Jesus gave. Abraham said:

فَمَنْ تَبِعَنِيْ فَاِنَّہٗ مِنِّيْ ۚ وَ مَنْ عَصَانِيْ فَاِنَّکَ غَفُوْرٌ رَّحِيْمٌ

"So whoever follows me, he is certainly of me; and whoever disobeys me – Thou art, surely, Most Forgiving, Merciful." (Surah Ibrahim, Ch.14: V.37)

Jesus, the Messiah, said:

اِنْ تُعَذِّبْهُمْ فَاِنَّهُمْ عِبَادُکَ ۚ وَ اِنْ تَغْفِرْ لَهُمْ فَاِنَّکَ اَنْتَ الْعَزِيْزُ الْحَکِيْمُ

"If You should punish them – indeed they are Your servants; but if You forgive them – indeed it is You who is the Exalted in Might, the Wise." (Surah al-Maidah, Ch.5: V.118)

Upon hearing this response, they felt ashamed and went on their way.

There was another Khawarij, his name Ad Dahhaq. He once came to the masjid and he said to him, "Repent." He said, "Repent from what?" Ad Dahhaq said, "I am told that you agreed to Ali. That when Ali said that having a dispute with Muawiyah; he decided to settle his dispute by having what they call an arbitrator." The Khawarij, they didn't agree with this and they also accused Ali (RA) of getting an umpire from his family. Like someone who is his friend. They said this is wrong. And you know what Abu Hanifa you agreed with what he did. So repent. If you don't repent the sword."

So, Abu Hanifa looked at him and he said, "Then let me speak." Ad Dahhaq said, "I want to debate you." Abu Hanifa said, "Okay if you want to debate me then how are we going to know who is right or wrong? We have to put an umpire, an arbitrator." He said, "Okay, put him." And the Khawarij pointed to a man who is also from the Khawarij. And then Abu Hanifa said, "You just did exactly what Ali (RA) did. So why are you disputing me?" And immediately and straight away the Khawarij person put his head down and he had nothing to say. He walked out and he never repeated what he said to Imam Abu Hanifa ever again.

In his time, the Umayyad Era was a time where Khalifas were coming, leaders of Muslims were coming and going. He lived with about 40 different leaders. One of them was Umar Ibn Al Aziz, a great leader, but the rest of them, they were corrupt.

He lived in a time where the rule was being corrupted by its leaders. He was fed up with them because Imam Abu Hanifa was a man of justice and fairness.

Khalifa Abu Jafar Al-Mansur was also a scholar, he was a scholar of Hadith and Scholar of Fiqh. But it goes to show; that not just because if a person has knowledge then he/she is necessarily a man of God. People use their knowledge for corruption, and people can use their knowledge to be God-fearing. Those who have knowledge but they have no good character, they are not the scholars which Allah Tala praises. If you have arrogance and proudness over what you know to show it off in front of people, you are not an Alim. If you learn knowledge only to debate people, and to make them look like they were wrong and you were right, you are not an Alim. If you have great knowledge and you abuse and disrespect, you are not an Alim. The Ulema are the ones who fear Allah Tala.

So, Khalifa Al Mansur was corrupt in his rule, gave land to family members and was unjust. When it came to courts, doing justice to members of the government, they gave them favors. But when it came from a person from the common people, they ruled against them with harshness. Corruption in the courts, corruption in favoritism, taking money from the people in Zakah and spreading it among their relatives and family, giving leadership and the seat to their sons or their relatives and so on and so forth. Imam Abu Hanifa opposed that tremendously and all the scholars did as well. But he stood up the most; he was the most vocal.

Abu Hanifa distanced himself from every kingdom or palace because he felt that they would attract him to say the wrong thing. And they could easily use him and today still many people use scholars for their own benefits, right?

He used to say to the people, "Be careful, be careful of going to the Khalifa; the leader. And fear him just like you fear fire. Don't go to him or to his courts except for some specific purpose, and if he's giving you a post or a judge, don't accept it. Unless you are sure he will accept that you exercise your personal judgment. You will judge even against him. If he doesn't accept, then don't accept to be a judge. So, you get pressured and never accept a position that you are not fit with." These were the words that Abu Hanifa used to advise his students and people.

An official one day said to Abu Hanifa, "Visit me, I want you to visit me at my house." Abu Hanifa asked him, "Why? What for?" Now normally you should visit people but this official, you see, he used to use the scholars. So, Abu Hanifa said, "Why should I visit you?" and he said to him, "Visit me, so I can get to know you more." Abu Hanifa said, "I do not visit people in power." He got angry with him. So, people in power began to resent Abu Hanifa. He had enemies and his enemies were people in power.

They wanted to use him to their advantage.

There was a governor of Iraq by the name of Yazid Ibn Amr Hubayra. He once called Abu Hanifa to him. And he said to him, "I want to give you the position of chief treasurer. Abu Hanifa immediately said, "Never." Yazid said to him, "Why?" Abu Hanifa said, "If you asked me to guard the doors of the mosque, I wouldn't listen to you. Let alone guarding the money of the Muslims. And standing up for you so that when you seal the death of a Muslim and you sign it; I have to carry it out.

Yazid got so angry with him that he ordered his imprisonment for going against him. And he ordered that he be whipped every day one hundred lashes. Abu Hanifa was imprisoned; until finally he found that his students were protesting for him. He had no other choice but after thirty days to release him.

Once, Imam Abu Hanifa visited the court of Abu Jafar Mansur where an official of Mansur, Abul Abbas Tusi, who held animosity against Abu Hanifa, was also seated. Abul Abbas Tusi found an opportunity to create mischief and intended to have him punished by any means necessary. In front of Mansur, he asked Imam Abu Hanifa, "If Amirul Momineen calls someone and orders him to smite another person's neck while they are unaware of their crime, should such a person follow such orders?"

Imam Abu Hanifa realized the mischief and asked, "In your view, does Amirul Momineen issue commands with justice and integrity, or are his orders unjust and without reason, bearing a thirst for the blood of others?" Abul Abbas Tusi immediately felt uneasy and abruptly answered, "Amirul Momineen's decision is just," to which Abu Hanifa replied, "A just order should be obeyed."

A person once made a will for Abu Hanifa in his absence.

According to the law, his property was handed to the court. When Imam Abu Hanifa finally arrived, he filed a lawsuit and explained the circumstances. The witnesses attested to the fact that the will was, in fact, in Abu Hanifa's name. Upon hearing this, the adjudicator said to Imam Abu Hanifa, "Can you swear on oath that what the witnesses are saying is the truth?" He replied, "How can I take an oath when I was not even present when the will was made?" To which the adjudicator responded, "Then you have lost this case."

Imam Abu Hanifa was very intelligent and so, when he assessed that the adjudicator was testing his intellect, he said to him, "If a blind man is beaten by someone and injured and witnesses attest that so and so was the one who beat the blind man and that they were present and saw it happen, would you require for the blind to take an oath that the witnesses are telling the truth?" Observing Imam Abu Hanifa intelligence and astuteness, the adjudicator was left stunned and called a decision in favor of Imam Abu Hanifa.

A mentally challenged lady would often walk the bazaar (market) of Kufa. Once, someone harassed the lady, to which the lady became enraged and started hurling foul language, calling him, "Ya ibnal-zaniyain" (son of two adulterers). This incident took place in the bazaar close to the main mosque and was witnessed by Kufa's qazi (judge) Ibn Abi Layla. He instructed for the woman to be arrested and sentenced her to twice the amount of the usual sentence of lashing.

When Imam Abu Hanifa came to learn of the injustice against the lady, he could not just sit by and observe. He criticized the sentencing and said that the qazi had made many blunders, for example:

1. The lady was insane and such people cannot be held accountable for their crimes and cannot be punished

2. The punishment was given inside the mosque, whereas the mosque is not a place for meting out punishments

3. When the lady had been punished, she was standing, even though women should be seated whilst being punished and cannot be punished whilst standing

4. By ascribing two crimes to the lady, the qazi issued two punishments, even though one punishment was enough. If a person falsely makes an accusation against an entire group of people, they would be punished once only and only that false accuser would be punished

5. The qazi issued both punishments together, even though the limits prescribed are that there should be a gap of a few days between such sentences so that the injuries sustained from first punishment can heal

6. Those who have been accused of being adulterers should also be present during sentencing and their refutation should be heard, rejecting any truth in the claim. It is apparent that in the case mentioned, this did not happen.

The qazi, Ibn Abi Layla, complained to the governor of the city about Imam Abu Hanifa's criticism, saying that he had defamed the court. Thus, the governor issued sanctions upon Abu Hanifa that prevented him from issuing any fatwas or answering any theological question.

Imam Abu Hanifa considered it acceptable to criticize issues surrounding the Shariah. He would himself criticize and would welcome criticism.

While at home, his son, Hamaad enquired about a certain matter, to which he replied, "The government has prohibited me from giving my view on any religious matter. If anyone from the government asks whether I issued any ruling, then how will I reply?"

Once, a qazi called Shurayk was presented with a question on what to do if a person was in doubt about whether they had divorced their wife or not. To this, Shurayk answered, "Such a person should divorce his wife and then do ruju' (seek to return to the wife) to remove any doubt."

Imam Thawri said that in such circumstances, divorce was not required as the husband's intention was equivalent to ruju'.

Imam Zufar said that their Nikah was certain and that doubt was not more credible than certainty. Therefore, she would remain his wife as she was prior to the doubt.

When Imam Abu Hanifa heard of these views, he remarked that Imam Zufar's views were closest to the principles of fiqh, Imam Thawri's fatwa was based on taqwa, while Shurayk's suggestion was similar to a person, who says that they are in doubt about whether their clothes were contaminated with urine, being told to urinate on their clothes and then to wash them. Shurayk was offended by Imam Abu Hanifa's strict criticism and never ceased in his spite for him.

Despite all of this, Imam Abu Hanifa never resorted to rebellion and never attempted to topple the government. He was of the view that one should help a government in their good works. He was always a well-wisher for others and tried to advise them for their betterment. He would say that rebellion was a form of disorder and that the bloodshed in this act was even worse than the individual cases of wrongdoings of those in authority. Therefore, he would always discourage rebellion as a means of seeing improvement.

We said that Abu Hanifa was against the corruption of Khalifa Mansur. One day he called him and he said to him, "I want you to be the chief judge of all Iraq." Imam Abu Hanifa said to him,

"Never because then I will have to rule in rulings in favor of the people in the right way but when it comes to you, will you accept my ruling even if it's against you?"

The Khalifah got angry at that stage, he didn't expect something like that. You don't talk to the leader like that. He said to him, "You must take the chief judge position." Abu Hanifa said, "I am not fit for that position." So, then the Khalifah said, "You're a liar." And then Abu Hanifa said, "Well that just proves my statement then; if I am a liar, a judge is not fit to be if he's a liar." The Khalifah got so angry at him that from that day onwards he resented him more and more. And because later on as he resented him and he kept on refusing these positions; he finally imprisoned him. Merely for the fact that he would not accept the position, the post of being chief judge. Why? Because he was afraid. This post, you're going to be questioned about, he didn't want to meet Allah (SWT) with lots of baggage. And he knew that the government was going to use him, so he got imprisoned for it.

Khalifa Al Mansur had to allow the students to come and learn from him behind bars. He had thousands of students coming to learn from him. While Abu Hanifa was inside the prison and he began teaching people while he was behind bars and the rest of his students were in front of him. He stayed in this way for three months. To the point where he kept talking against the corruption of the government, to the point where the narration says that the government got so annoyed with him that they poisoned his food. And he felt the poison in his food. He began to pray in prison for a few days and he died in his prayer. He was about seventy years old and died in the year 767.

Before he died, he had written a will. After warning people away from the corruption of the government he said,

"When I die, I request you not to bury me in any land which was given by the Khalifa to any of his relatives, his family. And that meant that the people opened their eyes and thought "What the Khalifah is giving land! Our land to his relatives and family?"

So, he made even more of a problem and it is narrated from Al Mansur who used to say, "Abu Hanifa, we are not saved from Abu Hanifa. Neither in his life, were we saved and even in his death I am not saved."

His funeral prayer, on the first day of his funeral, fifty thousand people came to attend it. People kept on coming from all around Iraq and even outside of Iraq. It was so much so that the body of Abu Hanifa had to be laid there for the whole day, from Fajr until sunset. Because six Janazahs were made for him and each time, the first was only fifty thousand and the rest were more. He died in Baghdad and was buried in Baghdad,Iraq.

The school of Hanafis is spread throughout the Turks. The Turkish sultans took it as the Hanifa Madhab. The Ottoman Empire followed the Hanafi Madhab. All the principles of Abu Hanifa, that scholars that came after him, ninety percent of them used the principles of Abu Hanifa to deduce and deduct rulings. Among them was Imam Shafii and this is what he said, "Anyone who wants to excel in Islamic Law cannot do so without referring to Abu Hanifa. Allah Tala has blessed him with the gift of wisdom and understanding."

Imam Ahmad, when he was asked about Abu Hanifa said, "SubhanAllah! In matters of knowledge, piety, abstinence from the dunya and preference to the hereafter; he was of the highest stages that nobody else would be able to occupy. He was lashed for the simple reason that he refused the post of a judge offered to him by Abu Jafar Al Mansur."

Quotes by Imam Abu Hanifa

"Who are we to wish for Paradise? It will be enough if Allah spares us his wrath."

"Practice what you have learned, for theory without practice is like a body without a soul."

"If you learn the sacred knowledge for the sake of this world, then the knowledge will be never rooted in your heart."

"Difficulties are the result of sin. The sinful therefore does not have the right to lament when difficulties befall him."

"A little action with knowledge is far more beneficial than a lot of action with ignorance."

"Show affection to people as much as possible and greet even blameworthy people."

"When a hadith is authentic, then that is my madhab."

"Knowledge without deeds is like a body without a soul. As long as knowledge doesn't embrace the existence of action it will not be enough, not agreeable nor sincere."

MU ʿTAZILAH

Muʿtazilah, (Arabic: "Those Who Withdraw, or Stand Apart") English Mutazilites, also called Ahl al-ʿAdl wa al-Tawḥīd, in Islam, political or religious neutralists; by the 10th century CE, the term had come to refer specifically to an Islamic school of speculative theology (kalām) that flourished in Basra and Baghdad (8th–10th century).

The name first appears in early Islamic history in the dispute over ʿAlī's leadership of the Muslim community (ummah) after the murder of the third caliph, ʿUthmān (656). Those who would neither condemn nor sanction ʿAlī or his opponents but took a middle position were termed the Muʿtazilah.

The theological school is traced back to Wāṣil ibn ʿAṭāʾ (699–749), a student of al-Ḥasan al-Baṣrī, who, by stating that a grave sinner (fāsiq) could be classed neither as believer nor unbeliever but was in an intermediate position (al-manzilah bayna manzilatayn), withdrew (iʿtazala, hence the name Muʿtazilah) from his teacher's circle. (The same story is told of ʿAmr ibn ʿUbayd [died 762].) Variously maligned as free thinkers and heretics, the Muʿtazilah, in the 8th century, were the first Muslims to use the categories and methods of Hellenistic philosophy to derive their three major and distinctive dogmatic points.

First, they stressed the absolute unity or oneness (tawḥīd) of God. From this, it was logically concluded that the Qurʾān could not be technically considered the word of God (the orthodox view), as God has no separable parts, so the Qurʾān had to be created and was not coeternal with God. Under the Abbasid caliph al-Maʾmūn, this doctrine of the created Qurʾān was proclaimed (827) as the state dogma, and in 833 a miḥnah, or tribunal, was instituted to try those who disputed the doctrine (notably the theologian Aḥmad ibn Ḥanbal); the Muʿtazilī position was finally abandoned by the caliphate under al-Mutawakkil about 849. The Muʿtazilah further stressed the justice (ʿadl) of God as their second principle. While the orthodox taught a certain determinism in which all actions, whether good or bad, are ultimately willed by God, the Muʿtazilah posited that God desires only the best for man, but through free will man chooses between good and evil and thus becomes ultimately responsible for his actions. So in the third doctrine, the promise and the threat (al-waʿd wa al-waʿīd), or paradise and hell, God's justice becomes a matter of logical necessity: God must reward the good (as promised) and must punish the evil (as threatened).

KHAWARIJ

There are many Muslims who are troubled by ISIS and their vicious rhetoric and vicious actions. But this is not the first time that a rebel group of Muslims has emerged with extremist tendencies. And as the saying goes, those who do not heed history are doomed to repeat it.

Prophet Muhammad, peace be upon him, warned his followers of a group of people who would arise after his death. The Prophet mentioned their arrival and characteristics no less than 10 times. Among the characteristics he mentioned were:

They would worship so much that "you shall consider your worship and your prayer and your recitation of the Qur'an to be nothing compared to theirs." Meaning, their outward actions, like praying and reciting the Qur'an, would be on overdrive. And yet…

"They shall recite the Qur'an but it will not leave their throats." Meaning that their understanding of the Qur'an will not go any farther than their recitation, and they will not have religious knowledge or insight.

"They are calling to the book of Allah, but they have nothing to do with the book of Allah." Meaning their call is great, but their actions are terrible.

"They are speaking the best speech that you will ever hear of any man. But they will leave Islam like an arrow leaves its prey."

Surely enough, less than 20 years after the death of The Prophet, this group came into being.

The Beginning of the Khawarij: During the time of the fourth Caliph, Ali (RA), (who ruled from 656 – 661 CE) there was a political war between him and another man named Mu'awiyah. Both were Companions (sahaba) of Prophet Muhammad, peace be upon him.

At one point, Ali and Mu'awiyah had ceased fighting and began a process of arbitration to bring about peace. Arbitrators were selected from the two sides to bring an end to hostilities, based on the Qur'an and sunnah (traditions of The Prophet). However, among these people was a group who believed that arbitration was a sin, based on their own understanding of the verse of the Qur'an which states:

The judgement (hukm) is Allah's alone, He relates the truth and He is the Best of deciders. Qur'an, 6: 57

The group accused Ali of sin and disbelief and told him to repent. He defended himself, and said of them:

"The sentence is right but what (they think) it means is wrong. It is true that law-giving (hukm, judgement) is God's alone, but these people say that governance is God's alone…In short, the law does not get put into practice all by itself; there must be someone, or some group, who tries to put it into practice."

The group was adamant that Ali had sinned. In short, they believed that if Ali was following the truth, he had to kill Mu'awiyah and all his men for their insurrection. And if he was not following the truth, then Mu'awiyah and his men should have killed him.

6000 of them split away from Ali's rule and formed their tribe. They became known as the Kharijites or Khawarij. The title comes from the Arabic word "khuruj", meaning "revolt" or "insurrection." This group was the first group to exhibit extremist tendencies and the first sect to split away from mainstream Islamic thought—even before the Sunni-Shia split.

Features of the Khawarij: Initially, Ali left the group alone. In his wisdom, he did not want to force people to reform their beliefs or overpower them. He told them that they could practice however they wished, so long as they did not spread corruption in the land.

However, the extreme, overzealous practices of the Khawarij are what drove them into constant conflict and bloodshed. They would kill anyone who did not believe in their extremist ideology. Some of the many features of the Kharawij were among the following:

They would pray so much that their foreheads would become calloused and their hands rough

They would be malnourished from fasting so much

They considered anyone who had committed a major sin (ie drinking alcohol, fornication, backbiting) to be a disbeliever, and that they should be killed

They believed only they were on the correct path and everyone else was a disbeliever and had to be killed

They questioned the religious scholarship of notables like Ibn Abbas, Ibn Masud, Aishah—and even The Prophet himself

They were narrow-minded and short-sighted

They lacked any sort of religious knowledge or scholarship

They acted without knowledge or insight into the consequences of their actions

They saw the need to openly fight whoever they considered to be an unjust ruler

In short, much of the Khawarij belief stemmed from an overzealous sense of righteousness. Their intention was noble: they were concerned for the purity of the religion. However, their extremist tendencies were incompatible with the realities of life and showed a disregard for the maxim of Islam that calls for mercy and peace first and foremost.

The decline of the Khawarij: Caliph Ali sent the scholar and Companion Ibn Abbas to the Khawarij camp to debate with them. Ibn Abbas noted that they were ceaseless in their worship to the point where their camp was buzzing with Qur'an recitation in the afternoon heat, and their shirts were reduced to tatters. He debated with them and, using his knowledge and wisdom, won the debate.

One of the points he mentioned was related to what caused their split in the first place—the issue of arbitration between people. Ibn Abbas mentioned that arbitration between people is mentioned as something acceptable in the Qur'an, and quoted the verse that discusses appointing an arbiter from a husband and wife if the two fall into disagreement (4:35).

2000 of the Khawarij agreed with Ibn Abbas's arguments and returned with him, reforming their ways. However, the remaining 4000 refused to acknowledge his logic and remained stubbornly ingrate.

The turning point was when a man named Abdullah ibn-Khabbab, one of the children of the Companions, passed by the Khawarij with his pregnant wife. The Khawarij captured him and his wife and questioned him on his beliefs. When they asked what his opinion was on Ali—whom they regarded as a disbeliever—Abdullah told them Ali was more knowledgeable than either of them, and was the Caliph.

With that, the Khawarij killed his wife in front of him, cut her open and killed the baby, then tied him up and slaughtered him like an animal.

Upon hearing this, Caliph Ali went to war with them. He fought them for many years in many battles until they were practically eradicated in the Battle of Nahrawan in 659 CE. Though the bulk of them were killed, a few stragglers dispersed and fled.

They were Muslims—and yet Prophet Muhammad, peace be upon them, called them "the worst of creation" and said they were "the dogs of Hell." He said if they were to rise up in his midst, he would kill them.

The trials and troubles they caused Muslims were so great that after the Khawarij had been defeated, one of the men in Ali's army said: "Praise be to God who gave us rest with the death of these people."

But Ali said in response: "No. There will be amongst the loins of people this ideology until you will find them that they will fight with Ad-Dajjal (the Anti-Christ)."

Modern Times

The Prophet, peace be upon him, said that this group would continue to come and go until near the Day of Judgement. He described the Khawarij of our times like so:

"There will come towards the end of time a group of people, young men, they have the most grandiose visions, they are speaking the best speech that you will ever hear of any man. But they will leave Islam like an arrow leaves its prey." (Muslim)

There are a few noteworthy things to take from that hadith:

They will be young men. Meaning they will be composed mainly of overzealous young men. You won't see the old and wise among their ranks.

They will have the most grandiose visions. They will, as young men do, dream of changing the world and will be able to inspire others with their dreams—though their dreams will be incompatible with reality.

They will be speaking the best speech. Meaning, as the Prophet said before, they will call to Islam and to the Book of God, but their actions will be outwardly evil.

FOUR ADVICE FROM THE QURAN

✓ Talk straight, to the point, without any ambiguity or deception (33:70)

✓ Always speak the truth. Shun words that are deceitful and ostentatious (22:30)

✓ Say with your mouth what is in your heart (Al-Qur'an-3:167)

✓ When you voice an opinion, be just, even if it is against a relative (6:152)

Narrated Malik: Similarly as above adding, "Who believes in Allah and the Last Day should talk what is good or keep quiet." (i.e. abstain from dirty and evil talk, and should think before uttering). (6135)

Always converse in clear, straightforward and decisive language, which contains no ambiguity: (Al-Qur'am 33:70)

"The reality of manners is that it results from beautiful

character. Thus, manners is the manifestations of the integrity and strength in one's inward personality into action." (Ibn Rajab)

A thought-provoking questions you should ask yourself every day

Am I living true to myself?

Practical Ways to Improve Yourself

Cultivate a new habit

Some good new habits to cultivate include reading quran, gain Islamic knowledge, start your day at fajr, constantly reflect on your actions.

Be honest

Being honest is one of the most important characteristics of a good person. When you're honest, you'll feel better about yourself and people will trust you more because you won't tell any lies; you'd be straightforward. This way, you'll feel comfortable about everything you say or do since you know that you're not hiding anything and everything is clear and simple.

📝 THE HEALTHY SELF-ESTEEM CHECKLIST 📝

Are you taking care of your self-esteem?

☐ 1) Sleep well (less sleep increases toxic triggers).

☐ 2) Exercise to look and feel good (even 20mins is plenty).

☐ 3) Smile often (releases positive neurotransmitters instantly & it's a Sunnah!)

☐ 4) Stay clean, groom yourself and look presentable every day.

☐ 5) Don't miss any obligatory prayers (poor spirituality = poor self-esteem as a Muslim).

☐ 6) Avoid major sins gifts (self-esteem suffers with major sins).

☐ 7) Replace perfectionism with effort and progress.

☐ 8) Aim to please Allah alone (don't stress over pleasing people).

☐ 9) Avoid toxic people (toxic trigger identification)

☐ 10) Don't over-plan your days. (Use The Muslim Productivity Planner)

☐ 11) Set goals efficiently so you can actually accomplish them & boost your self-esteem. (Use the Plan-to-Action Workbook)

☐ 12) Accept your insecurities, shortcomings, qualities, achievements and failures. (using The Self-acceptance Worksheet)

☐ 13) Daily SELF-TALK therapy (lighten up your negative thought tunnel)

☐ 14) Practice gratitude and self-love daily.

Imam Malik ibn Anas

The story begins like this; Imam Malik was about nine or ten years old. He was a cheeky little boy when he was a child, and he didn't listen to his parents much. They had a bit of a hard time with him. When he was sitting at the dinner table, his father tested his children with a Fiqh question; understanding of the laws. Malik didn't know the answer. But his older brother knew the answer. His father said to Malik, "The pigeons distracted you from knowing." Imam Malik had pigeons. And this struck Imam Malik right in the heart as a child, it angered him.

It angered him to make a decision. Not to fight with his brother or to get jealous. The anger was the motivation, the other aspect was his mother, when she saw that he was angry she took him and made him take a shower. Then she dressed him with really nice clothing, and she put perfume on him and she made him look well-groomed, presentable in the highest esteem. She said to him, "I'm going to take you to learn knowledge behind the Imams in Madina." He said, "But mother I want to become a singer." He had a nice voice but his mother was very smart and wise and said to him, "Son you know singing is not just about the voice. Singing comes with good looks and you don't have it. You don't have good looks." Even though Imam Malik was very good looking.

So, she took him to the Masjid al Nabawi in Madina. Over there he saw seventy Imams giving seventy different classes at once. She chose for him a particular scholar; she chose an Imam by the name of Rabiah Ibn Abd Ar Rahman. The first thing his mother said to him was this, she looked him in the eye and said to him, "Son, I put you with this Imam just so can learn his knowledge. Before you learn his knowledge, I want you to learn his Adab, his morals and his character."

It was Eid time and any students in Eid, they go to celebrate. Imam Malik, what's he doing? He's going to the house of Imam al-Zuhri. He waited outside the house of Imam al-Zuhri. He was about sixteen years old at that time. A servant of Imam al-Zuhri saw Imam Malik. And she told Imam al-Zuhri about him. They used to call him the blonde boy. She said, "Here is the blonde boy." Imam al-Zuhri said, "Let him in." So, he came inside. Imam al-Zuhri thought he's coming to eat Eid food with him. So, the Imam put food in front of him. Imam Malik looked at the food and said, "I don't want food." He said, "What do you mean, then why you are here?"

He said, "Teach me." Imam Zuhri said, "Sit down." He taught him forty hadith with the chain of narrations and Imam Malik writing them down. Then Imam Malik said, "Teach me more." Imam Zuhri said to him, "Go first and learn these and then come back. I'll teach you more." He said, "I've learned them." Imam Zuhri said, "Really?" He said, "Yes." He said, "Tell me." He said them all. With the chain of narrations without a single mistake at all just by writing them once.

When he did that, Imam Zuhri looked at him and he said, "Stand up. Stand before me. You are one of the vessels of knowledge. You are one of the exceptions which Allah made."

Allah Tala bears witness of greatness; to Himself that there is no God worthy of worship but Him. And He bears witness to the greatness of His creation of the angels. And He bears witness to the importance and greatness of those endued with knowledge.

Malik bin Anas bin Malik bin Abu Amer al-Asbahi was his name and his titles were Amirul Momineen fil-Hadith and Imam Dar-ul-Hijrat. He was born in the year 93 Hijri in Madina about the year 760.

The man of Aura, the man who when you looked at him, you

cannot help yourself but give him respect. And even though his origin was from Yemen and he lived in Madina, he really stood out. He was a tall man, wide chested, broad-chested man, wide eyes, strong-looking man. And he was blonde-haired, white face and some narration say he had blue eyes. His beard was long until it reached his chest, he wore the most elegant and eloquent clothing. When you looked at him, even if you didn't know that he was an Imam, his features strike you and you find something inside of you forcing you to respect this man.

His great grandfather Abi Aamer, who was from Yemen, embraced Islam in 2 AH and migrated to Madina. He participated in all the battles alongside the Holy Prophet (peace be upon him) except the Battle of Badr.

His father was a Tabiee, he had three brothers and one sister. One of his brothers, his older brother by the name of Al Nadir Ibn Al Anas; he was the man of knowledge. They used to say, Malik the brother of Imam Al Nadir. When Imam Al-Malik reached his position by the will of Allah, they started calling Al Nadir the brother of Imam Malik.

Imam Malik was a Tabiee at-Tabiee. He met the people who met the Sahabahs (companions of the Prophet). His grandfather Malik Ibn Anas was a friend of Uthman Ibn Affan (RA).

Imam Malik started his knowledge at the age of 10 years. He received his education in Madina and contacted about 900 scholars for collecting Hadiths. And he spent his whole life in Madina. In the land of the Prophet (peace be upon him). He never left Madina Al Munawwarah, only to Mecca when he went to do Hajj or Umrah.

He never even rode on a camel or any transport vehicle in his entire life when he was in Madina. Because in his righteousness and love for the Prophet (peace be upon him) and as a role model, he saw it disrespectable as an Imam representing his deen in the highest esteem to lift himself off the ground, out of respect for the messenger (peace be upon him) while his body was in the ground.

When he wanted to meet the rulers in Iraq, in Baghdad, in Kufa, in those areas; he never left to see them there. When he wanted to give them advice, he waited for them when they came to Hajj, to Mecca; if he was there, he'd meet them in their residential palaces. And when they came to Madina he would go to their residential palaces and meet them there and advise them.

He never went to a ruler for any need for himself or for any need of that ruler. The only time he ever went to the rulers or officials for only one reason; was to advise them when they had erred. And this is the trait of all the Imams. And especially the four Imams.

Imam Malik learned of his first teacher Rabiah Ar Rai for seven whole years, dedicated to him. After that, he started with the famous Imam, Abdullah Ibn Hurmuz. Abdullah Ibn Hurmuz was an ex-servant, slave. He graduated after 8 years from Ibn Hurmuz's school. There is another Imam that he learned of, his name was Imam Al Zuhri.

Jafar Sadiq was the grandson of Ali (RA) and he was a very important figure, he was the teacher of Imam Malik. There is a school of thought called the Jafari Madhab. I just want to mention Imam Jafar's very famous quote, he said, "Allah (SWT) destined for our things and he made them unknown and what he wanted from us he showed it to us. So why do you have to sit there thinking of the future? Don't think of the unknown, don't worry about the unknown and ask questions of the unknown. Think and worry about what you have that is known and work with it."

When he went to these scholars, he used to try and play a game to win the scholar for himself. So, he used to bring dates and stuff and he would assign some of his mates, his friends in the class and say, "I'll give you some dates to persuade the students to go back home today." So, it'd be him or one or two people with his teacher and so he'd have this teacher all for himself and that's where Imam Malik began.

He was the vessel of Knowledge and he loved Hadith, he loved his teachers. He used to stand outside and wait for his teachers in the heat of the sun, right in the middle of the Zuhr, when everyone else was at home and he'd wait for his Imam. So, one of his Imam, Imam Ibn Al Hurmuz, never liked people to stop him and ask him questions except at the time of his Dars (class). But Imam Malik didn't settle for that. He tried to always work his way around. He'd wait behind the rock. When Imam came out, he'd see him and he'd rush after him secretly and the first thing he'd do, he'd say, "As Salamu Alaikum Wa Rahmatullahi Wa Barakatuh." The Imam used to say, "Wa Alaikum As-Salam." Then he would say, "Ya Imam just about this hadith, can you just narrate that to me again?" He tried to get as many as he can from the Imam and the Imam would have to answer him as he was walking by.

In terms of acquiring knowledge, Imam Malik exerted a lot of effort. Despite the extremes of weather, he would visit his teachers and would try not to miss a single lesson. Acquiring knowledge of hadith was his primary goal. He excelled and mastered his knowledge but his sister became worried that he used to stand a lot of days, a lot of hours in the sun. Sometimes he's come back really sunburnt. Her father said to her, "Don't worry daughter, he'll be alright, he is learning the hadith of Rasulullah (peace be upon him), let him endure."

Through the likes of Ibn Shihab al-Zuhri, Ibn Hurmuz,

Rabi'atur-Ray and Yahya bin Saeed al-Ansari, he gathered hadith. He also gathered the fatwas [religious rulings] of Umar, Uthman, Abdullah Ibn Umar, Zaid bin Thabit and Abdur Rahman bin Auf.

When he was 21 years old, he became that mufti and he said, "I did not give any fatwa until I had seventy great scholars who had qualified me." These were seventy of the greatest Imams; Fuqaha, Jurisprudents, scholars of Madina; seventy who qualified him to be ready. They said, "You are now ready to make, derive your own opinions, obviously based on Daleel (evidence) from raw Quran and raw Hadith."

His way of thinking was a little bit different from Imam Abu Hanifa. In fact, very different from all the Imams; he didn't like to dwell into areas of controversial issues in Aqeedah and he didn't like to dwell into areas of ideological differences. Such as what used to happen in Kufa with Imam Abu Hanifa, with the Mu'tazila and the Khawarij. Philosophies of Greek theology and Aristotle's beliefs; such as saying today modernist views, he didn't like to dwell into them. In fact, he didn't need to do that because he was living in Madina.

Imam Malik was a traditional man. He taught according to the actions and practices of the people of Madina. He used to look at the companions who lived in Madina and his laws and school of thought revolve a lot around it. One of his students, Yahya Bin Yahya says, "A man entered into our circle one day and he asked the Imam a question, "Ya Imam, the most merciful rose above his throne. That's literally what it says in the Quran." He asked, "How did Allah rise?" Imam Malik put his head down and the students could see him sweating, sweating out of anger. He was angry at that question.

So, Imam Malik looked up and he said to him, "I don't know how above, but Allah is above, he's not below. And asking this question is an innovation." Then he looked at him and he said to his students, "Get him out!" They carried him out of the masjid quickly and he said, "I don't see you except an innovator or a mischievous person who wants to cause Fitna." That's how he dealt with these issues.

Imam Malik's fiqh like every other scholars such as Imam Abu Hanifa, Imam Malik; looked at the Quran for solutions. If there were no clear-cut solutions in the Quran then he would look in the Sunnah of the Prophet (peace be upon him). If there was nothing clear cut, he would look into the opinions of the Sahabas. Then if he couldn't find a clear-cut solution from the opinions of the Sahabah, he would look at something called Al Ijmah; the consensus of the companions and consensus of the scholars, the great scholars that existed. And up to here, all of the four Imams still followed up to this stage.

Now here was where Imam Malik differed, he looked at something which the other Imams didn't agree with him about; including one of his very close colleagues who studied with him, his name was Al Laith Ibn Sa'd. Imam Malik used to use the practices of the people of Madina, meaning he would look at their practices and how they acted. There were more than 120,000 companions in Madina that lived by the time Imam Malik came around. Laith Ibn Sa'd used to write letters to him saying, "Ya Imam you are right to use these great Sahabas of Madina, that's good, we don't see ourselves any better than them. However, not 200 years later, there are customs involved, traditions of your culture." Imam Malik respected his opinion but he stuck to his own, believing that this is the right one. If he couldn't find it among the people of Madina, he went to something which Imam Abu Hanifa used; and that is Qiyas to come to a ruling by comparison.

He'd look at a similar ruling and say, "Okay we'll say that it's like this, we'll practice it like this." The scholars used to say that smoking is Makruh; it's just disliked. But when they find out the effects of smoking and tobacco and how bad it is, we conclude that cigarettes and tobacco are haram like the way drugs or alcohol is haram.

Imam Malik also looked at a very unique way and this is where he really differed, something full of flexibility. In his Madhab, you will find three things that the other Imams didn't.

One of them was called Al Istihsan; which means the better of two fiqh matters. It had two fiqh matters, he'll take the easier or better one.

The second thing, he used to follow was Sadd Ad Dharai; which means something lawful or unlawful depending on what it will lead to. For example, if it leads to destruction, eliminate it.

Thirdly, Al Masalih Al Mursala; the benefits of the public; if something may lead to the harm of the public or community, even if it was something halal, they should stop it and this is to look at the benefits of the people at large.

Imam Malik's Madhab was actually the most flexible because of these three. The other Imams differed about that they didn't really agree on it; maybe Abu Hanifa to a certain extent.

Imam Malik produced a monumental book. It is called Al Muwatta. This book is a collection of prophetic hadith, and some companions saying etc. It contains currently about 1,720 hadith.

It was about 100 years before Bukhari and Muslim and the six books of Hadith that we know about. So basically, some scholars say this was probably the first book of hadith ever and it is one of the most authentic.

This Kitab Al Muwatta was spread by his students. Imam Malik didn't write Al Muwatta himself; he collected it and his students put it together. Imam Malik's daughter Fatima had memorized Al-Muwatta.

The way they put it was, first of all, there was a 100,000 hadith in it. From the 100,000; 9,000 were taken as being the most authentic and from the 9,000, we finally ended up with 1,720 most authentic hadiths till today.

Among them are several of them which Imam Malik narrated himself; we call it the golden chain. They are the most authentic hadith existing today. Any hadith of the Prophet (peace be upon him) that had the following chain, from Malik who heard it from Nafi who heard it from Ibn Umar who heard it from that Prophet (peace be upon him); if you see that chain before any hadith the scholars unanimously say this is the strongest chain of narration to existing in any form hadith. They call it the golden chain.

Imam Shafi says about Al Muwatta, "No book before the Book of Allah was more authentic and accurate than Al Muwatta." Keeping in mind that Bukhari and Muslim weren't existing at that time.

Imam Al Mansur who was the Khalifa at that time remember we mentioned him, he was at the time of Abu Hanifa. He came up to Imam Malik at the Kaba and he said to him, "Ya Imam, I want this book to be copied and printed and distributed and I want it to be the main source and every other book to be destroyed and burnt." Imam Malik said to him, "No, don't do that. For there are people who receive knowledge from their Imams and from different sources and there could be sources that are not known to me. To take only my book and refuse all the rest is a dangerous thing to do. Don't take away all the other knowledge just based on mine. For I am a man of knowledge and there's still more for me to learn." And this was the way the Imams always spoke.

Imam Malik's greatest fear, someone asked him a question and they've got to give them a verdict. Every time Imam Malik was asked for a verdict that didn't exist before he would tell the person to wait. He'd go to make Wudu (abultion). Then he'd come back. He'd sit down and he would start by saying, "There is no might and there is no power except Allah." Then he would give the answer to the best of knowledge. He used to say, "There is nothing harder upon me in life than when I was asked a question about halal or haram; is this permissible or not, because I am representing the ruling of Allah himself, the creator of the world."

So the scholars form a common motto, "I do not know." Ibn Hurmuz would say, "If you are not aware of the answer to a question, do not display unnecessary formality. You should clearly say that you do not know. Therein lies your respect." Imam Malik always lived by this advice. If he was ever asked a question that he did not know the answer to, he would simply reply, "La adri" – "I do not know."

Al Haithami, who was one of the students of Imam Malik says, "I witnessed Imam Malik being asked about 48 issues on separate occasions; he replied to 32 out of 48 of them, 'I do not know.'"

There is a story about a Moroccan, he had a question which all of the Imams of Morocco could not answer. So, he traveled for four months with a message from the Imam saying, "There is no more knowledgeable scholar on the face of the Earth than Imam Malik, go to him in Madina and get us the answer for your question."

So, he set out for four months. You can imagine the desert and the heat and the struggle. When he arrived, he asked Imam

Malik the question. Imam Malik went and made wudu (abulation) and came and sat down and said, "La Hawla Wa La Quwwata illa BillAhil Aliyyil Azeem (there is no might and power except Allah)" stood up and said to him, "Give me till tomorrow." The next day, he did the same thing and he sat down and he said to him, "My answer is, I don't know." The Moroccan student stood up and said, "Ya Imam, with all due respect, the imams of Morocco are waiting for my answer and I've traveled four months and I have to return another four months, so how many is that? Eight months to get the answer. I can't say to them that the great imam says, "I do not know." Imam Malik said, "Well then go and tell your scholars that Imam Malik says, "He doesn't know." The Moroccan went back and told the scholars, "This is what he told him, 'I do not know.'"

If Imam Malik knew that he had made a mistake, he'd gather his students, and then he'll clarify his mistake in front of all his students. That's something very heavy to do. "Listen students, I said this before and I've made a mistake; this is what the correct answer is."

In his circles, if anybody spoke while he was speaking, that would be forbidden. In his circles he never allowed someone, he didn't like people asking, "What's your Daleel (evidence)?" They're asking him things which they don't understand themselves. Opposite to Abu Hanifa's circles, Abu Hanifa used to encourage his students to discuss and debate. As for Imam Malik who lived in Madina, the knowledge in Madina was different. It was quite strict and straightforward and these ideologies of Khawarij and Mu'tazila and Greek philosophy and Aristotle believed and stuff; they weren't in Madina.

So Imam Malik was not interested in all those ideologies; anyone who asked him, "Does Allah have a hand? Where is He? Which face is he directed?" All those thoughts he never attempted to even answer them; except in one way; brief answers that made them quiet; take it as it is and walk away.

When he used to sit it was the same spot where the Prophet (SAW) used to sit and teach. It was the same spot where Umar (RA); the Khalifa sat and taught. He never in his life narrated a single hadith while standing. Imam Malik, before he ever said one hadith; he'll go and have a shower or he'd make wudu, then he prayed 2 rakats, then he'd wear the best of clothing, put on the best of perfume, enter the masjid quietly, would not say a word. Until serenity and peace befell him. He went to the seat where the Prophet (SAW) used to sit and he sat there. Then he'll look up at his students and he spoke the hadith with his narration. That's how Imam Malik Narrated hadith.

Imam Malik's family was not particularly affluent and survived on a meager income. He acquired education in very difficult circumstances. When he began teaching, even then his financial state was deficient. He had around 400 dinars, which he invested in a business. Whatever he earned from his business was what he would spend for domestic use.

He married a freed slave and lived a happy life with her. When he gained worldwide acclaim and people started to recognize him, statesmen and Khalifa began visiting him. In this way, Allah strengthened his economic status. He would not accept gifts from ordinary leaders. However, he happily accepted the gifts sent by Khalifa. He was of the view that if a Khalifa sent a gift and it had no strings attached, there was no harm in accepting it because those who had dedicated their lives for the proliferation of knowledge had a share from the bait-ul-mal (central reserve). Whatever monetary gifts were sent his way from Abbasid caliphs, he would spend most of it on students of his madrasah (school). Most of the expenses of Imam Shafi's education were covered by Imam Malik, as was the case with the rest of his students. As regards accepting monetary gifts from khalifa, Imam Shafi shared the same view, although because he belonged to the category of zawil-qurba, he preferred not to benefit from this.

In contrast, however, Imam Abu Hanifa and Imam Ahmad bin Hanbal held the view that any monetary gift sent by khalifa should not be accepted as such motives have strings attached. Imam Abu Hanifa never needed such gifts as he had a well-established business from which he earned thousands. However, Imam Ahmad's income was very basic. Imam Ahmad bin Hanbal would earn a small amount through the property and would live off that. If times were desperate, he would perform manual labor to earn money. After crops had been harvested, he would go to collect fallen wheat spikes as this was considered acceptable and a basic right for the less privileged. Despite all this, he never accepted any gift sent by khalifa of the time.

Imam Malik, he went against the norms. I'd like to say that all four Imams even though they had different ways of dealing with the government, all of them got imprisoned and all of them got tortured, including Imam Malik. Even with the way Imam Malik dealt with them.

Imam Malik witnessed the fall of the Umayyad Dynasty and the rise of the Abbasid Dynasty. He witnessed eight Khalifas in the time of the Umayyad Dynasty and five Khalifas in the time of the Abbasid Dynasty. He lived for eighty-six years. Making him the longest living among the four imams. The point is that Imam Malik was courageous and this is proof that him taking the gifts did not mean that he was a government puppet, like some of the scholars today. He was not a government scholar. Once Harun Al Rashid gave three thousand Dirhams to Imam Malik and he said to him, "When these three thousand Dirhams reach you, I want you to come immediately to my palace with my royal order." He had to leave Madina and go to Iraq, to Baghdad. Imam Malik never left Madina and he insisted on never leaving it. He said, "A letter to come to Baghdad because of the three thousand dinars?" He sent the three thousand dinars back saying to him, "I will never leave Madina."

So, what did Harun Al Rashid do, to show you how much they respected him? He sent him double, six thousand dirhams with no conditions. Imam Malik looked at the wealth and looked at his students and said, "The Prophet (SAW) says, "Whoever leaves something for the sake of Allah, Allah will give him something better." And he distributes the dirhams amongst his students and himself. To show you, that if he was a government scholar, would he say something like that? Never.

Now because of this truth, something happened, and he had to face a terrible ordeal; he clashed with the state. Every Imam clashed with the state. A revolution against Abu Jafar Al Mansur began. Imam Abu Hanifa was about in his sixties at that time. And the people who started this revolution were people from the Prophet's (ﷺ) family. And the leader of the revolutionist was led by Muhammad An Nafs Az Zakiyyah; who was a descendent of Imam Hasan Ibn Ali (RA).

Imam Malik, he supported the leader of this movement. If Imam Muhammad Na Nafs Az Zakiyyah; a great Imam, if he became the new ruler, then it would be better. That's what Imam Malik thought on the inside. What happened was the governor of Madina started going around; basically, forcing the people to pledge allegiance for himself. And the people didn't like this. So the revolution increased.

The fact is that Imam Malik was against any form of rebellion. His view was that the bloodshed caused by rebellion saw no limit, and even if the rebellion was successful, those who gained dominance were usually as bad as the previous rulers, if not worse. In such circumstances, there could be no hope of improvement or any sort of benefit.

When the Abbasids gained dominance, he had to endure certain difficulties. One was a result of the forceful oaths that were being taken by the new government from the public. From a Shariah perspective, the oaths had no bearing and whilst being questioned, he would openly express this opinion.

One day someone asked Imam Malik a question, which had a political motive behind it and Imam Malik knew this. The question was, "If a man was forced to divorce his wife and he divorced her, does the divorce count?" Imam Malik said, "In Fiqh and Islam nothing is valid out of force."

So, the Khalifa found out and he sent news for the Imam to stop saying what he was saying and never to repeat that rule; that verdict again. The Imam replied, "I cannot conceal knowledge if I know it."

So they sent a spy to one of his circles and the spy asked the question again. To check if this is what Imam really meant. So he asked the question, the Imam answered him exactly the same answer as before knowing the political consequence of it. The result of this was, there was an order to capture Imam Malik in Madina to the governor of Madina.

They captured him, imprisoned him and they tortured him. He was beaten so badly until his arms became disabled. And his shoulder, his right shoulder was dislocated. At that time, Imam Malik prayed a little with his arms down.

Then there was a second revolt when they heard about Imam Malik being tortured this way, his students got up, you mess with his students? So Khalifah Mansur came in-person to Madina and he said, "I apologize, I did not order this. Please tell me what you need and I'll give you and I'll sack the governor and I've humiliated him and so on," this is what he claimed. And Imam Malik, therefore, was not a government scholar.

Allah gave him long life and enabled him to make the best use of his time. In later years, he suffered from illnes, due to which he was unable to visit Masjid al-Nabawi for a long period and would teach his lessons at home. He never mentioned his suffering to anyone.

People raised many accusations against him when he was unable to visit the mosque. However, he would remain silent. As his final days approached, he mentioned the reason behind not visiting the mosque to some of his special students and said, "It is not necessary to be vocal about your illness in front of everyone. Everyone must return to their Lord eventually and everyone is answerable before Him."

His final illness rendered him extremely weak and resulted in his final hour. Imam Malik died on the 14th of Rabiul Awwal 179 AH. Amir of Madina Abdul Aziz Ibn Muhammad Ibn Ibraheem led his funeral prayers.

The whole of Medina gathered to participate in his funeral, a scene that was witnessed after a long time after the death of Umar (RA); no such event of mourning took place. He was buried in Jannatul-Baqi.

It is reported that the Holy Prophet had said: "Very soon will people beat the flanks of camels in search of knowledge, and they shall find no one more knowledgeable than the knowledgeable scholar of Madina" (Sunan Al-Tirmidhi). Scholars consider that the scholar referred to was Al-Malik ibn Anas. (May Allah's peace and blessing be upon them all).

Quotes by Imam Malik

"Verily, when a person starts praising himself, then his honor will leave him."

"A sign of a person's evil is his need to constantly argue."

"I have met people in my city who seem the most righteous but they went out and started exposing people. So Allah made their faults apparent. I know other people who have faults but because they are quite Allah causes people to forget their faults."

"Always be in a company that motivates you toward a positive direction."

"Knowledge is not knowing a large number of texts and quoting narrations. It is a light that Allah places in the heart."

Four Advice from the Quran

✓ So fear not mankind, but fear Me (5:44)

✓ And to your Lord alone turn all your intentions and hopes (94:8)

✓ Fear Allah (SWT), surely Allah (SWT) is aware of all your actions (59:18)

✓ Do what is beautiful. Allah loves those who do what is beautiful. (2:195)

"Do good deeds properly, sincerely and moderately and know that your deeds will not make you enter Paradise, and that the most beloved deed to Allah's is the most regular and constant even though it were little." (Sahih Bukhari, vol. 8, hadith 471)

When you meet each other, offer good wishes and blessings for safety. One who conveys to you a message of safety and security and also when a courteous greeting is offered to you, meet it with a greeting still more courteous or (at least) of equal courtesy (Al-Qur'an-4:86)

"The heart that beats for Allah (God) is always a stranger among the hearts that beat for the Dunya (world)." Anonymous

A thought-provoking questions you should ask yourself every day

What do I fear?

Practical Ways to Improve Yourself

<u>Be helpful</u>

Helping others is one of the best ways to make you a better person. When you help someone in need you will feel self-content and satisfied by your achievement. You will realize that what you do is worth something to other people and that you are bringing about good deeds with your help in'sha'Allah.

 BALANCE DEEN WITH CAREER

STEP ONE: IDENTIFYING INDICATORS OF POOR BALANCE.

So the first step is to identify the areas of your life that are being neglected more than others. Mark the indicators of poor balance in your life currently using the Balance Criteria below. This activity will show you how balanced your life is right now. Note: Don't be a perfectionist while marking your weak areas. Go easy on yourself & give yourself a tick for the activities that you're doing consistently (even if you're not doing them perfectly a 100% of the time!).

THE BALANCE CRITERIA

A) Ibadah (rights of Allah) being compromised

☐ Praying 5 Fard prayers on-time (not missing prayers)

☐ Praying salah with khushoo & in the earliest time

☐ Keeping all fasts in Ramadan

☐ Making dua and reading daily azkaar to remember Allah

☐ Reading Quran regularly

☐ Nafl Ibadah - Keeping extra fasts/ praying nafl salah (tahajjud, Ishraq etc.)

B) Fulfilling all your roles in the family with ihsan

☐ Taking care of the mandatory responsibilities

☐ Helping them with regular work with kindness and good akhlaq

☐ Having fun & playing with them

☐ Teaching each other and learning Islam together

C) Fulfilling all your responsibilities outside family with ihsan

☐ Earning a halal income if you're working

☐ Giving your best to your job

☐ Doing dawah to the best of your ability in your social circle

☐ If you've taken up other responsibilities, doing good service in each of the

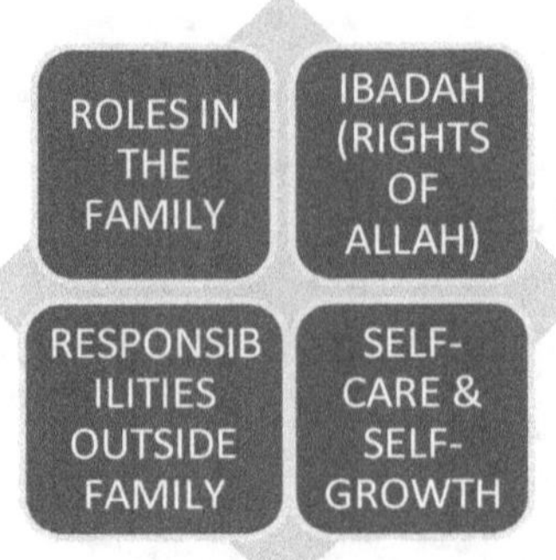

D) Having some time to yourself to recharge and relax

☐ Spending some time (even if little) to recharge yourself so you're not sleep-deprived, cranky or irritable most of the time

☐ Spending time on things you love (self-care, productive fun activities etc.)

E) Improving yourself as a muslim

☐ Taking up goals to advance in Islamic learning (Arabic, tajweed, tafseer of Quran...)

☐ Consciously improving your habits, routines, behaviours (akhlaq) etc.

After you've identified the areas that are the WEAKEST for you right now, it's time to move on to the next step! Also, don't worry... you don't have to work on all of those areas at once! I've an easy and really effective way for you to get started >>>>

IMAM ASH-SHAFI

When Imam Malik was in his middle ages, a young boy by the age of thirteen, his mother from Mecca, his mother said to him, "My son you are well known. You have memorized the whole Quran and you have memorized Hadith and you have memorized poetry. I want to send you to Imam Malik to learn his Adab, his character before you learn his knowledge."

So she got him ready and she wrote a letter to the governor of Mecca who happened to be her cousin. She writes a letter to him to send a letter to the governor of Madina, to go with her son to Imam Malik. Basically, to intercede for him, to become his teacher.

Young 13-year-old going through the deserts to Madina, seeking knowledge. He reached the governor of Madina and gave him the letter of the governor of Mecca. And the governor of Madina, his face changed and he started to sweat. The young boy looked at him and said, "What's wrong?" He said "Wallahi! If the governor of Mecca asked me to walk barefoot in the middle of the desert with nothing on my head, it would be easier than for me to go to Imam Malik's house. Because he had so much respect for him. So, the boy innocently said to him, "Well you don't have to go to him, make him come to you." The governor of Madina laughed and said, "Come on, let's go."

They went to Imam Malik's house, they knocked on the door and the housemaid of Imam Malik answered and they asked for Imam Malik. She said to him, "Listen if there is a religious question right now is not the time. Write it on paper and he will answer it for you. If you want to learn hadith, go to his circles of Dars (classes), if the government issues, it's not the time, there's another time for it." So, the governor of Madina says, "I have a letter for him from the governor of Mecca." The young boy says, "A big blonde, white, colored eyes, unexpected from the people of Madina, came to the door."

He says, "I looked up at him and the servant lady brought him a chair, he sat on it." And then he said, "What does the governor of Mecca want from me?" And the governor of Madina just gives him a paper without a word. When Imam Malik read this paper, he threw the paper away saying, "Lahawla walakuata illa billah, there is no might and power except to Allah. Has it come to this that knowledge now needs connections?"

He looked at the young boy and the young boy said to him, "May Allah straighten the path of the Sheikh. I am from the lineage of the Prophet (peace be upon him)." So now basically he forced, he obliged the Imam to listen to him. "I am a Qureshi, I have memorized the Quran at the age of seven and your Muwatta, the whole of it. I've memorized it with its chain of narrations. My mother sent me here to learn from you." The Imam looked at the boy for a long time as the boy was telling his story of how he sought knowledge so far. The Imam had an astonishing physiognomy and a penetrating insight; he told him:

"My son! By the Will of Allah, you will have a great future. Tomorrow comes to me and brings with you someone who could read the 'Muwatta' well as I fear you would not be able to read it by yourself."

The boy responded with politeness,

"Imam, I will read it myself from memory without a book."

Does anyone know who the young boy was? He was Imam Muhammad Ibn Al Idris Ash Shafi'i.

Allah bears witness of greatness; to Himself that there is no God worthy of worship but Him. And He bears witness to the greatness of His creation of the angels. And He bears witness to the importance and greatness of those endued with knowledge.

Imam Shafi, also known as 'Shaykh Al Islam', is one of the four great Imams of Sunni schools of law. He is also the author of several prominent works in the field. He has been titled 'Nasir al-Hadith' which means "defender of hadith."

Imam's full name is Abu Abdullah Muhammad bin Idris Shafi`i ibn Al-Abbas ibn Uthman ibn Syafie bin Ubaid ibn Abdu Yazid ibn Hasyim ibn Al-Muttalib [father of Abdul Muttalib grandfather of the Prophet (peace be upon him)] bin Abd Manaf. He is the Only Imam who is related to the Prophet (peace be upon him) as he belonged to the Qurayshi tribe of Banu Muttalib, which was the sister tribe of the Banu Hashim [the tribe of the Prophet (peace be upon him)].

Imam Shafi's mother reports of an incident before the birth of Imam Shafi, wherein her dream she sighted the Jupiter star emerging from her womb and embarking in the province of Egypt. She distinguished a radiant light emitting from this star illuminating the entire city. She questioned the wise men of the city to interpret this dream, who notified her that soon she was due to give birth to a learned scholar whose knowledge would be beneficial far and wide.

Imam Shafi was born in the year 150 AH (767 AC) in Gaza, Palestine. It was the same year in which the Great Imam Abu Hanifa had passed away. He lost his father during infancy and was raised by his mother under very poor circumstances. Fearing the waste of his son's lineage, his mother decided to move to Mecca where their relatives lived. Imam was very young at that time. It is quoted by some scholars that he was two years old when his mother migrated to Mecca. Therefore, he spent his formative years acquiring religious education in the cities of Mecca and Medina. According to some sources, he memorized the Quran by the age of seven or nine.

As for his features, Imam Ash Shafi was Arab looking, very healthy, he had a strong build, tall muscular. He had a strong presence when he walked in; everybody stopped and listened and looked at him.

His early education was marked by poverty because of which his mother could not afford to pay the fees for his education. Consequently, instead of participating in the classes, the young Imam would just sit on the sidelines and take it all in only by listening to what his teacher was teaching to other kids in the class. He became so adept at learning and storing knowledge even though just by listening, that on occasions when his teacher was unable to take a class, the young Imam would step in and take the class, teaching his fellow students. His teacher was so impressed by his abilities that he took him on as a formal student on a complimentary no fee basis. The Imam himself used to say:

"After I finished learning the Quran, I would go to the Mosque and sit with the Scholars of hadith and Islamic matters. I used to live in Mecca among tent dwellers in such a state of poverty that I could not even afford to buy paper to write, so I would write on stones and bones instead."

Imam Ash Shafi loved sports, he loved archery; that was his favorite sport. He was ten out of ten in archery. Once, he said, "Very few can stand against me in archery. If I want to shoot ten arrows at a fixed target, not one of them will miss."

Excellent horse rider and he would jump on his horse without needing to touch anything, maybe just the ear or the head. And he lived in the desert. It's very important for 17 years of his life. When he was a child his mother sent him to the desert for 5 years of his childhood; until he was 13. And then he spent another 12 years in the desert later on. Why? There was a tribe in the desert by the name of Banu Huzain. When you hear this name Banu Huzain all the Arab world, especially in those times know that Banu Huzain was where the original Arabic, Arabic is to be taken from there. They were the spring, the fountain of all the Arabic of the world.

During this period, he also gained familiarity with astronomy and medicine. He was a good poet and was considered a talented writer. His language proficiency was reflected in his writing and it is for this reason that his books are counted among the great works of Arabic literature, even though they are to do with fiqh-related matters and not literature per se. Imam Shafi had a very melodious and touching voice. When he would recite the Holy Quran, people would be overcome with emotion. He spoke Arabic clearly and was an eloquent speaker. He would make use of proverbs whilst speaking. The famous muhaddith, Ibn Rahwayh called him Khatib-ul-Ulema [orator of the scholars].

When he turned 20 and had completed his education with the scholars of Mecca, he desired to travel to Medina to study the Muwatta from Imam Malik and gain mastery in the field of hadith. This was at the height of Imam Malik's profession and it was very difficult to be admitted into his school.

Thus, he worked very hard to make himself worthy of being accepted. He acquired a copy of Muwatta and memorized the hadith narrated therein. He also had the governor of Mecca write a letter of recommendation to the governor of Medina. With this, he set off for Medina. When he arrived in Medina, the letter, unfortunately, made no difference.

However, using his speaking skills, he managed to acquire a place in Imam Malik's school. He then went on to get the attention of Imam Malik through his dedication and love for hadith. He stayed in Imam Malik's company for around ten years. He also benefited from the other leading scholars of

Medina, which enabled him to become a scholar of hadith and an unparalleled authority in fiqh.

After the death of Imam Malik, he returned to Mecca. In search of a job, he traveled to Yemen, where the maternal side of his family lived. With the recommendation of the governor, he acquired a position in Najran, which gave him financial stability. In terms of public relations, however, this post caused many problems for him. People were accustomed to dishonest recommendations and fulfilling selfish interests.

The rich people in the area were used to doing things their way. Imam Shafi would work with complete justice and integrity and would not care for how influential a person was. As a result, a bombardment of complaints was filed against him. The new governor of Najran was a cruel and harsh ruler and he too felt strongly against him.

At the time, the Abbasids were extremely concerned about the Alawites (rebellion) lest they gained influence. The governor of Najran, therefore, took advantage of this weakness on the part of the Abbasids and, through a conspiracy, complained to Harun al-Rashid that some Alawites had sought to stir up commotion in Najran, among whom was Imam Shafi.

Harun al-Rashid immediately took notice of this complaint and ordered the rebels to be captured and brought to Baghdad. Thus, the captives – among whom was Imam Shafi – were brought to Baghdad before Harun al-Rashid in shackles after suffering extreme cruelties. Rashid took everyone's statement individually, which involved very brief hearings. He would then order for each one of them to be executed.

Imam Shafi's turn came and Rashid said to him with a furious look, "You are dreaming of a caliphate and you think that we are not worthy of it."

At the time, people were drowning in their own blood; he was surrounded by a ghastly view. When it was his turn to talk, using his God-given faculty of wisdom, Imam Shafi said, "I am a victim of enmity and jealousy. Opponents have unjustly captured me. As the Amirul Momineen, you should ponder over how I can be a part of this when they consider me their servant and how I can go against your family, which considers me its brother."

Imam Muhammad bin Hasan was present in the court when Imam Shafi pointed in his direction and said, "I am a knowledgeable person and possess a thirst for knowledge. I have no interest in rebellions and this qazi knows it."

Rashid looked in Imam Muhammad's direction as if to confirm what Imam Shafi was saying. Imam Muhammad replied, "Shafi is speaking the truth. I know him. He is not a rebel, but rather is a scholar and holds a keen interest in teaching."

Imam Shafi's clarity of speech and Imam Muhammad's endorsement worked in his favor. Rashid said to Imam Muhammad, "Very well, keep him with you and I shall make a decision about him later."

In this manner, Imam Shafi came into the refuge of Imam Muhammad and began residing in his house. There, he studied the Hanafi fiqh and studied Imam Muhammad's books. This trying time became a means of excelling his knowledge further and thus, he became an imam of the fiqhs prevalent in Medina and Iraq. This favor of Imam Muhammad remained embedded in his heart forever and he would often mention Imam Muhammad with great reverence.

After living in Baghdad for around two years, Imam Shafi returned to Mecca and established his school in Masjid al-Haram. This school gradually excelled to the extent that Imam

Ahmad once said, "When I went to Mecca, I heard Muhammad bin Idris giving a lesson on hadith and fiqh."

He then said to his friend Ishaq bin Rahwayh, "I have just seen a young man giving a lesson and the more I listen to him, the more I become fascinated by what he says. Come, let me show you." Thus, Ishaq bin Rahwayh also heard his lesson and was intrigued.

Alongside teaching in Mecca, he also began writing. To explain his fiqh school of thought, he compiled a set of rules on deduction and thus founded his fiqh order. Here, he also wrote two books. One was Khilaf Malik, wherein he criticized his teacher, Imam Malik's fiqh-related views and expressed his views on the actions of Medina's dwellers. He also referred to Imam Malik's care in deducting hadith as "unnecessarily extreme."

The other was Khilaf al-Iraqiyeen, wherein he criticized Imam Abu Hanifa's views … In this manner, he served his duties of writing and teaching in Mecca for around 12 years. In 195 AH, when he was around 45 years of age, he traveled to Baghdad again. When he got there, he prayed at Imam Abu Hanifa's grave, offered two nawafil in the adjacent mosque and during the prayer, he only raised his hands at the beginning of the prayer. When asked about this, he replied that he had done this out of respect and recognition of Imam Abu Hanifa.

Whilst living in Baghdad, he authored two further books. One was called Al-Risalah, unique work on the principles of fiqh which had never been touched on previously, and the second was named Al-Mabsut, wherein he described the details of his fiqh. Both these books are famously known as Al-Kutub al-Baghdadiyah [the two books of Baghdad] and were narrated by his intelligent student, Al-Hussain bin Muhammad al-Sabah al-Za'farani (died 260 AH). Compiled with a few other booklets, this set is known as Al-Umm and is used even today.

When he traveled to Egypt in 199 AH and interacted with the Maliki scholars there, he made some amendments to some of his books, which were narrated by another of his brilliant students, Al-Rabi bin Sulayman al-Muradi (died 270 AH) and are called Aqwal-e-Jadidah.

This period, in which Imam Shafi was busy explaining his fiqh school of thought, was the period of compilation of knowledge. Whilst students of Abu al-Aswad al-Du'ali were occupied in compiling rules of Arabic grammar, Al-Asma'i and his students were busy collating Arabic literature and poetry. Khalil had just founded Ilm-ul-Urooz; Jahiz was busy explaining the methods of critiquing and investigating Arabic literature; Imam Abu Yusuf and Imam Muhammad bin Hasan al-Shaybani were occupied in collating the Hanafi fiqh; Imam Malik's efforts were gaining acclaim in Medina; narrating hadith was becoming an acquired skill; various groups were organizing themselves intellectually and Kharijites, Shiites and Mu'tazilites were engaged in combat with debates and conflicts erupting everywhere.

In such an intellectual climate, Imam Shafi was occupied in searching for the truth. He cited incredible arguments on the authenticity of akhbar-e-ahaad [hadith with a single narrator or very few narrators]. He earned the title of Nasir al-Sunnah [the Defender of the Sunnah] from the Muslim Ummah.

In terms of qiyas [deductive analogy], even though nobody could compete with Imam Abu Hanifa, the services rendered by Imam Shafi in the field of qiyas stand alone and have a unique status. He explained that even though akhbar-e-ahaad and qiyas were sources of deductive knowledge, it did not diminish their importance. They were of equal importance and all human life revolved around this deductive knowledge. Therefore, he explained, "when we solve most of our day to day problems using this, then why is it that we feel insecure about resorting to this in matters of Shariah?"

He would say that most problems could be resolved through the Quran and hadith, but if any question still remained unanswered by them, then one can resort to qiyas through the means mentioned in the nass [sources of ruling]. He would say that any intellectual mujtahid [a person who practices ijtihad – exerting one's mental faculty to find an answer] can answer such problems. In terms of hadith, his knowledge was sound.

Once, a person asked him, "I have heard that you answer all problems from the Quran and hadith. Tell me, is there any compensation for a person in the ihram who kills a wasp?"

Answering the question, Imam Shafi replied, "Allah says that whatever the Prophet (peace be upon him) says to you, you must act upon it and the Prophet (ﷺ) also said to follow his example and the example of his Khulafa. Tariq bin Shahab narrated that Umar once asked a person in the ihram to kill a wasp. From this, we can ascertain that there is no compensation for a person who kills a wasp."

As has been mentioned previously that aside from qiyas, Imam Shafi considered all other means of knowledge as improper, for example istihsan [making a ruling different from that on which similar cases have been decided, based on precedent], masalih-e-mursalah [consideration of public interest], etc.

In fact, he deemed such methods harmful. Despite holding differing views, Imam Shafi held other schools of thought in high regard and held no grudge against them. Once, a person asked him, "What do you think of Abu Hanifa?" He replied, "He was the leading figure of Iraq." When he was asked about Abu Yusuf, he replied, "He followed the hadith and revered them."

Imam Muhammad was an expert of the branches of fiqh and was gifted in the field of qiyas. Thus, he expressed his views concerning Hanafi imams with great reverence and clarity. Imam Shafi was not fond of kalam [argumentation based on Islamic scholastic theology], debates and such encounters. He would say that debates had no benefit and they only served to sharpen the tongue and entertain the mind and thus, they were futile.

He would say that true salvation was in following the Quran and Sunnah. He would say to his students: "Do not give any importance to matters of kalam and save yourself from pondering over it."

Imam Shafi lived in Baghdad for around three years, though he never really considered it home. The Mu'tazilites were gaining influence in the area and had submitted to Mamun al-Rashid. Aside from this, after the defeat of Al-Amin [son of Harun al-Rashid], the Arabic influence over the area began to diminish and Mamun al-Rashid gained the support of the people of Khorasan and Persia, who had great influence over him.

The people of the Quran and Sunnah, therefore, began to face difficulties. In such circumstances, Imam Shafi did not deem it suitable to continue living in Baghdad and after consulting some of his peers, he decided to shift to Egypt as it was far away from Baghdad, the Markaz, and also because the students of his contemporary, Imam Malik resided there, who he hoped to live peacefully with.

Egypt at the time still had an Arabic foothold. Another reason for his decision to move was that the Governor of Egypt, Abbas bin Abdullah Abbasi held him in high regard. Thus, bearing this in mind, he migrated from Baghdad to Egypt in 199 AH. The journey was extremely long and arduous. The situation he faced in Egypt was no less difficult as he faced many challenges.

During his journey to Egypt, in fact, he expressed his thoughts in a qaseeda, of which two couplets are:

"I wish to journey to Egypt, yet the path between is dangerous and full of desert.

By God, I do not know whether peace and tranquillity await me or if fate has something else in store; I am oblivious to this."

When Imam Shafi arrived in Egypt, he experienced immense success. The governor of Egypt approved a set allowance for him from the "Sahm-e-Zawil-Qurba" part of the treasury. A student of Imam Malik, Abdullah bin Abdul Hakam, who was affluent and an influential figure in the government, helped him a great deal and extended all sorts of comforts for him. Here, he got the chance to proofread his books and start a school.

Imam Shafi had no comparison when it came to argumentation and debates. Once, Imam Muhammad bin Hasan al-Shaybani somewhat teasingly said to him, "I have heard that you consider my view of ghasab [seizing] to be incorrect."

At first, Imam Shafi apologized and decided to avoid directly answering the question as he had immense respect for Imam Muhammad and also because he wanted to avoid any argument. However, Hanafis are of the view that debates should be pursued as they open up new avenues of knowledge and matters become clearer. When Imam Muhammad pressed a little harder, Imam Shafi became ready to debate on the topic. With regard to ghasab, Hanafis are of the view that:

1. If the item that has been seized is still intact, then it should be returned to the person from whom it had been seized

2. If the seized item has been rendered useless, then it should be paid for

3. If the seized item has been transformed into something else

(for example, a building is erected on a plot of land, the paper was seized on which a book has been written, gold was stolen and molded into jewelry, the cloth was seized and sewn into a shirt or trousers), then the owner will still be paid the full worth of the original item. However, if the originally seized item has something else now attached to it (for example, a cow was stolen which gave birth to a calf) then the originally seized item will be returned along with its by-product

Shafi's are against the third point. They say that in such a scenario, the rightful owner has the right to take back what belongs to them, however, if the one who seized the item desires, they may destroy the erected house and take the debris.

Nonetheless, the debate ensued in the following manner:

Imam Muhammad: If a person seizes another person's plot of land and builds a beautiful building, worth hundreds of thousands of dirhams, but the plot of land is worth a lot less, then what is your view?

Imam Shafi: The land should be returned to the rightful owner, however, if the one who seized the land wishes, they may take the debris with them. In any case, the owner cannot be forced to purchase the house or sell off the land.

Imam Muhammad: Let's say a person seized some planks of wood and fixed one of his boats with them and the boat has now set sail with passengers on board. If the person who owned the planks of wood demands for them to be returned in the middle of their journey, what is your verdict in such a case?

Imam Shafi: The owner's demand to return the wood immediately would be inappropriate in such a case. When the boat reaches the shore, however, then it will be the owner's right to have the planks returned, even if taking them apart from the boat causes harm to the structure of the boat. Similar questions were posed to t Imam Shafi, the contents of which are extremely detailed.

The final argument posed by Imam Muhammad was, "If the owner demands for the property [built on their land] to be destroyed and its debris to be removed, then it goes against the principle of … 'La dharara wa la dhirara [One must not harm themselves, nor harm others]'. To destroy such an expensive house is a waste of resources and the punishment for this outweighs the crime, especially when the person is prepared to pay for the original cost of the land and the owner has no loss to face."

Imam Shafi: Alright, then let us consider that a wealthy man belonging to an affluent and respectable family entices a slave-girl belonging to a poor family and marries her whilst the owner of the slave-girl does not give his consent. The slave-girl eventually gives birth to ten boys who go on to become successful and educated employees of the government. Tell me, if the slave-girl's owner demands that as the girl belonged to him, the girl should be returned to him, what would be your decree?

Imam Muhammad: The slave-girl and all the boys she gave birth to would be returned to the owner, who would become the property of the owner … The entirety of the slave-girl's wealth is the property of the owner.

Imam Shafi: Where has your "La dharara wa la dhirara" principle gone? Is the demolition of the property more harmful or is it more harmful to bring ten intellectual and well-educated young men into slavery and subject them to such degradation?

Imam Muhammad was unable to answer this and fell silent.

Imam Shafi was an expert in physiognomy and had studied it. Once, he had the chance to put this knowledge to the test. He visited Yemen to run some personal errands and arrived there in the evening. He was passing by the bazaar when he noticed a person with blue eyes and a peculiar look standing outside his house. Imam Shafi'i thought that person to be of an evil and impure disposition and nature. As dawn was approaching and he had to reside somewhere, he asked that man whether there was any place for him to stay. The person replied, "Why of course! I shall offer my house to you."

That person showed great hospitality and offered a nice, clean bed, appetising meals and fodder for the animals that brought him to Yemen. In this manner, he spent the night in immense comfort. His heartfelt great remorse over his earlier thoughts in that he had suspicions of a pious and sincere gentleman. Thus, he thought of the science of physiognomy as useless.

As he got ready to leave after breakfast, he thanked the gentleman for he had brought him great comfort. He prayed that God may bless him in return for his pious deeds. The owner of the house replied, "Don't thank me. The hospitality I extended to you cost me this much. My wife and I spent last night in great discomfort and sacrificed our comfortable room for your sake, for which the rent is this much, the food was this much and the fodder cost this much."

In this manner, he demanded a much higher price than what was reasonable. Imam Shafi'i later said that his physiognomic analysis was in fact correct and told his servant at the time to give whatever the man demanded and leave the place immediately.

Al-Shafi'i loved the Prophet (peace be upon him) very deeply. Al Muzani said of him, "He said in the Old School: 'Supplication ends with the invocation of blessings on the Prophet, and its end is but by means of it.'" Al-Karabisi said: "I heard al-Shafi' say that he disliked someone for saying 'the Messenger' (al-Rasul), but that he should say 'Allah's Messenger' (Rasul Allah) out of veneration for him." He divided his night into three parts: one for writing, one for praying, and one for sleeping.

Apocryphal accounts claim that Imam Ahmad said of al-Shafi, "I never saw anyone adhere more to hadith than al-Shafi. No-one preceded him in writing down the hadith in a book." Imam Ahmad is also claimed to have said, "Not one of the scholars of hadith touched an inkwell nor a pen except he owed a huge debt to al-Shafi."

Muhammad al-Shaybani said, "If the scholars of hadith speak, it is in the language of al-Shafi."

Shah Waliullah Dehlawi, an 18th century Sunni Islamic scholar stated: "According to many accounts, he was said to have a photographic memory. One anecdote states that he would always cover one side of a book while reading because a casual glance at the other page would commit it to memory."

Some accusations that have been raised against Imam Shafi. One accusation against him was that he was a Shia as he would often express his love for Ali (RA) and his offspring. However, history testifies against him ever being a Shia. Imam Shafi revered the Khulafa-e-Rashideen [four rightly guided Khulafa – Abu Bakr, Umar, Usman and Ali, may Allah be pleased with them all] and believed in their high spiritual ranks and supremacy. In contrast to other Sunni Muslims of the time, however, he would condemn Amir Muawiyyah's rivalry with Ali (RA) and considered his actions as disobedience.

Aside from this, whilst commentating on Islam's teachings for dealing with rebels, he referred to Ali's response as an example in his book Al-Siyar because it was Ali who had to deal with Muslim rebels for the first time. Some people have considered this interpretation to be inaccurate and have accused Imam

Shafi of being influenced by Shia Islam. In answer to similar accusations, he once cited the couplet:

"If love for the people of Muhammad is to be considered heresy, then I swear by the two things held sacred (in Islam; i.e. the Quran and the Ahl-e-Bait) that I am a heretic."

After returning from Medina, Imam Shafi married a paternal granddaughter of Uthman (RA) named Hameeda, from whom he was given a son. He called him Muhammad and he gave him the appellation of Abu Usman, which proved that he had immense love for Usman.

Imam Shafi was of average height, yet he had a towering figure and personality. He was extremely generous and loved giving to others. Whenever he received any monetary gift from a friend or the rulers of the time, he would distribute the amount among his students and those that deserved it or he would purchase books from it. The details of his school of fiqh have been mentioned earlier.

According to one narration, when Imam Mohammad Ibn Idris (Imam Shafi) moved to Mecca as a seasoned scholar in his later years he had nearly 10,000 dinars with him which was a huge amount of money in those days, however, on the outskirts of the city, he came across a group of people who were very poor and destitute which affected the Imam so much that he distributed that entire some of the money amongst them to the extent that he had to borrow some money in Mecca for his own expenses.

Imam Shafi views were based on the principle that the foundations of the Shariah were built on either nass (injunction) or qiyas (deductive analogy); all matters should effectively be based on evidence found in the nass and access to it should not be difficult for a mujtahid [a person who does ijtihad (exerting one's mental faculty to find an answer)].

One of his most remarkable achievements was the compilation of principles of fiqh and the determination of such regulations that form the commandments of the Shariah. Scholars have written that Imam Shafi was the founder of the science of fiqh principles. Other schools of thought focused their attention on his school of fiqh after he had passed away. This honor was given to him as he was the first to do it.

Imam Shafi remained to follow his daily routine until illness forced him to retire and stop teaching. In his last days before his death, Imam said:

"I feel that I am traveling away from this world, away from the brothers, drinking from the cup of death, and approaching Allah the Glorious. By Allah, I do not know if my soul will go to heaven so that I may congratulate it, or to hell so that I may lament."

Then he went into crying. He became very sick at the end of his life. Imam Shafi kept the company of learned people till the very end of his life, and he is reported to have spent his last days in the company of Abdullah Ibnul Hakam, a well-known scholar of his time.

Due to a severe bowel illness, he became extremely weak. There began rebellions in Egypt and he faced severe opposition on behalf of Malikis. As he faced these challenges, this star of knowledge left this world for the Hereafter. He is thought to have died on a Friday in the Islamic calendar month of Rajab aged 54 in the year 204 AH (820 AC). The Governor of Egypt of that time acknowledged his academic excellence by not only just attending his funeral but leading those prayers. His two sons Abul Hasan Muhammad and Uthmaan were present for the funeral rites.

Allah had blessed him with talented students and sincere

friends, both in Baghdad and Egypt. His students at Baghdad spread his school of thought to the regions of Persia, Khorasan and Ma Wara al-Nahr [Transoxiana]. Here, they faced the Hanafi school of thought, which gave them a tough time. Sultan Mahmud of Ghazni followed his fiqh order. The Sunni Kurds of Iran today are mostly followers of his fiqh school of thought.

The Shafi school is now predominantly found in Somalia, Eritrea, Ethiopia, Djibouti, eastern Egypt, the Swahili coast, Hijaz, Yemen, Kurdish regions of the Middle East, Dagestan, Chechen and Ingush regions of the Caucasus, Indonesia, Malaysia, Sri Lanka, Maldives, Kerala and some other coastal regions in India, Singapore, Myanmar, Thailand, Brunei, and the Philippines.

His students gained much acclaim in the East and had the chance to serve their nations on intellectual levels. Imam Ahmad bin Hanbal especially had this honor, who was a permanent imam of this order. Al-Za'farani had the opportunity to spread his Kutub al-Baghdadiyya in these areas. Apart from these, hundreds of world-renowned scholars associated themselves with his fiqh school of thought, for example, Imam-ul-Haramain Abdul Malik bin Abdullah al-Juwayni, HujjatulIslam Imam Muhammad al-Ghazali, Allama Fakhr al-Din al-Razi, Abu Hamid al-Asfara'ini, Taqi al-Din al-Subki, Allama al-Mawardi Sahib-ul-Ahkam al-Sultaniyya, Sultan al-Ulema Allama, Izz al-Din ibn Abd al-Salam, Ibn Daqiq al-'Id, Nizam al-Mulk Tusi and commentator of Sahih Muslim Allama Nawawi.

All these scholars were affiliated with the Shafi order and through their efforts, his school of thought spread far and wide.

Quotes by Imam Shafi

"True knowledge is that which benefits oneself or others, not information that is merely memorized."

"Don't love the one who doesn't love Allah. If they can leave Allah, they will leave you."

"You will never be able to please everyone, rather rectify what is between you and Allah and do not care about the people."

"And tire yourself out, because it makes life worth living! I have seen that water stagnates when it stands still, yet when it runs it is sweet and pure."

"If you see a man walking on water and flying in the air, then do not be amazed by him until he demonstrates that he follows the commands of the Book (Quran) and the Sunnah."

"Fools are those who Debates with ignorants"

"If you are on the way towards Allah, then run. If it's hard for you then jog: even crawl, but never stop or go back."

"There is a verse in the Quran that every wrongdoer should be terrified of." He was asked, "Which verse is that?" He replied, "And your Lord never forgets.'"

"Don't you see that the lion is silent and yet feared, while the dog barks constantly and is despised?"

"Increase in worship before your responsibilities increase. Then you won't have time to worship as much."

"When the foolish one speaks, do not reply to him, for better than a response (to him) is silence, and if you speak to him you have aided him, and if you left him (with no reply) in extreme sadness he dies."

"The more I learn; the more I learn of my ignorance."

"When you correct a fool, he will hate you. When you correct a wise man, he will appreciate you."

"My heart is at ease knowing that what was meant for me will never miss me and that what misses me was never meant for me."

"The Dua made at Tahajjud is like an arrow which does not miss its target."

"Despair not from your Lord's blessings, If He had wished that you reach the hellfire eternally, He would not have inspired your heart towards Him."

"Be hard on yourself, easy on others."

"If you have a friend who helps you to"Nobility has four pillars: good character, generosity, humility, and piety" obey Allaah, hold onto him."

"The first squeeze of the Grave will make you forget every warm hug you had in your life."

"My silence towards the idiot is indeed an answer."

"Seek understanding before you lead. When you lead, then there is no way to seek understanding."

"If you don't occupy your soul with the truth, it will occupy you with falsehood!"

"Time is like a sword, if you don't cut it, it will cut you."

"Whoever gossips with you (about others) will also gossip about you (to others)."

FIVE ADVICE FROM QURAN

✓ Peace, a word from a Merciful Lord (36:58)

✓ Choose best words to speak and say them in the best possible way [Al-Qur'an-17:53, 2:83]

✓ And say to My slaves that they should (only) say those words that are the best. (Because) Shaitan verily, sows disagreements among them. Surely, Shaitan is to man a plain enemy. (17.53)

✓ And your Lord has decreed that you worship none but Him. And that you be dutiful to your parents. If one of them or both of them attain old age in your life, say not to them a word of disrespect, nor shout at them but address them in terms of honour. (17.23)

✓ Avoid all absurdities. One of the qualities of the believers has been stated as [Al-Qur'an 23:3] "They avoid vain talk". The word "Laghwa" means vain as well as meaningless. In Surah Al-An'aam (6th Chapter of the Qur'an) it is said: (6:151) this includes all sorts of immodesty -- even an immodest talk as it arouses lewd passions.

Narrated Sahl bin Sa'd: Allah's Messenger (ﷺ) said, "Whoever can guarantee (the chastity of) what is between his two jaw-bones and what is between his two legs (i.e. his tongue and his private parts), I guarantee Paradise for him." (Al-Bukhari, 6474)

Narrated Abu Huraira: The Prophet (ﷺ) said, "Whoever believes in Allah and the Last Day, should not hurt his neighbor and whoever believes in Allah and the Last Day, should serve his guest generously and whoever believes in Allah and the Last Day, should speak what is good or keep silent." (Al-Bukhari, 6136)

"Speak only when your words are more beautiful than the silence." Anonymous

A thought-provoking questions you should ask yourself every day

If I were to die tomorrow, would any of this matter?

Practical Ways to Improve Yourself

<u>Self-Restraint</u>

We as humans are bound to commit error, however, this fatal flaw in our nature does not mean that we don't need to control ourselves, rather we need to practice self constraint as much as possible. It is this practicing of self-restraint that keeps us on the right track and prevents us from going stray on a path that leads to total darkness.

<u>Be a role model</u>

Being a role model to someone will encourage you to constantly strive for the better because you wouldn't want to disappoint whoever is looking up to you. You will always find ways to improve yourself and be more careful how you behave because you'll always want to set a good example to others. Just like when parents want to be role models to their children, they'll try their best to make decisions and take actions that their children will respect.

▸ BALANCE DEEN WITH CAREER ◂ 

STEP TWO: DEFINING YOUR VERSION OF AN IDEAL BALANCE

What does a good, balanced routine look like to you? Define your ideal day (use the balance criteria above to decide between your goals in the order of priority). Make sure your ideal routine has goals from all areas of your life. You can use the example below as a guide. Have a look at the example given below. This is the ideal routine for 'Salama'. She is a 28yo registered nurse. Currently, she's working 40 hours a week while pursuing an online post-graduate diploma in Palliative Care

Example Routine

Salama's Ideal Day: I wake up early at 4:30 and pray Tahajjud before Fajr. After Fajr prayer, I recite my morning azkar and make duas. I read Quran for half an hour. Then I do a little streching/ yoga before planning and organizing my day. I look at my work schedule, have my breakfast with coffee and go to work early. At work, I give my best to my job. I keep checking my planner in my work-breaks and try to get other tasks done in the free time-pockets at work. I pray dhuhr and Asr at my workplace during breaks and maghreb as soon as I reach home after work. All throughout the day, I recite the daily azkar whenever I can. I actively try to stay in a positive mood all day. After I come home from work, I spend some time with my family. Sometimes I take a quick nap on my couch to freshen up. I have tea in the evening to freshen up and then I cook dinner for my family. Then I just relax and catch up on some reading. After I feel fresh, I spend 40mins studying materials/ doing research work/ taking online classes for my diploma. At the end of the day, I do a little review with myself about what I did well today and what I could have done better. I eat dinner after Isha and then read Surah Mulk. Then I spend some quality time with family and call my relatives/ friends before going to bed early. Example Routine Let's break down Salama's ideal routine>

EXAMPLE ROUTINE TEARDOWN

IBADAH: Salama's Ideal Day: I wake up early at 4:30 and pray Tahajjud before Fajr. After Fajr prayer, I recite my morning azkar and make duas. I read Quran for half an hour.

SELF-GROWTH: Then I do a little streching/ yoga before planning and organizing my day. I look at my work schedule, have my breakfast with coffee and go to work early.

NON-NEGOTIABLE: At work, I give my best to my job. I keep checking my planner in my work-breaks and try to get other tasks done in the free time-pockets at work.

NON-NEGOTIABLE FARD SALAH: I pray dhuhr and Asr at my workplace during breaks and maghreb as soon as I reach home after work.

SELF-GROWTH: All throughout the day, I recite the daily azkar whenever I can. I actively try to stay in a positive mood all day.

FAMILY-TIME: After I come home from work, I spend some time with my family.

SELF-CARE: Sometimes I take a quick nap on my couch to freshen up. I have tea in the evening to freshen up and then I cook dinner for my family.

SELF-GROWTH: Then I just relax and catch up on some reading. After I feel fresh, I spend 40mins studying materials/ doing research work/ taking online classes for my diploma. At the end of the day, I do a little review with myself about what I did well today and what I could have done better.

IBADAH: I eat dinner after Isha and then read Surah Mulk.

FAMILY-TIME: Then I spend some quality time with family and call my relatives/ friends before going to bed early. I recite all the bedtime azkar before sleeping.

NOTES:

Notice how Salama has added goals using the 'Balance Criteria' from all areas of life to her Ideal Routine. This routine has a good healthy balance. You want to make sure you add goals to your routine using the 'Balance Criteria' so you're not focusing heavily on one area of your life (for e.g. setting lots of career-related goals or Islamic goals) while ignoring other areas (for e.g. leaving no time for family or yourself). Leaving time for self-care and family is a part of the Prophet's Sunnah. The Prophet's day had a beautiful combination of activities in all areas of life.

My Ideal Routine

ASK YOURSELF >Have you ever had this kind of 'ideal balance'? If yes, for how long? Do you believe you can bring your definition of an ideal balance in your days with your current work & family responsibilities? If no, revisit your ideal routine and make changes so it's realistic. If yes, proceed to the next step

Imam Ahmad ibn Hanbal

He was a scholar; an expert in Quran, Hadith. He studies in Yemen, Morocco, Khorasan, Allahu Akbar! He used to travel distances for more than 2 months, 4 months, with his friends to learn knowledge. And on top of that, he had extreme financial difficulties to the point where he never asked for any money from anybody. People offered him, scholars, the government, the Khalifa, friends, Imam Ahmad never accepted anything from anybody until he died.

His uncle used to work for the government and he used to write letters to the Khalifa Harun Ar Rashid. A long time passed, and Harun Ar Rashid sent a letter to his uncle saying, "Where are all the letters? You're meant to report to me." He's writing reports about people, what they're doing, what they're not doing, so like spying. The uncle said, "I sent them all through Ahmad." The Khalifa said, "I never received anything."

So they called Ahmad along. Now imagine 12/13-year-old boy coming before the Khalifa and he's asking him, "Where are all the letters?" Uncle said, "I gave you them all from 5 years ago." Imam Ahmad said, "I threw them all in the Tigris River." He said, "Why?!" Imam Ahmad said, "In it are backbiting and spying on other people, this is Haram. I refuse to do it." The uncle got a little bit upset. The Khalifa looked at him and said, "Don't be upset, if this young boy has that much piety, how we can compare ourselves to him? He is an example to us."

Allah Tala bears witness of greatness; to Himself that there is no God worthy of worship but Him. And He bears witness to the greatness of His creation of the angels. And He bears witness to the importance and greatness of those endued with knowledge.

Imam Ahmad was born in the year 164 Hijri, born in Baghdad,

died in Baghdad and he was born in the year when Imam Malik died. Imam Ahmad was one of those just like Imam Ash-Shafi and Imam Malik, his inspiration and his channeling to knowledge was his mother.

Imam Ahmad was raised by his mother. Imam Ahmad came from a tribe called Banu Shayban. The mother of Imam Ahmad was extremely wise. She spent so much on her son, in knowledge and wisdom, she stayed single all her life after the death of her husband, raising and teaching her son Imam Ahmad.

Imam Ahmad loved his mother so immensely, he had a special part in his heart. He was 21 years old and one day he was walking with one of his friends and he said to him, "Let's cross the Tigris River," for some reason. He said to him, "No, my mother told me never to cross the Tigris River." If today a 21-year-old who says my mum doesn't let me, imagine what would happen to him?

She gave up her life, you won't believe this but Imam Ahmad because he loved his mother so much and he knew the sacrifice she had done for him; he did not marry as long as his mother was alive. Because he also wanted to dedicate his time and his years to his mother. His mother died when he was at the age of 40. He married at the age of 40, SubhanAllah!

His first wife was Aisha; Umm Saleh. She lived with him for 30 years. In these 30 years, they never disagreed on a single word. After she died, Imam Ahmad married another wife. Her name was Rayhana and from her was his second son Abdullah. Saleh and Abdullah became scholars and muhaditheen. After Rayhana died he married again and he had 2 children at the age of 74. He died at age of 77. And his kids were still babies when he died.

There is a beautiful story about his first marriage. When he decided to get married, he went to his aunt for help. He said, "Go to such and such family. I was told they're a righteous family. And look into the two daughters." So the aunt came back and she was so much impressed with the younger daughter. She said, "Allahu Akbar! She has beautiful eyes, long curly dark hair and very light skin." Imam Ahmad asked, "What about the older daughter?" She said, "Oh, no, she has short curly hair; she's dark." Imam Ahmad asked, "What about their deen?" She said, "The older daughter has better deen." Imam Ahmad said, "I want to marry the older daughter." Then he married her. When she died, he looked at the grave and said, "May Allah mercy on Umm Saleeh. She didn't disagree with me one single day. She didn't upset me for once."

From a very young age, Imam Ahmad was extremely intelligent, modest, sensible and had an earnest desire for worshipping Allah. Imam Ahmad memorised the Quran at an early age, and as he was directed by his uncle and his mother to pursue his studies, his serious nature and early pious attitude ensured that he sought to study Fiqh, or Islamic jurisprudence. Imam Ahmad study of Fiqh, reading under Abu Yussuf, the best known student of Abu Hanifa. This means that his early studies took him into learning Fiqh that gave scholarly discretion a very high rank and relied much on analogy. But soon afterwards, he decided to pursue the study of hadith, delaying Fiqh study for a while.

Imam Ahmad started his pursuit of the study of hadith in Baghdad at the age of 15, and continued to give it his full attention there for seven years. He realised that the main scholars of hadith did not all live in the capital. So he decided to seek them wherever they lived. He began to travel to Basrah, Kufah, Hijaz and Yemen. He is said to have travelled five times to Basrah, and paid a similar number of visits to Hijaz. However, in the latter trips he combined offering the pilgrimage with his studies.

His trip to Yemen was one such effort. He was keen to meet Abdurrazzaq ibn Hammam, an eminent scholar of hadith who was at the time, and remains today, widely famous. In fact, he had met Abdurrazzaq during pilgrimage, and he could have learnt from him whatever he wanted to learn, sparing himself a long journey to Yemen, but he preferred to learn from the scholars of Makka and Madina while he was on pilgrimage, and to go to Abdurrazzaq in Yemen later. That way, he would hope for God's reward for his arduous journey and get all that he could from the Yemeni scholar in his home surroundings.

It was Imam Ash-Shafi, who was his greatest and most influential and loved teacher. He said to his son, "My son Ash-Shafi was like the sun to the world. And he was the medicine and health for people. So look, can you live without the sun and health? No." He also said about Imam Ash-Shafi, "I make dua for Ash-Shafi in my Salah every prayer for 40 years." He used to say, "Oh my lord, forgive me and my parents and Muhammad, son of Idris Ash-Shafi."

In Makka, Imam Ahmad went there one day and he was still in his 20's. So he's a young man and Imam Ash-Shafi was still in his early times, he wasn't very popular yet. Imam Ahmad had a friend by the name of Yahya Ibn Muayn. And he was his friend in study lessons. When he used to go to Makka, there was a teacher named Sufyan Ibn Uyaynah. So one day his friend Yahya Ibn Muayn, he noticed that Imam Ahmad was not in the circle with them. Sufyan Ibn Uyayanah an extraordinary scholar of his time and even till today. He looked and he saw Imam Ahmad the young man sitting in the circle of Imam Ash-Shafi. Now at the time, Yahya did not know who Imam Ash-Shafi was, he wasn't popular yet. He just looked like a Bedouin. He thought why Imam Ahmad is sitting with a Bedouin. He went there and sat with Ahmad, just a few people around his circle. He said, "What are you doing here Ahmad?" He said, "Listen to this man?" He said, "It's impressive but why'd you leave Imam Sufyan Ibn Uyaynah to come to a Bedouin?" He said, "With Imam Sufyan, if you listen to him and if you miss out on something, you can ask him tomorrow. As for this man, the words you hear from him, if you don't hear them the first time, you will never hear them from anyone again. This man is something different." Yahya said, "But okay." He went and sat back with Sufyan. Afterward only in a matter of about two-or three-years Imam Ash-Shafi's circle was the largest in all of Makka and everybody left all the circles and sat with Imam Ash-Shafi. What does that tell you about Imam Ahmad? He had the foresight.

Imam Ahmad bin Hanbal had offered Hajj several times. On some occasions, he offered the Hajj traveling from Baghdad to Mecca on foot, whilst studying along the way. During those journeys as a student, he faced many challenges. He experienced financial problems but always considered it secondary to the wealth of knowledge that he desired to gain. At times, he would work as a casual laborer for subsistence.

Once, when he was in Yemen and was experiencing financial difficulties, his tutor, Abdur Razzaq expressed the desire to help him financially. However, he was not prepared to accept any financial help. He would sew caps and sell them, living off the profit he made from this business.

One day, his clothes were stolen and for many days he could not leave his house. One of his fellow students, who was also a friend, got to know of this and wanted to offer him some money, which he declined. His friend persisted and asked, "How long will you remain hidden in your house? Take this as a loan and when you have the means, you may return it." Even at this,

Imam Ahmad was not prepared to accept the money. Eventually, they reached an agreement that Imam Ahmad would rewrite his notes neatly for his friend, and his friend would pay him in return. Thus, he purchased new clothes from that money and was able to leave his house once again.

He survived on a meager income, which was earned through letting properties. Some have narrated his income as being 17 dirhams a month. As has been mentioned above, he would work even as a laborer, so much so that after crops were harvested, he would go to collect fallen wheat spikes. However, he would never accept gifts from the Khalifas (rulers) or the governors of the time.

It was not until Ahmad was 40 years of age that he had a circle where he taught and gave rulings on any question put to him. This does not mean that he would not have given rulings earlier than that. Indeed, he would answer when a question was put to him, because abstention meant suppression of knowledge and that is forbidden in Islam. But he would not sit for teaching and issuing rulings until he was 40. He had two reasons for that: the first was to follow the Prophet's example, who received his revelations and became a teacher for mankind at that age, and the other his respect for his teachers meant that he would not teach while they were alive. It was a coincidence that Imam Ash-Shafi died in 204, when Ahmad was 40. A point to remember is that Imam Abu Hanifa did the same, starting his study circle at the age of 40.

It did not take long for Ahmad to become widely known. Indeed his circle was soon very large, with some reports putting the number of students and listeners attending it at 5000, among whom one tenth wrote what he taught. While this may be rather exaggerated, even a circle one-fifth that size, i.e. 1000 students, is very large by any standard. People loved his teaching because they recognised in him a teacher of wide knowledge, and a highly pious man who spared no effort in the pursuit and dissemination of knowledge.

Three factors enhanced Iama Ahmad's popularity as a teacher. The first was that his serious attitude to learning and teaching was coupled with exemplary humility and contentment. Secondly, he was always keen to report only that of which he was absolutely certain. Hence, he did not rely on his memory, fine and sharp as it was. He always referred to his books, which he had written with his own hand, when he learnt from his teachers. He feared that if he would report from memory, he might be mistaken and he would attribute to the Prophet (peace be upon him) what the Prophet did not actually say. Thirdly, he taught his students to write down what they learnt of hadith only. He did not allow them to write anyone else's views or teachings. To him, true knowledge that deserved to be documented was the Quran and the hadith.

This meant that despite the numerous trends of scholarship with which Baghdad was bustling at the time, Ahmad rejected any study that was not based on the Quran and hadith only. Thus, he would not take a logical approach to faith, nor would he discuss matters of faith in a purely rational or philosophical way. He rejected any involvement in debates of theological nature, such as whether God's names and qualities mentioned in the Quran were purely attributes of His, or they were the same as Himself. To him, that was a pursuit that brought no useful results.

Ahmad ibn Hanbal combined qualities that are always certain to ensure a degree of exceptional excellence. The first of these is one, he shares with all hadith scholars of repute; that is, a sharp memory coupled with penetrative insight. In this regard Ahmad is rated by many scholars who knew him well as having the clearest, sharpest and most reliable memory of all his contemporaries.

The other quality that stands out when we discuss Imam Ahmad's personality is his endurance and perseverance. This is the fruit of a strong will, sincerity and an aspiration to achieve only what is best. It gave him a most pleasant personality that combined poverty with generosity and dignity, self-respect with willingness to forgive those who caused him harm and injury, and a willingness to undertake difficulties in the pursuit of his goals. We will see how these qualities stood him in good stead during his long and hard trial when he was subjected to much persecution. As we try to delve deeper into his character, we find a person who derives his dignity from faith, relies on none other than God, aspires to nothing that a human being can confer, and fears God alone. Hence, he was a model of humility; always ready to overlook other people's mistakes and forgive whatever they might have caused him of hardship.

Imam Ahmad's third quality was purity of heart in the broadest sense of the word. He never touched anything belonging to someone else, nor did he ever succumb to a desire. Moreover, his faith was pure, acknowledging no authority other than that of God. We find this quality rubbing off onto his scholarship. In beliefs and thought, he would not take any course other than that of the Prophet (peace be upon him) and his companions. In Fiqh, he would not even try to weigh up the different views of the Prophet's companions. If they differed on one questions, he would consider their differing views as equally acceptable. He treated the tabieen, or successors to the Prophet's companions in the same way.

Imam Ahmad also maintained a high standard of honesty in everything he pursued. Thus, all his scholarship was for God's sake. He sought no recognition or position. Even when he was young, he would not carry his writing material in a visible way; he would hide them so that people would not say that he was going to study, or that he was a scholar.

During his old age, one day he was traveling to As-Sham; to Syria. He walked into a Masjid to spend the night. The guard of the Masjid told him to get out; Masjid closing.Owing to his humility, he hadn't introduced himself to anyone thinking that if he did, he would be welcomed by many people.Failing to recognize Ahmad bin Hanbal, the caretaker/guard of the mosque refused to let him to stay in the mosque. He said, "I have nowhere to go." He said, "Get out." So, Imam Ahmad picked up his stuff and he slept on the steps of the Masjid. The guard said, "You can't even sleep here, go, move away. Imam Ahmad like, where am I going to go? The guard picked up Imam Ahmad by his legs and he dragged him to the middle of the street and dropped him. A baker who owns a bakery across the street; he came to Imam Ahmad and said, "You can come to sleep in my bakery."

Imam Ahmad observes this man. He sat there, putting the dough together and putting them in the oven. Everything that he does while he's making the dough, he's saying: SubhanAllah, Alhamdulillah, La ilha illah, Allahukbar. The entire night, he's making Tasbeeh.

Imam Ahmad was shocked. Imam Ahmad asked, "How long have you been doing this?" He said, "My whole life, this is what I do." Imam Ahmad asked, "What have you seen from Allah (SWT) as a result of all this Tasbeeh that you make?" He said, "I never made a dua to Allah (SWT) for anything except that He answered it." Imam Ahmad said, "You never made dua to Allah (SWT) except He gave it to you?" He repeated, "I never made dua to Allah (SWT) for anything except that He gave it to me." He said, "Except for one thing." Imam Ahmad asked, "What is that?" He said, "To have a chance to see Imam Ahmad." Imam Ahmad brought tears and he embraced this man. He said, "SubhanAllah! Here is Allah, He brought to you Ahmad, dragged him by his feet to your Bakery."

He went through a trial more than any other Imam went through. This issue is called the creation of The Quran. There was a group called Al-Mu'tazila, and they started even before in the time of Abu Hanifa but they never came up until the time of Imam Ahmad, where they really started to show. Now, what happened?

It was the period of religious polemic and philosophical debate. Mu'tazila, the founders of Islamic scholasticism, was gaining a foothold. As a result, many questions being raised were: Does man have free will or is his destiny predetermined? Are God's attributes part of the divine essence or distinct? Is speech an attribute of God? Is the Quran uncreated or created?

One major issue Al-Mu'tazila raised was that of the position of the Quran in relation to God. It is well known that all Muslims believe that the Quran is, literally, the word of God, but Al-Mu'tazila added that it was 'created', in the sense that it did not share God's attribute of being 'ever-present'. This attribute belonged to God and to no one and nothing else.

Debates on such topics occupied everyone. Khalifa Mamun al-Rashid himself enjoyed such debates and the Mu'tazilites would press him to extensively promote such doctrines. For this reason, the conservative scholars faced a predicament.

So, Al-Mamun was the first, he first didn't believe in that. But there was a man who came out, he was a Faqi, he was a scholar and religious man but he was affected by the philosophy and dialectics of the Greeks and so on and so forth. He came to the Khalifa Al-Mamun and he convinced him about the Khalq of the Quran. And Khalifa Al-Mamun unfortunately even though he was a very learned man, he influenced and he believed. At first, Al Khalifa Al-Mamun did not impose it on people.

In his later years, however, Mamun al-Rashid's persistence grew in that he would force people to accept that the Quran, being the Word of God, was a creation.

He said, "Everybody must accept it." He came to all his workers and his government officials and he said, "Okay start with my judges and the scholars that work for me. They have to believe in it." About 30,000 Imams. It's Halal because of their lives, yielded. They all said the Quran is created. Some of them did a trick, they said, "The Quran, the Zaboor, the Psalms, and the Torah, these 4 are created." Meaning my four fingers.

Finally came Imam Ahmad and a few friends of his who were contemporaries. They came to them and they asked them the question, "What do you say?" They said, "The Quran is the word of Allah, not created." The Khalifa ordered that they would be put in chains and brought as prisoners. When they came to do that, two of his friends, The Ulama, yielded. They couldn't withstand it. They said, "Our family, our children and they were left behind." The two stand firm were Ahmad ibn Hanbal and Muhammad ibn Noah. On the journey to the Khalifa as prisoners, Muhammad Nuh died, a martyr.

On his way Imam Ahmad, this is now where the karma comes in, on his way he made a dua, he said, "Oh Allah, Oh Allah, do not let me meet Mamun." The second day, they came back and they said, "The khalifa died."

After spending a few nights in a prison cell, he was taken to the new khalifa, Abu Ishaq Al-Mu'tasim. Al-Mutasim was not a scholar. He was a military commander. So he was tough, he was ruthless. His brother Al-Mamun loved him a lot. And Al-

Mamun before he died requested him, he said, "Make sure that there is no Alim or judge except that you make sure that they believe and say that the Quran is created." He even wrote in his will that he bears witness that 'God is unlike anything else. He is One, the Sovereign of the universe with no partner. Everything else is a creation of His. The Quran cannot be anything other than the rest of creation, having the same qualities as everything else, while God is one with nothing like Him.' He also urged his brother, Al-Mutasim, who was to succeed him, to follow his ideas.

Al-Mutasim did not care about anything else. All he wanted is to carry out his brother's order.

And so, Imam Ahmad is brought into chains one more time. On his way, Subhan Allah! It was not an Alim, it was not a scholar or a sheikh or a judge who came to him to give him strength; a simple Bedouin who hardly knows anything, hardly can read or write. He came up to him and he said, "Ya Imam, I hear that you have been summoned to say that the Quran is created. Ya Imam, stand strong, never say these words." Imam Ahmad said, "Allah, this is from Allah, a support. Allah is sent a Bedouin from the desert. When all the scholars said we yield."

So he was brought before the Khalifa in Baghdad. It was hot. It was deadly. It was Ramadan. On the first day, Al Mutasim tried to yield. He said, "Ya Imam, you are a respected person, I'll let you go, if you say what your friend said; Yahya." Imam Ahmad said to the Khalifa, "Ya Khalifah, Ya Amir Al Mumineen." So, he acknowledged his Imama (leadership). He said to him, "Give me one evidence from the Quran that the Quran is created. I cannot find any evidence. Give me evidence and I will accept it." Al Mutasim couldn't find anything. Then he said to his guards, "Take him to the prison."

In terms of politics, Imam Ahmad considered the obedience of rulers of the time as mandatory and to raise the sword against them as strictly prohibited because the sword disturbs the general law and order and control. On the other hand, when appropriate, there should be no shortage in promoting righteous deeds, preventing wrong, suggesting alternative solutions and speaking the truth, as these are also mandatory.

He went, the second day, he came out. And this time Ahmad Ibn Abi Duad and his scholars were around there, Ahmad Ibn Abi Duad went into a debate with him. He said, "I have evidence from the Quran that the Quran is created." Imam Ahmad said, "Which one?" He said, "Allah Tala says we have sent this Quran down in the Arabic Language." Imam Ahmad looked at him and he said, "Allah Tala did not say we have created the Quran in the Arabic language. He said; We have sent down the Quran in the Arabic language. This does not mean it's created." Then they went into a debate and the debate went on and there is no evidence and Imam Ahmad is reciting his evidence as if he could read them before his eyes. Even though he was in chains. As for Al-Mutasim, he's watching, he didn't care whether he's right or wrong. All he cared about was carrying out the request of his brother, that's it. They put him back in the prison.

The third day, the fourth day, the fifth day, Al-Mutasim is trying to yield, "Please, I'll let you go with your family. Just say it and I'll let you go." Imam Ahmad determined, "I will not say it. This is Deen, this is not my religion, this is the religion of Allah (SWT)."

The whip was brought out, they whipped him and he would resort to dua and supplications and he would go unconscious. The doctor would say, "I would have to take the remnant of the rope out of his body with knives and sometimes I would have to cut out meat by the knives of his back. But he stood firm."

He was fasting in Ramadan while being whipped and his back

was seeping puss and blood. He would not break his fast and people would give him water, those who were whipping him they'd say, "Drink." And he would say, "Wallahi! I will not drink while I am fasting. I wish to meet my lord if I die like this, I wish to meet him fasting." A man of determination, I mean this is something unbelievable. But he didn't lie.

After a few days of whipping, they saw him say some words, they wouldn't understand it. But one of the writers, later on, said, "I understood what he was saying. He was saying, "Oh Allah, do not let my Awra (private part) show." His pants were slipping off, all this mattered not to him except that his Awra would show." The person whose writing said, "Wallahi! I saw his pants by themselves somehow make their way up and they were tied on his body and never fell."

When he entered the prison with his pain and torture, he would stay up in the night praying. Another support from Allah came to him, a man who was imprisoned for drinking alcohol. He came up to him and he said to him, "Ya Imam, I have been whipped 40 lashes each time for drinking alcohol. I have now been imprisoned for 4 years because I drink alcohol. And I cannot resist my alcohol but I have resisted the whipping for four years for something haram; alcohol." He said, "You are resisting the whipping for the sake of Allah, do not give up. If I resisted for Alcohol, you can resist it for something Fillah." Imam Ahmad said "Allahu Akbar! This is more support from Allah. No scholar, no pious person, no one. A drunk; an alcoholic and a Bedouin from the middle of the desert; this is where supports come from."

So, he made friends with all the prison inmates. A man from prison said to him, "Ya Imam, just get yourself out of this. We can't bear seeing you like this." He said, "Look outside through the window of this small door of this prison. He looked outside.

Imam Ahmad said, "What do you see?" He said, "I see people I cannot count in numbers. Thousands and thousands of people waiting outside. They are carrying pens and paper." He said to him, "They all want to know what Imam Ahmad says on this issue. If I conceal what I believe to be the truth in order to spare myself, this wrong idea will spread and flourish for generations to come. I will not meet my Lord having helped to spread it." He remained steadfast bearing excessive torture. This was carried out repeatedly over a period of 28 months, but Imam Ahmad would not budge.

Imam Ahmad's popularity increased, as people admired his resolute stand. Therefore, he was released, but placed under house arrest. He was banned from teaching or meeting other people. This continued for the rest of the reign of Al-Mutasim and his son, Al-Wathiq.

The Khalifa Al Mutasim died. And Al Wathiq, his son took over. The same thing was affected by. One day, Ahmad Ibn Abi Duad came up to Imam Ahmad, "Just say it, whisper it to my ear. Whisper it, I have a connection with the Khalifah." Imam Ahmad said to him, "Ya Ahmad, give me one evidence and I will follow you." He said "The most merciful, he taught the Quran." Imam Ahmad said, "Allah Tala did not say Ar Rahman created the Quran. He said He taught the Quran. This is not an evidence."

Then Imam Ahmad said to him, "Ar Rasul (peace be upon him) was silent about it, Abu Bakr was silent about it, Umar was silent about it. And you think you are better than the Prophet (peace be upon him) and Abu Bakr and Umar. They stayed silent, why can't you stay silent?" And that's when it was the last straw, Al Wathiq started to think with his head. It says in the narration that Al Wathiq started laughing so badly that he fell back, lifted his leg up saying, "Ya Ahmad Ibn Abi Duad, the Prophet (ﷺ),

and Abu Bakr and Umar stayed silent and you had to open your big mouth." Until finally Al Wathiq looked at it and said, "This is rubbish" Al Wathiq died but he didn't release Imam Ahmad.

Al-Mutawakkil succeeded Wathiq and he said, "What is this?" He released Imam Ahmad. Al-Mutawakkil announced that the Mutazilla are rejected and refused. And this Imam had shown their wrong. Imam Ahmad announced, "I forgive every person, every Khalifa, every person instigated this, every person who whipped me and I forgive them with all my heart except the Mu'tazila."

When he was dying on his deathbed, he was unconscious and Abdullah, his son heard his father saying, "Not yet, not yet" and his son said, "What do you mean not yet, you don't want to meet Allah yet?" Then when he awoke, he said to him, "The shaytan came to me saying to me you have gone away from my trickery, I couldn't do anything to you." And I said to him, "Not yet, the war between you is not over yet. You're trying to trick me so I can put my guards down." Imam Ahmad even to the last minute, determined, and said, "The war between me and you is not over yet, don't flatter me."

When he passed away at the age of 77 in 241 AH, the whole of Baghdad went into mourning. Hundreds of thousands of people flocked for his funeral and felt as though a great imam had departed them.

What happened after him, was a disaster. His students became overzealous and they began to become too rigid, too strict beyond measure saying some of them even went to the extent of saying, "After the Prophet (peace be upon him) no one is more important or valuable or pious than Imam Ahmad." They went to the extent of saying, "There is no greater Faqi than Imam Ahmad on the face of the Earth." So much so that taking the law into their own hands going beyond the Khalifa; they would instigate something in order to prove the Madhab of Imam Ahmad to be right. Just to pick up a fight.

His son Saleh married a wealthy woman and he bought some expensive furniture for about 4,000 dirhams. One day a fire lit up his house and burnt all the furniture and everything. And this was after his father's death. Imam Saleh said, "I am not upset because my furniture was burnt; but because I kept this garment which my father used to wear and he gave it to me after his death. Every time I prayed; I wore it. Every time I went to the Masjid I wore it. Every time I gave a Halaqa I wore it." So, he entered his house and he says everything burnt, he looked and guess what? He found the garment unburnt.

His monumental service to hadith is preserved in the form of his magnum opus, Al-Musnad. The book contains between 30,000 to 40,000 hadith and narrations of Companions. His book was considered a foundation for future muhadithin.

Imam Bukhari, Imam Muslim and other acclaimed muhadithin referred to this book while preparing their compilations, and in selecting authentic hadith, they got considerable help from it.

Suffice it to say that when Al-Bukhari completed his Sahih collection, he chose Ahmad to review it for him, and Ahmad raised questions only on four hadiths in the book that was destined to become the best known in the Muslim world for 12 centuries so far. Hence, Ahmad's fiqh is closest to the Sunnah and hadith.

Instead of focusing on the subject-matter, the Musnad lists hadith in order of narrators. For example, first are the hadith narrated by Abu Bakr, followed by hadith narrated by Umar, then by Uthman, and in this manner, all the Companions' narrations have been compiled.

There have been efforts to collate the narrations of Musnad

subject-wise but have not been published in its complete form as of yet.

No doubt, there are some hadith that are weak in the Musnad, but scholars have elucidated that there are no fabricated traditions in the Musnad. Imam Ahmad's belief was that after the Quran and Sunnah [practices of the Prophet (ﷺ)], hadith is one of the sources of Shariah, regardless of whether the traditions are authentic, weak, have narrators omitted in the chain of narrators or have a continuous chain of narrators.

He considered the sayings of the Companions as an authority and would cater for the views of the tabi'een [those that followed the Companions]. When necessary, albeit rarely, he would rely on qiyas [deductive analogy], istislah [seeking the best public interest] and istiswab [seeking consultation]. He did not believe in the lawfulness of any other ijma' [concencus] other than the consensus of the Companions. In his opinion, the concept of a general consensus was incorrect as there could have been opponents among them who the people were not aware of.

According to the Hanbali school of thought, it is necessary to carry out qiyas in the absence of a decisive dictum. However, in their opinion, the meaning of qiyas is vast as compared to the Hanafi and Shafi schools of thought. It includes all the means of deduction i.e. istihsan [application of discretion in a legal ruling], masalih-e-mursalah [a consideration that secures benefit and prevents harm] and istishab [logical reasoning through the presumption of continuity]. For example, according to the Hanafis, the validation of bay' salami [sale agreement by advance payment] is contradictory to qiyas as it is against the decisive doctrine of:

"Do not trade with that which you do not have", and it falls under the category of bay' al-ma'dum [sale of non-available goods], whereas in view of the Hanbalis, the legitimation of this sale's agreement is based on qiyas because it has been permitted by keeping in view the interest, demand and custom of the public.

For the public interest, Imam Ahmad saw it permissible to deport malicious and disorderly elements and to compulsorily reside the needy in people's homes when there was no other solution. The same applies to force someone to learn a skill when no one in that profession is available.

Thus, the Hanbali school is no less in favor of using a medium, but it discourages the usage of a medium when the outcome can lead to disorder. People with contagious diseases can be discouraged from visiting public places. In times of public disorder and unrest, the buying and selling of weapons can be halted. Talaqqi al-Rukban [manipulative trade, where a city dweller buys goods from a villager for a small price and sells it at a much higher price, exploiting the villager's ignorance] is, for this reason, considered an illegal practice.

In this regard, the intention and the outcome will come into play. For instance, if a person shoots their gun at a person with the intention of killing them, but instead of the bullet Hatting the intended target, it kills a snake, then although the outcome may be considered good, in reality, it was ill-intended. In the sight of Allah, such a person would have sinned and they may be summoned in this world also.

If a person imprisons another in their home and as a result, the captive dies of starvation and thirst, in Imam Ahmad's view, the captor would have to pay compensation. To let one's apartment for dance parties is, under the aforementioned condition, considered prohibited.

The Hanbali school has sought immense help from istishab. Under this principle, they believe that doubt cannot end certainty. For example, water is pure and until there is the certainty that it has been contaminated, it will be deemed pure and any doubt will be shunned.

Quotes by Imam Ahmad ibn Hanbal

"If you desire Allah to be persistent in granting you the things you love, be persistent in doing the things He(Allah) loves."

"If you claim that you are amongst those who seek refuge from the Fire and desire Paradise, then strive for that which you seek and do not be misled by your worldly desires."

"Beware of developing a view that you have never heard from any scholar."

"If you see a man speaking ill of any of the Sahaba, then have doubts about his Islam."

"I left trying to please people and from that moment I got the energy needed to speak the truth."

"People need knowledge more than they need food and drink because they need food and drink two or three times a day, but they need knowledge all the time."

"I worshiped Allah 50 yrs and I didn't find the sweetness of worshiping until I left 3 things. (1) I left pleasing people and I got the energy of talking the truth (2) I left the company of evil people till I found the company of righteous people (3) I left the sweetness of World until I found the sweetness of the hereafter."

"Intend good, for you will always be in a good state as long as you intend good."

"The best of my days is when I awaken and find my cupboards bare. For that is a day my reliance on Allah is complete."

"It is a most amazing thing that you should continue to be unmindful, chasing after vain desires, wasting your time in disregard of this most important matter, for you are being driven at a fierce pace (towards death) day and night, hour by hour, like the blink of an eye."

"…and in no way is Allah to be described with anything more than what He – the Mighty and Majestic – has described himself with."

"For everything, there is a blessing; the blessing of the hearts is being pleased with Allah, the Almighty, the All-powerful."

"People need politeness and kindness, and enjoining what is good without harshness, except a man who does evil openly, who must be told and stopped (harshly)."

"Occupy yourself with every good deed and hasten to do it before something prevents you from doing so."

FOUR ADVICE FROM THE QURAN

✔ Verily, after every difficulty there is relief (94:5-6)

✔ So be patient. Indeed, the promise of Allah is truth (30:60)

✔ Pardon gracefully if anyone among you who commits a bad deed out of ignorance, and then repents and amends (6:54, 3:134)

✔ Allah is sufficient for us & He is the best disposer of affairs (3:171)

"Whoever abstains from asking others, Allah will make him contented, and whoever tries to make himself self-sufficient,

Allah will make him self-sufficient. And whoever remains patient, Allah will make him patient. Nobody can be given a blessing better and greater than patience." (Al-Bukhari, 1469)

"The more you let go, the higher you rise." Anonymous

A thought-provoking questions you should ask yourself every day

Do I treat myself with the love and respect I truly deserve?

Practical Ways to Improve Yourself

Thoroughness

The reason why we as humans are not able to stick with the right path or do anything good in our life is that we do not pursue it with thoroughness.

Forgive

When someone hurts you, try to forgive them. I know that might be hard but just try. If you don't forgive them for whatever they did and hold that against them for the rest of your life, you'll just be hurting yourself more because it's unhealthy to hold a grudge. That would only affect your body and mind negatively.

💼 BALANCE DEEN WITH CAREER 💼

STEP THREE: START BY WORKING ON THE NON-NEGOTIABLES

No matter how many amazing goals you're currently pursuing, if your 'standard nonnegotiables' are being compromised, then that's not a healthy balance. You won't feel satisfaction and confidence in yourself as a Muslim. That's why before you fix other habits and work on other goals, begin by working on your standard non-negotiables.

<u>STANDARD NON-NEGOTIABLES</u>

After observing the Prophet's day in detail, I've come to recognize that there are three non-negotiables for every Muslim (regardless of how many responsibilities you have or how busy you are).

1. PRAYING ALL 5 FARD PRAYERS ON-TIME: We can forget about creating balance as a Muslim if we're barely praying the fard prayers. Prayers have integral value in the disciplining of the Nafs and they form the cornerstone for all behavioral change in Islam.

2. GIVING TIME TO THE QURAN REGULARLY (EVEN IF LITTLE): If we don't make Quran a 'non-negotiable', then we'll never find the time for it. And without having the superior guidance from Quran, we can never truly feel satisfied with ourselves as Muslims. No matter how many other amazing goals we achieve in life, if we have a poor relationship with the Quran, it'll affect all areas of our life. Giving time to the Quran (even if little) is a mandatory part of achieving balance.

3. GETTING A HEALTHY SLEEP: A healthy sleep means sleeping 'enough' (this could mean 5- 8 hours) and getting a good night's sleep so you aren't drowsy and cranky all day. If you're compromising your sleep to achieve more goals, then you'll compromise your productivity over all areas of your life. Your mood will be low, you'll be in a negative energy state all day and that'll affect your inter-personal relations, focus at work as well as khushoo in Ibadah. Allah has made sleep a necessity for everyone, so no need to push yourself to burnout by compromising your sleep. (Note > Staying up till late a few nights here and there is fine as long as you don't miss fajr)

STEP FOUR: DEFINE NON-NEGOTIABLES 'SPECIFIC' TO YOU

Here you'll write all the other non-negotiables that are unique to your situation. Revisit your ideal routine and pick all the activities that are so important for you to follow regularly that they are 'non-negotiable' to you. Meaning, you'll try to do these activities, come rain or shine. These also include your responsibilities in the family that you have to do no matter what (maybe you have to take care of your old parents or you have toddlers). These can also include me-time (leaving some room in your day for yourself) so you can be in a positive energy state to 'give' to others during the rest of your time. If you feel like you need to spend some time doing things you love or just relaxing at the end of each day, then you can include this as your non-negotiable. An example of a non-negotiable act of Ibadah (besides the Fard Ibadah) could be reading your bedtime and morning azkar. Another example of a non-negotiable for a working Muslim could be giving your best to your job. Maybe you deal with people's lives every day (work with patients) or you deal with customers... in that case, giving your best (not missing work, having good inter-personal relationships and being mentally present at your work etc.) could be a non-negotiable for you. The reason why you're identifying your non-negotiables is so that you can create and set goals according to the time and energy available to you after your non-negotiables. One big reason why we feel like our day does not have balance is when we take time and energy from our non-negotiables and give it to less important goals. Or when we 'give up' all our non-negotiables during periods of high-stress. We take the 'all-or-none' approach even with the habits and activities that are really important to us, aka, our non-negotiables.

WRITE ALL THE DEFINE NON-NEGOTIABLES 'SPECIFIC' TO YOU

<< PRO TIP >>

Hold on to your non-negotiables even in periods of high-anxiety and low growth.

There'll be times in your life when you're being tested with a difficult challenge. During such high-stress, difficult periods, it can be very easy to lose all sense of control and let go of all our good habits. The key is to make sure that even during such difficult phases of life, when your routine is all messed up, you hold on to your non-negotiables. For example; Having a tough period at work, being in between jobs, family crisis/ health emergencies, exams, pregnancy/ childbirth, travel etc. Even in such 'high-stress' phases, don't stop doing everything you worked so hard for. If the 'high-stress' period is really tough, then at least continue practicing the non-negotiable habits EVEN IF ON A MINIMAL LEVEL. So that could mean you read Quran for 5 minutes instead of the usual 30 and pray only the Fard Salah without the Sunnah Nafl for each prayer (these 2 non-negotiables keep your emaan from falling too low during periods of stress and protect your relationship with Allah). This way you won't have to start working from scratch on your habits once the tough period is over.

Imam Al-Bukhari

Muhammad ibn Ismail al-Bukhari al-Jufi was born after the Jumu'ah prayer on Friday, 21 July 810 (13 Shawwal 194 AH) in the city of Bukhara in Transoxiana (in present-day Uzbekistan).

During his infancy, Imam al-Bukhari (RH) had weak eyesight that manifested into full-blown blindness. Desperate for her son, his mother made excessive, sincere, and constant dua for her son. This period extended for a lengthy two to three years. One night, Imam al-Bukhari's mother received the glad tidings of Ibrahim (AS) in a dream, who said that Allah (SWT) had granted Imam al-Bukhari vision because of her dua. The eyesight was not even restored at a lesser degree, but at full strength. It is reported that Imam al-Bukhari (RH) would write books without a candle but only from the light of the moon.

He memorized the Holy Qur'an at the age of 9. Then began to learn Hadith from scholars of his region. At the age of 16, he traveled to Mecca and stayed there for 16 years collecting Hadiths. He visited Egypt and Syria twice, Basra four times, spent many years in Hijaz and went to Kufa and Baghdad many times. It is said that he learned about 600,000 Hadith from more than 1,000 scholars.

Imam Bukhari (RH) had an extremely strong memory from an early age and his memory was considered to be inhuman. His brother Rashid bin Ismail stated that in his childhood:

"Imam Bukhari used to go with us to the scholars of Basra to listen to Hadiths. All of us used to write Hadiths down except Imam Bukhari. After some days, we condemned Imam Bukhari saying that you had wasted so many days work by not writing down Hadiths. Imam Bukhari asked us to bring our notes to him. So, we all brought our notes, upon which Imam Bukhari began to read Hadiths one by one from the top of his head until he narrated to us more than fifteen thousand Hadiths. Hearing these Hadiths, it seemed that Imam Bukhari was re-teaching us all of the Hadiths we had noted."

He did not depend on pen and paper as much as he relied on his sharp memory which was a result of Allah Tala's gift of intelligence and superb memory to him.

There is one remarkable incident that took place in Baghdad when Imam Bukhari (RH) visited the place. The people having heard of his many accomplishments, and the attributes which were issued to him, decided to test him to make him prove himself to them. In order to do that they chose one hundred different Hadiths and changed the testimonials and the text of the Hadiths. The Hadiths were recited by ten people to Imam Bukhari (RH). When the Hadiths were recited, Imam Bukhari (RH) replied to all in one manner, "Not to my knowledge." However, after the completion of all the Hadiths, he repeated each text and testimonial which had been changed followed by the correct text and testimonial.

Imam al-Bukhari (RH) was someone who upheld his credibility and dignity, knowing that he was trusted by the people to narrate hadith. On one occasion, he was traveling by boat while carrying 1,000 gold coins. There was another traveler who devised a plan to steal the coins. In the middle of the night, the traveler woke up screaming that he had lost his gold coins and described the bag that he had "lost" identical to that of Imam al-Bukhari (RH). The other travelers on the boat searched for the bag but none could find it, and when they could not locate the bag, they became upset with the traveler for waking them up. The traveler came to Imam al-Bukhari (RH) and asked him where the bag of coins was. Imam al-Bukhari (RH) said that he had thrown the bag, his life savings, overboard. When further questioned on his actions, Imam al-Bukhari (RH) said, .”..don't you know that I have spent my life collecting the hadith of the Prophet (ﷺ), and the world knows me as trustworthy? And that they trust me and take my hadith? Do you want me to sell all of that for a thousand dinars?”

The father of Imam Bukhari, Muhaddith Ismail ibn Ibrahim was enormously rich and Imam Bukhari had inherited a huge share of his wealth. He used to give his wealth on the basis of silent partnership (e.g. if a person is in possession of a shop, the profits are shared equally, but only one partner does all the work). Abu Sa`id Bakr ibn Munir states: "Once Abu Hafs sent some goods to Imam Bukhari and when traders learnt of this, they came and offered five thousand dirhams. He told them, 'Come in the evening.' A second group of traders came and offered ten thousand dirhams, but he told them, 'I have already made an agreement with someone else. I Don't want to change my intention for the sake of ten thousand dirhams.'"

From the point of view of his character, Imam Bukhari was a simple and hard working person. He would fulfill his own needs by himself. Despite having a lot of wealth and status, he always kept the minimum number of servants required and never indulged himself in this matter. Muhammad ibn Hatim Warraq, who was one of his main disciples, says: "Imam Bukhari was establishing an inn near the city of Bukhara and was placing the bricks with his own hands. I came forward and said, 'Leave the laying of the bricks for this building to me.' But he replied, 'On the day of judgement, this act will be of benefit to me.'"

Just as he was generous with this wealth, he was also greatly generous with his heart. Sometimes, he would give three thousand dirhams as a donation in one day. Warraq says that Imam Bukhari's earnings were five hundred dirhams per month and he would spend all of it on his students.

Imam Bukhari kept himself away from all worldly desires and temptations. Sometimes, in his quest for knowledge, he passed his time eating dried grass (hay). Usually, he would eat only two or three almonds in a whole day. Once he became ill and the doctors told him, "Your intestines have become dry because you have been eating dried leaves." It was at that moment that Imam Bukhari told the doctor that he had been eating dried leaves for forty years and during this span of time he never even touched any kind of curry.

He was bestowed with the highest rank of piety and righteousness. He feared Allah Tala very much inwardly and outwardly. He prevented himself from backbiting and suspicion and always respected the rights of others. Bakr ibn Munir relates that Imam Bukhari said, "I am hopeful that when I meet my Lord, He will not take account of me because I never backbited."

Imam Bukhari was so vigilant in his worship, that he would pray Nawafil and keep fasts in abundance. He would complete the recitation of the whole Qur'an daily in the month of Ramadan and also recited ten chapters of the Holy Qur'an deep in the night. He would complete the Holy Qur'an in the Tarawih prayers and always recite twenty verses in each rakat. He was very courteous, tolerant and gentle. He never became angry if mistreated by other persons and prayed forgiveness for those who attributed evil to him. If he needed to correct any person, he would never embarrass him in public.

In 250 AH, Imam Bukhari decided to go to Nishapur. After hearing this news, a wave of happiness spread among its people. In those times, Muhammad ibn Yahya adh-Dhuhli was the head of the literary kingdom of Nishapur. He advised and led the inhabitants of the city to gather together for the welcoming of Imam Bukhari. A huge crowd went to the outskirts of the city to receive Imam Bukhari, with extreme magnificence and honour.

Imam Muslim ibn Hajjaj says that in all his life, he had never seen such a reception ever given to a scholar or even a ruler.

Imam Bukhari began to deliver lectures on Hadith in Nishapur. At every session, a huge crowd always packed the area to listen and many included people who had arrived specifically to learn the science of Hadith. However, some unpleasant people were envious about the reputation and popularity of Imam Bukhari. These people set up Muhammad ibn Yahya adh-Dhuhli to become his opponent. In this incident, Muhammad ibn Yahya considered the pronunciation of the Qur'an as eternal and was firmly rooted with this concept.

Once, a man approached Imam Bukhari and asked him whether the Qur'an was created (makhluq) or not created (ghayr makhluq). Imam Bukhari paused for a while. The man insisted on a reply, upon which he was told, "The Qur'an is the words of Allah and they are not created (ghayr makhluq)." The man posed some more questions about the words of the Qur'an, upon which Imam Bukhari said, "Our actions are created and the pronunciation is one our actions."

[Comment by G.F. Haddad: The above is inaccurately translated. It should read: "Muhammad ibn Yahya considered the *pronunciation* of the Qur'an as eternal..." and "Imam Bukhari said, 'Our actions are created and the pronunciation is one our actions.'"

The disagreement was only over the pronunciation (lafz) of the Qur'an, not the words of the Qur'an, although lafz also means "wording." Al-Dhuhli and other people close to the Hanbali madhhab considered that the pronunciation is uncreated just like the Qur'an itself. Others, like Bukhari and Muslim, also al-Karabisi the companion of Imam Shafi and others considered the pronunciation created since it is part of one's acts and acts are certainly created. There was no disagreement that the words of the Qur'an are not created since they are what is meant when we say that the Qur'an is Allah's Speech.

What possibly reconciles the different views on this subject is that lafz is used by some to mean the revealed, uncreated words and contents of recitation, while others mean thereby the mere act of pronunciation, which is created; hence the extreme caution shown by some, such as Imam al-Bukhari, who fell short of saying: "Lafz is created" even though he used it in the second sense, since he said: "Lafz is an act of human beings, and our acts are created." This lexical ambiguity is a proof of sorts that the differences on this particular question were largely in terminology rather than essence. Added to this is a fundamental difference in method around the appropriateness of such dialectic (kalam), which poisoned the air with unnecessary condemnations on the part of Imam Ahmad's followers - and Allah knows best.]

After this, mass propaganda started against Imam Bukhari, which led to accusations that he believed the words of the Qur'an to be created. When Dhuhli heard these rumours, he disconnected his ties with Imam Bukhari and became his foe. He started warning people by announcing that they should not attend the lectures of Imam Bukhari. As a result, people refrained from sitting in his lectures, except Muslim ibn Hajjaj. At last, due to his disappointment, Imam Bukhari left the city of Nishapur and returned to Bukhara.

When the people of Bukhara learned that Imam Bukhari was coming back to his homeland, they became extremely overjoyed and erected tents many miles outside the city to welcome him. They greeted him with splendour for his return. He established a school there where he spent a great deal of time teaching with satisfaction.

Even here, there were envious people who did not leave him

alone. They met the governor of Bukhara, who was a representative of the Khalifa `Abasiyya, Khalid ibn Ahmad. They told him to call Imam Bukhari to his house to teach his son. When the governor put this suggestion to Imam Bukhari, he was told, "I do not want to abuse knowledge and carry it to the footstep of the rulers. If anybody wants to learn, they should come to my school." The governor replied, by stating, "If my son was to attend your school, he should not sit with ordinary people. You would have to teach him separately." Imam Bukhari answered, "I cannot stop any person from hearing hadith." Upon hearing this, the governor of Bukhara became angry with him and got a fatwa (verdict) from the time wasting opportunist (ibn al-waqt) Ulama against Imam Bukhari to banish him from the city.

Imam Bukhari was distressed at the thought of being banished from his homeland. Not even a month passed, before the Khalifa of Baghdad dismissed the governor of Bukhara, Khalid ibn Ahmad adh-Dhuhli. The governor was expelled from his palace in extreme disgrace and dishonor, being mounted on a she-ass and then thrown into prison, where he died in a space of a few days. Similarly, all the supporters of the governor also died in disgraceful ways.

After returning from Bukhara, Imam Bukhari decided to travel to Samarqand. He was still many miles from the city when he heard that the people there had two views about him. So he decided to stay in a village along the way called "Kharteng." Here, he made the following invocation one night after the late-night prayer: "O Allah, the Earth despite its grandeur is becoming narrow and is troubling me greatly. So take me back to You." After this invocation, he became ill. Meanwhile, the people of Samarqand sent a messenger to bring him there. Imam Bukhari got up and was ready to travel, but his strength gave way. He began to invoke Allah at length, then he took to his bed and his soul passed away to his Lord - may Allah have mercy on him.

His prayers were answered and at the age of 62, he died at Khartang, a place between Samarqand and Bukhara. It was on the night of Eid Al-Fitr, the first night of Shawwal 256 A.H. He is buried in Muhammad Al-Bukhari mausoleum at Khartang near Samarkand, in Uzbekistan

Abd Al-Wahid ibn Adam Awaysi states: "I saw the Holy Prophet (peace be upon him) in a dream standing with a group of Sahaba and asked, 'For whom are you waiting?' He replied, 'For Bukhari.' After a few days, I heard the news of Imam Bukhari's death. He had died at the very moment that I saw the Prophet (ﷺ) in my dream."

QUOTES BY IMAM AL-BUKHARI

"I never did backbiting against anyone since I came to know that backbiting is prohibited. Verily I hope that I meet Allah and He doesn't take me to account for ever backbiting anyone."

"Knowledge precedes expression and action. This is confirmed in the divine verse 'Know therefore that there is no God but Allah, and then repent your sin.' (47:19). God requires of us first knowledge and then action."

"Earn virtues in your spare time, because your death might come upon sudden, Many healthy people I have seen who were free of disease, But then their soul parted upon a sudden."

"One night Imam al-Bukhari was praying, when a wasp stung him seventeen times. When he completed his prayer, he (didn't complain but instead) simply said, 'Look and see what has harmed me during my prayer.'"

"I have discarded ten thousand Hadith narrations from a man simply because I had reason to doubt him. And I discarded a similar amount or even more from another narrator for the very same reason."

"I wrote down Hadith narrations from more than 1,000 trustworthy scholars. And I remember the chain of narrators of every single Hadith that I know."

SAHIH AL-BUKHARI

The Sahih Bukhari collection of Hadith is considered to be the most authentic collection of the teachings and sayings of the Prophet (ﷺ).

These Prophetic traditions, or hadith, were collected by the Uzbek Muslim scholar Muhammad al-Bukhari (RH), after being transmitted orally for generations.

Al-Bukhari (RH) traveled widely throughout the Abbasid Empire from the age of 16, collecting those traditions he thought trustworthy.

At the time when Bukhari (RH) saw [the earlier] works and conveyed them, he found them, in their presentation, combining between what would be considered sahih (correct) and hasan (good) and that many of them included da'if (weak) hadith.

He memorized 70,000 Hadiths at an early age and later in his life, this figure reached 300,000. Among those 100,000 Hadiths were Sahih and 200,000 were Hasan, Da`if, etc.

This aroused his interest in compiling hadith whose authenticity was beyond doubt. What further strengthened his resolve was something his teacher, hadith scholar Ishaq ibn Ibrahim al-Hanthalee – better known as Ishaq Ibn Rahwayh had said.

Muhammad ibn Ismaa'eel al-Bukhari (RH) said, "We were with Ishaq Ibn Rahwayh who said, 'If only you would compile a book of only authentic narrations of the Prophet.' This suggestion remained in my heart so I began compiling the Sahih."

What makes Sahih al-Bukhari so unique was Imam al-Bukhari's meticulous attention to detail when it came to the compilation of hadiths. He had far stricter rules than other hadith scholars for accepting a hadith as authentic. The chain of narrators for a particular hadith had to be verified as authentic and reliable before Imam al-Bukhari would include that hadith in his compilation.

Imam al-Bukhari also studied the lives of narrators, to make sure they were trustworthy and would not fabricate, or change the wording of a hadith. If he discovered that someone in a chain openly sinned or was not considered trustworthy, that hadith was immediately discarded and not included in his book unless a stronger chain for it existed.

Using his strict guidelines for hadith acceptance, Imam al-Bukhari was the first to make a systematic approach to classifying hadith. Each hadith he analyzed was labelled as either sahih (authentic), hasan (good), mutawatir (recurrent in many chains), ahad (solitary), da'eef (weak), or mawdu' (fabricated). This system for hadith then became the standard by which all hadiths were classified by other hadith scholars.

Imam al-Bukhari's collection of hadiths is a monumental achievement and an irreplaceable cornerstone of the science of hadith scholarship. Through his work, hadith studies became a science with governing laws that protected the field from innovations and corruptions. However, his Sahih is not just a simple collection of hadiths. Al-Bukhari organized his collection in a way that it can also be used to help deduce rulings within Islamic law – fiqh.

Bukhari (RH) also said, "I saw the Prophet (peace be upon him) in a dream and it was as if I was standing in front of him. In my hand was a fan with which I was protecting him. I asked some dream interpreters, who said to me, 'You will protect him from lies.' This is what compelled me to produce the Sahih."

Najm b. Fudail said, "[In a dream,] I saw the Prophet (ﷺ) come out of his grave, and I saw al-Bukhari walking behind him. Whenever the Prophet (ﷺ) took a step, al-Bukhari placed his foot over the footprint of the Prophet (ﷺ)."

FOUR ADVICE FROM THE QURAN:

✓ Do not lose hope, nor be sad (3:139)

✓ Do not be sad, indeed Allah (SWT) is with us (9:40)

✓ And do good as Allah (SWT) has done good to you (28:77)

✓ And do not let your dislike of a people lead you to be unjust. (5:8)

If anyone travels on a road in search of knowledge, Allah will cause him to travel on one of the roads of Paradise. (Sunan Abu Dawood, 1631)

He who issues forth in search of knowledge is busy in the cause of Allah till he returns from his quest. (Ibn Malik in Al Tirmidhi, 420)

"When you meet each other, offer good wishes and blessings for safety. Thus it is said: (4:86) "One who conveys to you a message of safety and security and also when a courteous greeting is offered to you, meet it with a greeting still more courteous or (at least) of equal courtesy. When you enter your own house or the house of somebody else, compliment the inmates. "[Al-Qur'an 24:61]

"When was the last time you read the Quran? If you want to change, start with the book of Allah." [Anonymous].

A thought-provoking questions you should ask yourself every day

What am I most passionate about?

Practical Ways to Improve Yourself

<u>Focus</u>

No matter whether it is a worldly objective or something that is in Islamic preaching, the achievement of it all depends upon focus. When a Muslim is focus, he or she sees thing clearly and when the destination is clear in the eyes, the ultimate result is a person arriving at the destination successfully.

<u>**Do things that you usually don't do**</u>

Sometimes, there are things that you normally wouldn't think of doing. You just don't want to take that risk. However, doing those things that you usually wouldn't do would increase your chance of becoming a better person because you'll be challenging yourself to try something new, something you might have been scared of in the past. Be open-minded and try to get over your fears and doubts.

💼 BALANCE DEEN WITH CAREER 💼

FINAL STEP: MAKING THE BEST USE OF YOUR TIME OUTSIDE THE NON-NEGOTIABLES

In this final part of the exercise, you'll set goals according to the time and energy you're left with after all your non-negotiables. This step is what I like to call the 'next-level discipline'. You should only worry about this stage IF you have time left after doing all your non-negotiables. You may not have any time & energy left after your non-negotiables (for example, maybe you have a day job and a part-time job in the evenings. Or you're in the 'Wahnan Ala Wahn' phase of motherhood (pregnancy/ breastfeeding). Or your day job takes 10+ hours from your day)... in such circumstances, if you can give your best to all your non-negotiables, you're already doing better than most Muslims! So don't worry about this stage. Now for the rest, if you started following your ideal routine by fixing your non-negotiables, then reaching this 'next-level discipline' will become easier for you. One of our biggest mistakes can be trying to do everything all at once. If we try to bring a lot of new behavioral changes in our day all at once, we'll inevitably suffer from burnouts. The smart way of following a new routine is to double-down on your non-negotiables first and once they're in a stable state, start using the time-pockets outside your non-negotiables in the most productive way you can. Most of the times, we simply waste all our free time-pockets on meaningless things that bring us no real self-satisfaction (such as scrolling through social media). In this step, I'll show you how you can recognize these free time pockets and block them for your goals in your schedule so there's no room for time-wasters.

1. How many hours does your job take? Write them down.

2. Write the remaining time in your day after your job.

4. Identify all the free pockets of time outside your job and all your other non-negotiables. Also, write all the time-wasters that are taking up those free time-pockets.

<< FREE TIME POCKETS >>	<< TIME-WASTERS >>

5. Which of the goals/ habits from your ideal routine do you want to get started on over the next 30 days? Pick only as many goals as you can realistically do with the time and energy available to you in the present (this is all the time you have outside your non-negotiables including the free pockets of time that you might be wasting).

TO DO NOW << (MOST IMPORTANT GOALS) >>	DESGINATED TIME -BLOCK

6. Which of the goals/ habits from your ideal routine will you do later? SAYING NO TO SOME GOALS is an important part of prioritization. It reduces overwhelm and prevents burnouts.

<< TO DO LATER >>

"

Saying NO to some goals

(purposeful procrastination) reduces

overwhelm and burnouts."

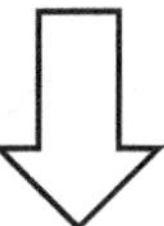

LISTEN UP GO-GETTER,
YOU'VE GOT WORK TO DO!

I believe we all have our unique potential to achieve SO much in life while also securing an Akhirah for ourselves... And the only way we can be a winner in dunya and Akhirah is by having a good balance between our dunya-goals and Deen.

Now tell me - after having all the first steps laid out in front of you... does getting a Sunnah balance in your life suddenly appear totally achievable? It does, doesn't it? It's exciting to know that you can create a different kind of life even as a busy career Muslim.

Can you be a good Muslim and a good Professional? YES! You totally can.

It's high-time we bust the myth that busy professionals can never be as spiritual or as productive as Muslims who're not working. Stick with me and I'll take you behind-the-scenes into the life of other professionals who have successfully achieved 'next-level discipline' despite their many responsibilities. I'll show you how to find that 'sweet balance'... that allows you to do the things you love while being consistent in the things you have to do as a Muslim. You'll learn what it really takes to go from being overwhelmed, stressed and frustrated to becoming a self-content and confident Professional Muslim. This starter kit is only the 'start' of an amazing transformation waiting for you! :)

IMAM AL-NAWAWI

We know him as Imam An-Nawawi, but his full name is Abu Zakaria Yahya Ibn Sharaf Al Hizami An-Nawawi. He was born in 631 A.H, that's roughly 800 years ago. In the small town of Nawa from which he gets his eponym, which is in Syria. He had a very short life of 45 years but during this short period, he had written a large number of books on different subjects and his every book has been recognized as a valuable treasure of Islamic knowledge.

The 7th century Hijri was a very turbulent time in Muslim history. On one hand, from one end you had the crusaders that were waging conflicts on the Muslim lands in Jerusalem. But was conquered for a large portion of Imam An-Nawawi's time. And in fact, Muslim re-conquered Jerusalem in 1245 (642 AH), he was a young boy when it was re-conquered. And on the other hand, in the year 1258 (656 AH), this is a watershed moment in Muslim History. When the Mongols come from the east and invade and sacking Baghdad. ***

Baghdad was the center of learning in the entire world at that time. As much as the conditions for the Muslims now are terrible, we certainly pray and comfort for Muslims all across the world; if you read the history and the accounts of what happened in Baghdad it pales in comparison to anything that we see today. Because they say that the Tigris and Euphrates, that one of the rivers were running red with the blood of Muslims that were killed and the other river was black with the ink of all the books that were tossed in the river.

That this was a turbulent time, this was a very difficult time and at the same time 2 years later, the year 1260 (658 AH) is the famous Battle of Ain Jalut** when the Mongols are defeated for the first time. At the same time, the Muslims establish rules in Mali and they establish a kingdom or a state in Indonesia.

So, why is all of this important, is that we see that in the heartland of the Muslim empire there's conflict and turmoil? But on the border on the hinterlands; to the south and to the east there's the expansion and there's spreading of Islam. And it's a very ironic and very fitting mirror of what's happening today in the Muslim world. We see that the Muslim lands, the traditionally Muslim lands that they're under attack both internally and externally. And we find that Islam is on the hinterlands, out in the West and out in the East that it's spreading and it's expanding and people are coming to Islam like never before. So, what should be appreciated is that despite this turmoil, despite all of these conflicts that were going on; that scholarship within the Muslim lands not only thrived, not only persisted but it thrived and flourished despite all that was going on.

Now Imam An-Nawawi (Rahimahullah) was born in the village of Nawa which is in Syria near Damascus and his town was not a very scholarly city. It was not known for having huge Madrasas or all these famous scholars that lived there. But even from a very young age Imam An-Nawawi was very attached to learning. And it's related to him that he was remarkable even as a child as somebody who had a great degree of seriousness to him; his personality. So, you'll notice the average 3/4/5-year-old, they love running around, they love playing with toys; Imam Nawawi was not like that at all. In fact, as a young child, he was known to be a child that would often contemplate and just think. So, while the other boys are running around and playing, Imam An-Nawawi would just be sitting there and watching and observing.

And there's a very interesting incident that Al Marrakushi, one of the historians from Nawa narrates about Imam An-Nawawi.

What was this incident? That the other boys in the town were just running around and playing and they were chasing him and teasing him or taunting him, as children will do. To try to get him to join in their games and he was sitting aside and running away from them and then sitting aside and crying and weeping. This person asked, "Why don't you play with the children?" He said, "But it wasn't for this that we were created." You see from a very young age that, SubhanAllah! Imam An-Nawawi had a completely different outlook on life than the other children that were around him. From this event, Al-Mrrakushi went to speak to Imam An-Nawawi's Quran teacher, who went to speak to Imam An-Nawawi's father and told him, "Look, your son has this special gift from Allah (SWT) make sure he's given that nurturing that he deserves." Imam's father was a virtuous and pious man. Keeping in view, the learning quest of his son, he decided to dedicate the life of his son for the service and promotion of the cause of Islamic Faith.

So, Imam An-Nawawi finished his hifdh of the Quran while he was in Nawa. Imam An-Nawawi lived in Nawa till the age of 18 years. In the year 649 AH, he went to Damascus which, at that time, was considered the center of learning as there were more than three hundred institutes, colleges and universities in Damascus. He studied Hadith, Islamic jurisprudence and principles from many great Islamic scholars.

In Damascus, this is where his life of scholarship really takes off. And you'll see that in these 45 years he's written so many books. One of the books he wrote Al Majmu he actually died before he finished it. And this book within itself is thousands of pages long. Now the scholars took an approximation that if Imam An-Nawawi started writing at the age of 18 till the day that he died, on an average how many pages did he write? He wrote an average of over 40 pages per day, in order for him to have achieved everything that he wrote; it would have been 40 pages a day from the age of 18 till the age that he died. That is how much he would've written each day. So, it shows you his great level of scholarship.

What made him so unique, just to say a little bit about his qualities; That he had immense and tremendous piety, they say that he would fast every single day. He would never eat from any of the public gardens because he didn't know if there were somehow some rights that were transgressed in the acquiring of that food. So, his father would have to send food from his village and that would be the only food that Imam An-Nawawi would eat. He was tremendously studious, that he would go to 12 classes a day (which were an hour each) and he would review the notes from those classes. He was engaging in tremendous amounts of Nawafil and Tahajjud. So, one asks how exactly was he able to do this. And the only answer we have is that you can't reproduce this in a laboratory. But rather that he had tremendous barakah, tremendous blessing in his time. Al-Qutb Al-Yauneeni said about him,

"He would not waste any moment of the day or night but he would spend it busy with attaining knowledge. Even when he is walking in the streets, he will be busy going over what he had remembered and reviewing his notes. He continued gaining knowledge in that way for a period of six years."

Imam An-Nawawi the way he would treat his guest, he would have a plate ready in the middle of his house. That anytime someone wanted to come, they were more than welcome. However, they would go through two things. Number one, he had so many books that there was no place to sit except for Imam An-Nawawi himself. So, if you wanted to sit down, you would have to lift some books and place them somewhere else. They didn't have bookshelves like we have today. So, they'll say what is important and then they'll leave and that's it. Imam An-

Nawawi's students mentioned that it was when the guest would come, he would then take the time to sharpen his pencils. That is the way he would keep himself busy, he didn't want anything to distract him from seeking knowledge. So when the guests would come he would be speaking to them at the same time sharpening his pencils so that no time would be wasted whatsoever.

He led a very austere, simple and modest life although it would have been possible for him to live otherwise, given his teaching position and influence. Some narrations state that all the clothing he possessed was a turban and a long gown. He did not desire any of the pleasures of this world. At one point in time, he would not eat anything except some cake and olives that his father would send him from time to time from Nawa. One of the reasons for this was that he was certain that such food came from permissible sources.

He did not accept a stipend for his teaching. Nawawi's only material possession of this world was books as his small room was like a warehouse of books and his goal was not simply to possess a large library. His books were not for decoration or display. Instead, he benefited greatly from those works and, from his lectures and writings, numerous people have benefited from them since then.

He himself said that he didn't sleep for two years lying down. That he would just be sitting and reading and he would fall asleep on his books and he would wake up a few, 30 minutes later or whatever it was and he would continue to do what he was doing. Imam An-Nawawi didn't get married. He said, "I fear that if I was to get married, I would fall into something haram." Meaning that I wouldn't be able to fulfil the rights of my wife. Because he loved knowledge so much, he loved teaching so much. This is why he didn't get married.

He lived at a time where a transition was taking place from the Ayyubid Dynasty to the Mamluk Dynasty. This has been the greatest fitnah that struck the Muslim Ummah. The attack of the Mongols. That if you look at what they did with Baghdad, Subhanallah; in that time, they said that they killed over 500,000 Muslims. They would just take their heads and they would pile them up in the city. That you would see blood flowing in the streets of Baghdad, flowing into the river. And then who does Allah (SWT) choose to stand up and defend the Muslim civilization? It is a group of slaves and that is where the title of Mamluks came from, that they were possessed. The head of the Mamluks at that time, who stood up was this individual by the name of Zahir Al-Baibars. He ends up becoming Khalifah. Now, unfortunately, Subhanallah! You would think that an individual that comes from a very humble beginning, not having any wealth, any property; he would appreciate wealth and be thankful to Allah (SWT). Yet unfortunately, this Muslim Ummah has been plagued with rulers and leaders that over indulge in this dunya, Subhanallah! So, Al-Zahir Al-Baibers defeats the Mongols and this new Mamluk Dynasty starts up and then again it becomes very, very oppressive.

So, when this starts to happen who is at the forefront of the opposition? It is Imam An-Nawawi. He writes a letter to Al Zahir Al-Baibers. He mentions that "Oh Zahir Al-Baibers, you started as an individual that had nothing, and Allah (SWT) now made you the leader of the Muslim Empire. Do not abuse your rights over the people. This waqf doesn't belong to the ruler but it belongs to the Muslim state and that is the way it should remain."

This is one of the first times that a tax is levied upon the people without reason. So, in Islamic history, the general concept of tax is that the Muslim ruler is not allowed to tax the civilians until there's a need for it. For example, the Muslims are going to war and they need that wealth, then they can be taxed. Or there's a need for the community then they can be taxed. But the general case is that they are not to be taxed.

So, now when the war is completely over, everything is finished, their need for the money is finished; Zahir Al-Baibers instead of decreasing the tax on the people, he increases it. And again, what does Imam An-Nawawi (Rahimahullah) do? Writes a very powerful letter, that "Fear the day where you will stand in front of Allah (SWT). Where in this dunya you are taxing the people and in the akhira (hereafter) it is your deeds that will be taxed by Allah (SWT)." Another very powerful, staunch and harsh letter that he wrote to Al Zahir Al-Baibers. Now, when this letter was sent he asked, "Who wrote this letter?" And it was told to him Imam An-Nawawi wrote this letter. But Al-Zahir Al-Baibers never actually physically did anything to him. And it is said in the books of history that Al-Zahir Al-Baibers was asked, "Why is it that you never imprisoned Imam An-Nawawi? Why is it that you never had him exiled? Why didn't you do anything?" He said, "Anytime I would think of Imam An-Nawawi, I would find a fear inside of myself, a fear that I couldn't do anything to him." The scholars commented that this is a sign of the hadith of the Prophet (peace be upon him) where Allah SWT says, "That whoever tried to harm one of my Awliya (friends), one of my close slaves, then I will wage war against this individual." And this is why Al-Zahir Al-Baibers never actually harmed Imam An-Nawawi.

Because of his persistence on justice, the Imam was removed from Damascus and returned back to his hometown of Nawa. After returning to his hometown in Nawa, he fell ill and passed away. He died on the 24th of Rajab, 676 AH (1277 AD). However, by the grace and mercy of Allah, his accomplishments during his short life span were equal to or greater than many who lived even twice as long as he did.

When the news of his death reached Damascus, the people were very saddened. Tears flowed from their eyes. One of the greatest scholars and the greatest leaders of the people had passed away. Indeed, one who was greatly beloved by almost everyone.

Some of his famous works that bear mentioning; number one, he has a very famous commentary on Sahih Muslim which they say is second only to Ibn Hajar Al Asqalani (Rahimahullah)'s commentary on Sahih Al Bukhari. He wrote the Bustanul Arifin, another famous text. And then of course the most well-known is the famous text Riyad As Salihin; The gardens of the righteous which is another collection of hadith which primarily deal with At Targheeb Wat Tarheeb; about encouraging and admonishing people towards going righteous actions and staying away from harmful actions. And of course, perhaps the most well-known of all of his texts is the Arbain of An-Nawawi.

As I mentioned he dies at a relatively young age, he's only 45 years old when he passes away. And yet the works he left behind are tremendous. Tremendous amounts of work that he left behind. They say that when he passed away that all he owned was a thawb, a staff, and a turban. Just these 3 items of clothing were all he had.

Imam An-Nawawi didn't want to have any marker over his grave, he didn't want his grave to be celebrated. And yet what ended up happening is that a tree grew from his grave. This is a sign, and the tree as we know is a very powerful metaphor. It's a symbol of life that even after he passes away that a tree that symbolizes life grows from his grave nonetheless; despite him not wanting to have a marker.

He is buried in his hometown of Nawa, Syria. Al-Nawawi wished that his grave would be according to the Sunnah i-e it was to be leveled and not prominent. However, some people decided to build a dome over his grave. However, Allah willed that Al- Nawawi's wish is fulfilled. Every time they tried to build something over his grave, it was destroyed. His grave, after many attempts, was finally left flat, slightly marked and according to the sunnah. His grave is still well-known and recognized today. May Allah reward Imam Al-Nawawi for all of his efforts and striving for the sake of Allah.

Now Adhahabi (Rahimahullah) when he concludes the biography of Imam An-Nawawi; mentions three important points. He says that Imam An-Nawawi (Rahimahullah) has three characteristics that he was at the pinnacle of, that he excelled at. And if any scholar of Islam had just one of these characteristics, he would be considered a great Imam within his own right.

Number one, his level of scholarship. That learning, reading, writing and most importantly disseminating; he was at the top of his game at that.

Number two, his level of asceticism. That his lack of love for this dunya was unparalleled. Someone constantly worshiping Allah (SWT); someone taking advantage of his time, someone always doing some sort of dhikr.

And then the third thing that he mentions is Imam An-Nawawi enjoining good and forbidding evil.

And Subhanallah! These are the characteristics that all the scholars are meant to have; these are like fundamental elements. And it was Imam An-Nawawi that excelled in all three of them; was the pinnacle at all three of them, that made him the great Imam that he was. We pray that Allah (SWT) has mercy upon him and forgives him for his shortcomings and raises us with him in Jannatul Firdaus (Ameen).

Quotes by Imam An-Nawawi

"If a person falls into the same sin a hundred times or a thousand times or even more, and he repents after each time, his repentance will be accepted and his sins nullified. Even if he was to repent after all his sins just one time, his repentance would still be sound."

"I love you because of your religion. If you let go of your religion, then I have to let go of my love for you."

"To keep the presence of Allah in your heart in public & private;

To follow the sunnah of Prophet SallAllahu Alaihi WaSallam by actions & speech;

To keep away from people & from asking them;

To be happy with what Allah gave you even of it is less;

To always refer your matters to Allah.!"

"Intention is the measure for rendering actions true, so that, where intention is sound, action is sound, and where it is corrupt, then action is corrupt."

"As for myself, threats do not harm me or mean anything to me. They will not keep me from advising the ruler, for I believe that this is obligatory upon me and others."

MONGOL INVASION OF BAGHDAD

In 1242, al-Musta'sim succeeded to the position of Khalifa, not knowing that he would be the last Abbasid to rule in Baghdad. Contemporary chroniclers, all of whom had the benefit of hindsight, are almost universal in their contempt for al-Musta'sim. One writer described him as "devoted to entertainment and pleasure, passionately addicted to playing with birds, and dominated by women. He was a man of poor judgment, irresolute, and neglectful of what is need for the conduct of government." Another chronicler summed up the Khalifa this way: "Undoubtedly he was not fit for kingship and greatness was beyond him."

The Khalifa's court was not much better, as it was portrayed as being a bunch of schemers who spent most of their time fighting against each other. This included a Vizier who, being a Shi'ite, was despised by the rest of the predominantly Sunni court. There was also the commander of the Khalifa's military, known as the Dawatdar, who was also looking to usurp power for himself.

In the summer of 1256, with the Mongols campaigning in neighboring Iran, major flooding hit Baghdad after heavy rains caused the Tigris River to overflow its banks. Before the waters receded, anarchy and sectarian violence broke out between Sunnis and Shiites. One of the Khalifa's sons led a group of soldiers to the neighborhood of Karkh, where they slaughtered many of Shiites living there. The Vizier protected hundreds of his co-religionists, letting them take refuge in his own palace. Sunni chroniclers often allege that it was this event that led Vizier to later secretly support the Mongols.

The Mongols set out from western Iran in November of 1257. By all accounts the size of Hulagu's army was massive. The

Mongol leader commanded between 15 to 17 tumens, which are theoretically units of 10 000 men. This would give him as much as 150 000 soldiers. One can add an almost equal number of local auxiliaries such as Armenians and Iranians, for a total of around 300 000 men available for the invasion. Of course, the entire Mongol army would not be able to take part in the invasion, as they still had to guard their recently conquered territories, but several chroniclers state that the Mongols took 200 000 troops for this invasion.

On January 11th, the Iraqi army encountered lead elements of the Mongol forces in Anbar, about 30 miles northwest of Baghdad. The Abbasid army defeated this group, but decided not to pursue. Instead, the Abbasid army stayed out in the fields and celebrated their victory with eating and drinking. An Armenian chronicler added that the Dawatdar sent messengers to the Khalifa, saying, "I defeated all of them, and tomorrow I will do away with the few survivors."

But the Mongols who were defeated were only a small reconnoitering troop that had been sent ahead to scout the Abbasid army. Before the end of the day, the main force had arrived. While the night passed, the Mongols encircled the Iraqi troops and destroyed several dykes and canals. When the Dawatdar and his soldiers awoke the next day, they found themselves in big trouble, as water flooded into the area all around them.

The Mongols were now attacked in full force, and the Abbasid army was routed. One chronicler stated that 12 000 Iraqi soldiers were killed or drowned here, while another reported that only three men, including the Dawatdar, managed to get back to Baghdad. After the Dawatdar's defeat, no further attempts were made to engage the Mongols before they reached Baghdad. Instead, work was done to prepare the city's defenses, such as setting up catapults and other siege machines. One source estimated that eighty thousand men were defending the city.

To make matters worse for Baghdad, tens of thousands of refugees were swarming into the city, trying to keep ahead of the advancing Mongol armies. With all these destitute arrivals coming into Baghdad, the city's food supply would become stretched and the streets extra crowded and filled with rubbish.

On January 18, 1258, Hulagu and his forces converged on the outskirts of Baghdad. The city was encircled, and several pontoon bridges were built over the Tigris by the Mongols using captured boats. The Mongols did not immediately attack Baghdad. Instead, they spent a day and a night building their own wall around the entire city. In front of this wall, they dug a trench, parts of which were filled with water to make moats. Behind their walls, the Mongols built mounds made of bricks and rubble, on top of which they set up their siege machines, including catapults and naphtha throwers.

While the Mongols made their preparations, the Khalifa made a final attempt to obtain a truce. He sent his vizier and the patriarch of Baghdad's Christian community to Hulagu with some gifts. They met the Mongol leader, but the efforts proved fruitless. On January 29th the Mongols began their attack.

The western part of Baghdad, which had no walls, fell on the first day of fighting. Shia dominated neighborhoods, like Karkh, may have welcomed the Mongols instead of fighting them. Even if they didn't, they were not well protected and could offer little resistance. Meanwhile, Hulagu had his siege machines concentrate their attack on Ajami Tower, which was at the southeast corner of the city. Because there was a lack of suitable stones around Baghdad, the Mongols cut down palm trees and hurled them at the city with their catapults. On February 1st, just three days after they began the attack, the Ajami Tower was destroyed. As the tower fell, the Mongols tried to storm the walls, but the defenders fought them off.

The Mongols also had scribes write messages for Baghdad's population, which were then fastened to arrows and shot into the city. The messages promised that no harm would come to several groups of people, including Shiites, Christians, Jews, merchants, scholars, and anyone else who was not involved in the fighting.

On February 1st, the Dawatdar commanded a force of up to ten thousand men into ships and sailed down the Tigris River, either in an attempt to escape or to land away from the Mongol forces and attack them from behind. Some reports suggest that the Khalifa was with the Dawatdar, having been convinced to flee the city. But significant preparations had been made along the river to prevent any such attempt, and when the Iraqis came, they attacked the fleet with catapults, arrows and naphtha. The Dawatdar was forced to return to Baghdad, leaving three of his ships behind to be captured.

Two days later, Hulagu commanded that the walls of Baghdad be taken. A Georgian chronicler proudly noted that his fellow countrymen led the assault. They and the other Mongol soldiers managed to overrun the ramparts around Ajami Tower shortly after sunrise, but other parts of the Mongol army had difficulty gaining their sections of the wall, and it was not until that evening before the rest of the city walls were held by the Mongols. So far, the fight had taken just six days.

With the Mongols in control of the walls, Hulagu did something very interesting – he had his men just sit there. No attempt was made to go into the city. Perhaps the Mongols did not want to get sucked into fighting in the crowded urban streets, where casualties would be high. Instead, Hulagu said, "The Khalifa can do what he wants. If he wants, let him come out; if not, let him not come out. But the Mongol troops will remain on the walls where they are until they come out."

While some fighting continued for the next several days, it seems clear that resistance by Baghdad's defenders was collapsing. Groups of soldiers, civilians and courtiers began to abandon Baghdad and surrender. Some were granted amnesty, others were taken away and executed. The Dawatdar himself tried to give up, was sent back to the city to convince others to stop fighting, and the next day returned to the Mongol camp and was executed. His head was sent to Mosul, as a gentle reminder to Lu'lu to stop being tardy and get his men down to Baghdad. The Khalifa remained in his palace, unsure of what to do, but the vizier convinced him that his only chance was to surrender and hopefully be given another chance to rule the city.

On February 10th, the Khalifa walked out of Baghdad with his family and three thousand courtiers and surrendered to the Mongols. He soon met Hulagu, who did not display any anger at the Khalifa, but instead asked about his health. He then requested al-Musta'sim to "tell the people of the city to throw down their weapons and come out so that we may make a count." The Khalifa agreed, and soon the remaining defenders of the city, thousands in all, marched out of the city and gave up their weapons. Once all of them were unarmed, the Mongols drew out their own swords and attacked the helpless soldiers. No one was spared. The Khalifa looked on this spectacle, watching his helpless countrymen being slaughtered. He wept, regretting that he did not continue to fight, and said to himself, "My enemy has succeeded. I have fallen into a snare like a clever little bird."

THREE TERRIFYING FIRST-HAND ACCOUNTS OF MONGOL INVASIONS.

Ata Malek Juvayni (Persian Historian and governor of Baghdad): Gengish Khan proceeded to Bukhara and at the beginning of Muharram he camped for the gates of the Citadel. His troops were more numerous than ants or locusts being in their multitude beyond estimation or computation. Detachment after detachment arrived each like a billowing sea and encamped round about the town.

At sunrise, 20,000 men from the Sultan's auxiliary army issued force from the Citadel together with most of the inhabitants being commanded by Kok Khan. Kok Khan was said to be a Mongol and to have fled from Gengish Khan and joined the Sultan.

When these forces reached the banks of the Oxus; the patrols and advance parties of the Mongol army fell upon them and left no trace of them.

On the following day from the reflection of the Sun, the plane seemed to be a tray filled with blood. The people of Bukhara opened their gates and closed the door of strife and battle. The Imams and notables came on a deputation to Gengish Khan who entered to inspect the town and the citadel.

He rode into the Friday mosque and pulled up before the maqsura. Whereupon his son Tolui dismounted and ascended the pulpit. Gengish Khan asked those present whether this was the palace of the Sultan? They replied that it was the house of God. Then he too got down from his horse and mounting two or three steps of the pulpit. He exclaimed the countryside was empty of fodder. Fill our horse's bellies. Whereupon they opened all the magazines in the town and began carrying off the grain. They brought the cases in which the Qur'an were kept out into the courtyard of the mosque. Where they cast the Qur'an left and right and turned the cases into manges for their horses. After which they circulated cups of wine and sent for the singing girls of the town to sing and dance for them. While the Mongols raised their voices to the tunes of their own songs.

When Gengish Khan left the town he went to the festival musala and mounted the pulpit and the people having been assembled asked which were the wealthy among them. 280 persons were designated. A hundred and ninety of them being natives of the town and the rest strangers. He then began a speech in which after describing the resistance and treachery of the Sultan, he addressed them as follows, "Oh people know that you have committed great sins. And that the great ones among you have committed these sins. If you ask me what proof I have for these words, I say it is because I am the punishment of God. If you had not committed great sins God would not have sent a punishment like me upon you."

Ali ibn al-Athir (Arab historian and biographer): For some years, I continued to averse from mentioning this event. Deeming it so horrible that I shrank from recording it. And ever withdrawing one foot as I advanced the other. To whom indeed can it be easy to write the announcement of the death blow of Islam and the Muslims? Or who is he on whom the remembrance thereof can weigh lightly? Oh, would that my mother has not born me. Or that I had died and become a forgotten thing air this befell. Yet with all the number of my friends urged me to set it down in writing. I say therefore that this thing involves the description of the greatest catastrophe and the direst calamity. Which befell all men generally and the Muslims in particular. For even Antichrist will spare such as to follow him though he destroys those who oppose him. But these

Tatars spared none. Slaying women and men and children. Killing unborn babies. These were people who emerged from the confines of China. And attacked the cities of Turkestan like kashgar and and Vala según. And then advanced on the cities of Transoxiana such as Samarkand, Bukhara. And they like taking possession of them and treating their inhabitants in such a way as we shall mention. All this they did in the briefest space of time. Remaining only for so long as their March required and no more. Moreover, they need no commissariat nor the conveyance of supplies. For they have with them sheep, cows, horses and the like quadrupeds the flesh of which they eat nor tell. As for their beasts which they ride, they dig into the earth with their hooves and eat the roots of plants knowing naught of barley. And so when they are liked anywhere they have need of nothing from without. As for their religion, they worship the Sun when it rises and regard nothing as unlawful. Stories have been related to me which the hero can scarcely credit. As to the terror of the Tatars which God Almighty cast into men's hearts. So, it is said that a single one of them would enter a village or a quarter wherein there were many people and would continue to slay them one after another, none daring to stretch forth his hand against this horsemen. And I've heard that one of them took a man captive but had not with him any weapon wherewith to kill him and he said to his prisoner lay head on the ground and do not move. And he did so. And the Tartar went and fetched his sword and slew him therewith

Kirakos Gandzaketsi (Armenian Historian): Now Hulagu commanded all those subjects to him to go against the Tajik capital Baghdad. Which was the seat of the Tajik Dominion. The king who sat in Baghdad was not called Sultan or Melek as the Turkish Iranian or Kurdish autocrats customarily are. But Khalifa is a descendant of the Prophet (peace be upon him). The great Hulagu went against the Khalifa with a countless multitude. Composed of all the peoples subject to him. This was done in the autumn and winter seasons because of the severe heat of that country in the summer. Before his departure, he ordered by Juno yin and the troops with him in the land of the Sultan of Rum to go and surround the Great Tigris River. On which the city of Baghdad was built. So, that no one could flee by boat from the city or to the more secure Basra. They immediately obeyed the command tying pontoon bridges across the Great River and sinking between the river and its bed sturdy fences with iron hooks and pipes. So, that no one could depart the city swimming without them knowing about it. Now the Khalifa who resided in the city proudly and presumptuously sent many troops against those guarding the river. They were under the command of a chief named Dawatdar. Dawatdar went and first triumphed, killing some 3,000 Tatars. When evening fell he sat eating and drinking without a care. And he sent messages to the Khalifa saying I defeated all of them and tomorrow I will do away with the few survivors. Now the crafty and ingenious tartar army spent the entire night arming and organizing. They surrounded the Tajik army. Daybreak they put their swords to work destroying the entire group. And throwing them into the river. Only a few men escaped. That same morning the great Hulagu surrounded the city of Baghdad. Stationing everyone at arm's length from the wall and telling them to demolish it and guard well that no one escaped. He sent valiant emissaries to the Khalifa so that he would come out obediently and pay taxes to the Khan. The Khalifa gave a stern reply full of insults. Claiming to be Lord of the sea on land, "You were a dog, a Turk. Why should I pay taxes to you or obey you." However, Hulagu did not become aggrieved because of the insults nor did he write any boasts. He merely said, "God knows what he does." Then he ordered the wall demolished and they demolished it. He said to rebuild it again and guard it carefully and they did so. The city was full of soldiers and people. For seven days they stood on the walls but no one shot arrows at them nor were swords used either by the citizens or by the Tartar soldiers. But after seven days the citizens began to request peace and to come to Hulagu with affection and submission. And Hulagu ordered that this be done that peace be made. Then the countless multitude came through the city gates climbing over each other to see who would reach him first. Hulagu divided up among the soldiers those who came out. And ordered the soldiers to take them far from the city and to kill them secretly so that the others would not know. They killed all of them. Four days later, the Khalifa also emerged with his two sons with all the grand ease and much gold silver and precious stones as fitting gifts for Hulagu and his Nobles. But first Hulagu honored him, reproaching him for dallying and not coming to him quickly. But then he asked the Khalifa, "What are you God or man? And the Khalifa responded, "I am a man and the servant of God." Hulagu asked, "Well did God tell you to insult me and to call me a dog and to not give food and drink to God's dog?" Now in hunger, the dog of God shall devour you. And he killed him with his own hands. That he said is an honor for you because I killed you myself and did not give you to another for killing. He ordered his own son to slay one of the Khalifa's sons. While he gave the other son as a sacrifice to the Tigris River. Saying it did not harm us but was our collaborator in killing the senseless ones. Hulagu then ordered the troops guarding the walls to descend and kill the inhabitants of the city great and small. The Mongols organized as though harvesting a field and cut down countless innumerable multitudes of men, women and children. For forty days they did not stop. Then they grew weary and stopped killing. Their hands grew tired and they took the others for sale. They destroyed mercilessly. Hulagu ordered all his soldiers to take the goods and property over the city. They all loaded up with gold, silver, precious stones, pearls and costly garments. For it was an extremely rich city unequaled on earth.

BATTLE OF AIN JALUT

In the 13th century, a new power emerged on the Mongolian steppeled by Genghis Khan, who mobilized his people for war and conquest.

He carved out a vast empire and upon his death in 1227, his descendants carried on his mission to conquer the world, leaving a permanent mark on history – one characterized by slaughter, destruction, and savagery.

Forays into Europe reached all the way into Poland, Hungary and the Balkans, while the advance into the Middle East brought the Muslim communities to the brink of extinction.

Now, the Mamluk Sultanate stands as the last bastion of Islam against the feared Mongol horde. The battle that will change the course of history is about to take place...

In Egypt, the Mamluks were a warrior caste of slave origin, trained from a young age as warriors that were very capable in battle, forming a military elite of Ayyubid Sultans of Egypt and Syria.

Over time their power grew and by 1250 they overthrew the Ayyubids and formed the Mamluk Sultanate. 10 years on, as the hot summer of 1260 rolled on, Cairo was the glistening jewel on the banks of the river Nile.

The city's inhabitants went about their daily routines, unaware that, in the palace, four Mongol envoys had the full attention of Sultan Saif al-din Qutuz and his generals.

They arrived on behalf of Hulagu Khan, carrying a letter that contained an unequivocal ultimatum: In short, the Khan threatened with the terrible destruction, vowing to shatter all mosques and kill all Muslim children if Qutuz refused to submit to Mongol rule.

For a time, the Sultan and the envoys looked at each other in silence. Then, Qutuz withdrew to consult with his generals, while the Mongols confidently smirked.

The hastily gathered council of war was a grim affair as the high ranking officers reminded Qutuz of the sobering Mongol advance into the Middle East…

Over the past 35 years, the unrelenting advance of the Mongols brought destruction to the Islamic world. Countless cities were leveled, their populations killed or enslaved.

Finally, the Great Khan Mongke, grandson of Genghis Khan, gave his brother Hulagu command of what could have been the largest single army ever assembled by the Mongols, ordering him to conquer the remaining Islamic countries of the Middle East and North Africa.

In 1258, they marched on Baghdad with 15 tumens, equal to 150,000 troops. The Abbasid Khalifate, although no longer the center of political power in the Islamic world, was still its' intellectual heartland.

In February, the Mongols took advantage of the treachery in the Abbasid court, as well as Khalifa's own foolishness, and cunningly captured Baghdad, a city of one million inhabitants, effectively putting an end to the once-glorious Abbasid Empire.

Hundreds of thousands of people were put to the sword or sold into slavery, the city sacked and burned to its' foundations, the Grand Library of Baghdad set on fire, the ancient irrigation systems destroyed, with the devastation so extensive that agriculture took centuries to fully recover.

A year later, as the aftershocks of the fall of Baghdad were still felt throughout the Islamic world, Hulagu moved into Syria with a detachment of 6 tumens, equal to 60,000 troops. The speed of the Mongol advance was frightening. By January 1260, the Mongols were at the gates of Aleppo.

The walls were breached after 6 days with the help of catapults and mangonels. As they stormed the city, the Mongols were joined by their vassal Armenian and Frankish forces, killing all Muslim and Jewish men in the ensuing massacre, while most women and children were sent to the slave markets. Christian King of Cilician Armenia and the Prince of Antioch and Tripoli were handsomely rewarded for their cooperation in the sacking of the city.

After hearing of the horrific fate that Aleppo suffered, the rest of Syria capitulated by late March. With the destruction of major Muslim cities, the Mamluk Sultanate was now left as the last true stronghold of Islam.

And for the Mongols, Egypt was the next target…

Back in Cairo, Mamluk commanders agreed that it would be wise to capitulate to Mongol demands.

Qutuz's opinion… differed.

Although he admitted that the Mamluks faced impossible odds against the vast Mongol army, he was a proud and strong-willed leader. To submit would be an act of cowardice.

"Egypt needs a warrior as its' king", he exclaimed.

"If no one else will come, I will go and fight the Tatars alone!"

And with that, the Sultan ordered the envoys seized, cut in half at the waist, then decapitated and their heads displayed on Cairo's imposing Zuwila Gate.

Qutuz's message to Hulagu was irrevocable – The Mamluks will not bow to the invader. The killing of envoys enraged the Khan and the preparations for a full-scale war began at once.

Qutuz had a difficult task ahead of him. He was vastly outnumbered. The Mamluk sultanate was divided into 24 districts, each charged with supplying 1000 troops, which placed the total number of Mamluk cavalry at 24,000, of which 4,000 were royal mamluks, 10,000 were emirs' mamluks, and 10,000 were more regular troops of various origins. Meanwhile, Hulagu had 60,000 troops across Syria.

Nevertheless, Qutuz began defensive preparations. Perhaps most importantly he could call upon his rival Baibars, one of the best military commanders of his time, to join him, promising to give control of Aleppo to him after the war.

Baibars was of Turkic origin, either a Kipchak or a Cuman. He was part of the Barli tribe that lived north of the Black Sea and, while still a boy, he was enslaved by the Mongols during their invasion of Europe and eventually sold to the Ayyubid Sultan of Egypt and Syria.

In Cairo, he was educated in accordance with the Mamluk Furusiyyu Code. He underwent years of extensive military training and received an excellent education. Even at a young age, Baibars displayed exceptional military prowess and upon completing his training he was appointed as commander of an elite group of Sultan's personal bodyguards.

He distinguished himself in battle during the Seventh Crusade and, alongside Qutuz himself, was one of the commanders who destroyed the Crusader army at the Battle of Al-Mansurah in 1250, where King Louis IX himself was captured. After the fall of Damascus in 1260, Baibars was invited by Sultan Qutuz to lead the elite Mamluk vanguard against the Mongols.

As defensive preparations in Egypt continued, word reached Qutuz that Hulagu postponed the campaign against Egypt and withdrew most of his troops east. The death of the Great Khan Mongke prompted Hulagu to return to the Karakorum for the election of the new Great Khan.

Hulagu left his trusted lieutenant Kitbuqa in charge of defending Syria until he returned to continue the campaign against Egypt.

Kitbuqa, who was now governor of Aleppo, was given command of 1 tumen of 10,000 troops. Additional 2,000 troops of Cilician Armenians, Georgians, the garrison from Aleppo, as well as locally recruited nomads were added to Kitbuqa's command, increasing his total force to around 12,000.

Hulagu correctly estimated that Palestine could not sustain an army larger than 15,000 for a prolonged period of time. Furthermore, intelligence gathered from captive and allied soldiers suggested that the Mamluks would be able to field no more than 15,000 troops in Palestine.

And indeed, for the offensive Qutuz prepared 14,000 of his best mamluks, including Bedouins, Turkoman Mamluks, Mongolian deserters and members of the Hawwarah tribe of Libya, assigning 10,000 troops to stay behind and guard Egypt against a possible Christian invasion.

Baibars left Cairo first, in late July, commanding the large vanguard contingent, force-marching to secure Gaza. Both Qutuz and Baibars saw the departure of Hulagu's main army as an opportunity to attack the Mongol rearguard.

Qutuz sent urgent letters to Latin crusaders, asking them to join him. However, the Crusaders, fearing ex-communication, as well as Mongol reprisals, opted for the middle ground, by giving the Mamluk army safe passage and allowing them to purchase supplies as they passed through Christian territory.

Once news reached Kitbuqa of the approaching enemy, he marched out to meet the Islamic army. Having received reports that Qutuz will pass through Christian territory, he planned to intercept the Sultan.

Meanwhile, Qutuz reached Acre and encamped outside the city to purchase provisions for his troops. Mongol spies reported the size and position of the Mamluk army, and Kitbuqa hastened his march, hoping to surprise the Muslims.

The Mongols marched along the eastern side of Lake Tiberias. Once they passed the lake they crossed the river Jordan and proceeded west towards the Spring of Goliath, where, according to legend, David slew Goliath.

Mongols marched in two columns, wanting to intercept and surprise the Mamluks. Cilician Armenian and Frankish troops were placed in the vanguard because they knew the terrain and could guide the rest of the army.

The Jezreel valley was surrounded by Mount Gilboa in the south and the hills of Galilee to the north. As the Mongol army crossed the river Jordan they were surprised by Baibars' contingent.

Sudden volleys of Mamluk arrows opened the engagement. The Christian heavy cavalry moved to close the distance. Baibars caught the Mongols off-guard. Just like the Crusaders, leading the enemy's vanguard, he too knew the lay of the land and he moved his troops into position to launch a surprise attack, while skillfully avoiding detection by Mongol scouts. Cilician armored cavalry made contact with the Muslim line, instantly breaking up their formation. A seemingly chaotic skirmish erupted as the Mamluks were being pushed back.

Further back, Kitbuqa's line of sight was blocked by the gentle ridge running north-south, where fighting was taking place and, not being able to see how many Mamluk troops are deployed beyond the ridge, he sent more troops to bolster the Christian charge, and ordered the rest of his troops to form the battle lines.

With Baibars' exceptional leadership the Mamluk vanguard is able to maintain discipline during a series of manoeuvers – rotating between intense brief hand-to-hand clashes, followed by short retreats and arrow volleys – thus managing to hold back the entire Mongol army with a significantly smaller force, while gradually giving ground to the enemy.

Despite taking considerable losses the Mamluk commander kept his line stable as he rounded the mountain slopes, maintaining a fighting retreat under increasing Mongol pressure.

Baibars' troops have reportedly used early forms of handguns to shoot at the enemy. These weapons, while very inaccurate, were very effective at scaring Mongol horses, thereby disrupting and slowing their advance, with some animals galloping off the field in panic with their riders.

After hours of holding back the overwhelming Mongol advance, tiredness set in and Baibars' contingent began taking heavy losses. But by now it became clear that his force was only a part of the Mamluk army.

From the surrounding hills, hidden in the trees, Qutuz watched and waited for the enemy to come to him. Seeing the Mongols pushing Baibars back Qutuz bolstered the moral of his troops with a rousing speech, which historians say elicited tears from the eyes of his soldiers, and he reminded them of the Mongol savagery, saying:

"There is no alternative to fighting, except a horrible death for all of you, your wives, and your children!"

Kitbuqa ordered an all-out charge, aiming to finish off Baibars' vanguard before they could rejoin the main Mamluk force.

Qutuz countered by ordering his right flank to charge out of the treeline into the Mongol left. Recognizing that he is surrounded on three sides, Kitbuqa ordered his troops to charge-shoot and break away, in an attempt to lure the Mamluks into giving chase.

But Baibars and Qutuz recognized the feigned retreat ruse. They ordered the men to hold their ground and shoot their arrows at the enemy from where they stood.

Aware that Mamluk bows and arrows are much deadlier at longer range, and seeing that the feigned retreat didn't work, Kitbuqa quickly adapted.

He ordered the bulk of his cavalry to swing across the valley and charge the Mamluk left flank while instructing the rest of his troops to close ranks and hold against the Mamluk center and right flank.

His plan was to use the gentle slope to mount a mass-charge that will smash the Mamluk left flank and encircle their army.

As Qutuz's left flank met the Mongol charge, they were in trouble almost straight away. By overloading the flank, the Mongols pushed back the Muslim line.

Seeing that his left flank was in danger of collapsing, Qutuz ordered a detachment of troops to follow him and he rushed to reinforce his troops on the left.

In the center, Baibars consolidated his lines after his fighting retreat and began pushing back the Christian heavy cavalry. The fighting was bloodiest in the center as the mounted Mamluk and Crusader troops locked in bitter hand-to-hand combat.

Baibars personally led his contingent from the front, urging his men to defend their country against the invader!

Meanwhile, Mamluk's left flank was in dire straits. Sections of the line faltered under the weight of the Mongol attack and some troops began fleeing.

As the Mamluk left flank began collapsing, the Mongols pressed forward, seeing their chance to rout and envelop the enemy. Galloping up the hill, Qutuz urged his men to stand and fight as he rushed to shore up the ranks. He took off his helmet so that his soldiers could recognize him.

"O, Islam!!!" he shouted three times and charged into the enemy line with his personal retinue.

This act of courage invigorated the troops, who rallied to his banner. After another hour of fighting, the Mongol push slowed as the Sultan managed to stabilize the flank.

Kitbuqa now found himself in a dangerous situation. When his attempt to overrun the Mamluk left stalled, his own position became exposed after he sent his last reserves to try and stop Baibars' attack in the center. Seeing that Mongols have committed all of their troops, Baibars sent urgent messages to the right flank, ordering them to push the Mongols at all cost, seeing his chance to encircle them from the right.

Meanwhile, more troops reinforced the Mamluk left flank and Qutuz at last managed to turn the tide. Less suited to hand-to-hand combat the Mongols could not withstand the determined Muslim cavalry and, despite their numerical advantage they began falling back.

Kitbuqa's other flank also began collapsing inward and now the danger was real that his position would soon be completely surrounded. One of his officers suggested to him to retreat, but Kitbuqa replied:

"We must die here and that is the end of it. Long life and happiness to the Khan."

And with those words, he too joined the fighting. Bolstered by the presence of their commander, the resolve of the Mongol troops hardened.

But as the Mamluks encircled the invaders, Kitbuqa was captured by Baibars' troops amidst the fighting.

By now the Mongols were tactically outmatched on the field and seeing their leader fall into enemy hands, they realized that the battle was lost.

The rest of Kitbuqa's troops began breaking out and retreated towards Bisan.

On that day, the Muslim army achieved a great victory at Ain Jalut. By halting the westward Mongol expansion, and thus saving the three Holiest cities, Mecca, Medina, and Jerusalem from destruction, Qutuz became the savior of Islam and, arguably, he saved his Christian enemies in the West from the "Devil's Horsemen", a name attributed to the Mongols.

For had they managed to conquer Egypt, the way across northern Africa, all the way to the Strait of Gibraltar, would've been open.

In theory, this would've enabled the Mongols to form a ring around Europe and invade on multiple fronts, making it difficult for any European army to be positioned in order to hold them back.

But Qutuz, who became known as the "Lion of Ain Jalut", did not get to enjoy this triumph. He was assassinated a few days after the battle, while the army was returning to Cairo.

Having been loyal to the Aybak faction, Qutuz certainly had a few enemies and rivals. Baibars, a member of the Bahri faction, was the most powerful of his rivals, and it is possible that he was responsible for Qutuz's death as retaliation, because the late Sultan refused to give control of Aleppo to Baibars as he had promised, fearing Baibars' power and ambition.

Upon the army's triumphant return to Cairo, he became the new Mamluk Sultan. Sultan Baibars was an equally capable ruler as Qutuz, continuing the strong Mamluk traditions.

Irrespective of their political rivalry, Qutuz and Baibars were men whose deeds on the battlefield at Ain Jalut preserved Islam from destruction…

FIVE ADVICE FROM THE QURAN

✓ Indeed He does not like the proud (16:23)

✓ Do not kill your children for fear of poverty (17:31)

✓ O you believe! Do not consume usury, doubled and multiplied, and keep your duty to Allah (SWT) that you may successful (3:130)

✓ O you who have believed, indeed, intoxicants, gambling, [sacrificing on] stone altars [to other than Allah], and divining arrows are but defilement from the work of Satan, so avoid it that you may be successful. (5:90)

"(God) has revealed to me that you should adopt humility so that no one oppresses another." (Riyadh-us-Salaheen, 1589)

The Prophet (s) said, "Shall I inform you about the people of Paradise? They comprise every obscure unimportant humble person, and if he takes Allah's Oath that he will do that thing, Allah will fulfill his oath (by doing that). Shall I inform you about the people of the Fire? They comprise every cruel, violent, proud and conceited person." (Al Bukhari, 6071)

"Be like a diamond, precious and rare, not like a stone, found everywhere." Anonymous

A thought-provoking questions you should ask yourself every day

What do I regret about yesterday?

Practical Ways to Improve Yourself

<u>Avoid negative people</u>

Wherever we go, there are bound to be negative people. Don't spend too much of your time around them if you feel they drag you down.

PRACTICAL TIPS FOR DEVELOPING THE GOOD MUSLIM MINDSETCHEATSHEET

5 TIPS FOR DEVELOPING THE GROWTH MINDSET

1. Continue learning (gaining knowledge and applying it. There's always room for more.

2. Get out of your comfort zone and set up challenges for yourself: Become comfortable with being uncomfortable.

3. Accept failure. Don't let failure keep you from getting up after the fall and moving forward.

4. Accept and appreciate others. Help others reach the same place where you want to be, rather than compete with them to reach there.

5. Accept negative feedback and constructive criticism. Stay clear of unhealthy, nonconstructive criticism that is coming from someone who's jealous of you.

5 TIPS FOR DEVELOPING CONTEMPLATING MINDSET

1. Understand your energy levels and contemplate accordingly.

2. Read less pages of Quran and contemplate more. Take your time with each Ayah.

3. Tahajjud is a great time to do contemplation.

4. Recite a verse multiple times to understand its deeper meaning.

5. Go outside after Fajr and let nature induce a deep thought process.

Ibn al-Haytham

Dozens of inventions come to mind that possibly created the largest transformation in modern human history. But there is one such invention that has completely revolutionized the 21st century; the camera.

The camera is now part-and-parcel of our lives, and even the latest mobile phone launch boasts its "new camera specs" as a unique selling point. Today, according to research by Pew, of the five billion people who own a smartphone around the world, approximately 90% have only taken a picture with a smartphone as opposed to a purpose-built camera, thus making the camera on the smartphone one of the most used functions.

From selfies to family group photos, our phone cameras have enabled us all to become photographers in some way or another. However, one question which almost never crosses one's mind is, where, when and who invented the camera?

What scientific research was necessary for mankind to get here? Who opened the gateway to such an invention? How far did science need to progress for someone to invent such a glorious image-capturing and breathtaking machinery?

Picture this: The year is 965. The world has seen inventions such as the windmill and gunpowder among many more and they seem to be the most advanced inventions of their time. If someone was to attempt to explain to people of that time the concept of a machine that can capture a moment and save it as an image forever, instant laughter would break out.

However, during the late 900s, a man by the name of Abul Muhammad ibn al-Hasan ibn al-Haytham, through his research paved the way for mankind to ultimately invent the camera. Ibn Haytham was a Muslim born in Basra, an Iraqi city located on the Shatt al-Arab, who spent most of his life in Cairo. He was an astronomer, mathematician and one of the most renowned scholars of the Islamic Golden Age.

Al-Hasan Ibn al-Haytham (known in the West by the Latinised form of his first name, initially "Alhacen" and later "Alhazen") was a pioneering scientific thinker.

The story of Ibn al-Haytham's life and discoveries is truly extraordinary. He made significant contributions to our understanding of both vision and light, bringing important new insights into both of these subjects. His brilliant breakthrough, however, came at a time of the darkest episode of his life.

He is known to have said, "If I would be given the chance, I would implement a solution to regulate the Nile flooding." This claim reached al-Hakim, the Fatimid Khalifa in Egypt who invited him to Cairo. Confident of his own abilities, Ibn al-Haytham boasted that he would tame the great Nile River by building a dam and reservoir. But when he saw the extent of the challenge and the marvelous remains of ancient Egypt on the river banks, he reconsidered his own boast thinking. If such a huge project could be done, he reasoned, it would have been done by the brilliant builders of the past who had left us such fantastic architectural relics. He returned to Cairo to inform the Khalifa that his solution was not possible.

Knowing that that particular Khalifa did not entertain failure and that his life would be at risk if he were to disappoint him, Ibn al-Haytham feigned madness to avoid the Khalifa's wrath. He knew that Islamic law would protect a mad person from bearing responsibility for his failure. Despite the Khalifa's wild swings of mood, he nevertheless abided by Islamic law. Rather than executing or expelling Ibn al-Haytham from Cairo, the Khalifa decided to put the scholar under permanent protective custody. That was required by law in order to ensure his safety and that of others. Ibn al-Haytham was placed under what amounted to house arrest, far from the lively discourses and debates to which he was accustomed.

Yet it just as life was at its bleakest moment. Ibn al-Haytham might have made the dazzling discovery for which he is best remembered. Legend says, one day he saw light shining through a tiny pinhole into his darkened room – projecting an image of the world outside onto the opposite wall. Ibn al-Haytham realized that he was seeing images of objects outside that were lit by the Sun. From repeated experiments, he concluded that light rays travel in straight lines, and that vision is accomplished when these rays pass into our eyes.

Ibn al-Haytham confirmed his discovery by experimenting with his dark room (calling it Albait Almuzlim)- translated into Latin as camera obscura, which simply means "dark room."

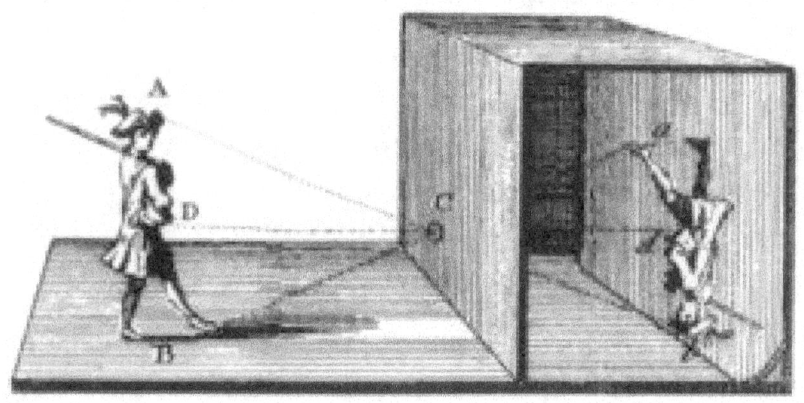

Camera obscura

After many additional experiments using the special apparatus of lenses and mirrors which he built, he laid down his new ideas about light and vision in his seven volumes Book of Optics. He was released from prison on the death (disappearance) of the

Khalifa.

Ibn al-Haytham died at the age of 74 in 1040. His greatest work, the Book of Optics, had perhaps begun from the confines of imprisonment and was completed around the year 1027- but its impact rippled out across the whole world. Both his optical discoveries and the fact that they had been validated using hands-on experiments, would influence those who came after him for centuries.

So how did that influence shine its light on later generations? In the early 12th century, Toledo in Spain was the focus of a huge effort to translate Arabic books into Latin. Christian, Jewish and Muslim scholars flocked to the city, where they lived alongside one another and worked together to translate the old knowledge into Latin and then into other European languages. Ibn al-Haytham's Book of Optics as well as some of his other scientific works were translated into Latin making them available to European scientists including Roger Bacon, Johannes Kepler and even Leonardo da Vinci.

Ibn al-Haytham's discoveries in optics and vision overturned centuries of misunderstanding. In his experiments, he observed that light coming through a tiny hole traveled in straight lines and projected an image onto the opposite wall.

But he realized that light entering the eye was only the first step in seeing. He built on the work of Greek physician Galen who had provided a detailed description of the eye and the optic pathways. Today the oldest-known drawing of the nervous system is from Ibn al-Haytham's Book of Optics, in which the eyes and optic nerves are illustrated.

Ibn al-Haytham suggested that only the light rays that hit the surface of the eye head-on would pass into the eye, creating a representation of the world. It was Kepler in the sixteenth century who corrected this and proposed that the object of sight – what is seen comes from both perpendicular and angular rays that hit the eye to form an inverted image on the retina.

Among Ibn al-Haytham's other insights was his understanding of the crucial role of visual contrast. For example, he realized the color of an object depends on the color of the surroundings, and that contrast of brightness levels explains why we can't see the stars during the daytime.

Ibn al-Haytham also subscribed to a method of empirical analysis to accompany theoretical postulates that is similar in certain ways to the scientific method we know today. He realized that the senses were prone to error, and he devised methods of verification, testing and experimentation to uncover the truth of the natural phenomena he perceived. Up until this time, the study of physical phenomena had been an abstract activity with occasional experiments.

In search of evidence, Ibn al-Haytham studied lenses, experimented with different mirrors: flat, spherical, parabolic, cylindrical, concave and convex. His practical results were clear:

"Visual objects seen by us through light refraction – across thick material such as water and glass – are bigger than their real size", he wrote.

After his death, Ibn al-Haytham's writings were more influential in Latin than Arabic. The only significant work in Arabic that built on Ibn al-Haytham's ideas was produced in the early part of the fourteenth century (in present day Iran) by Kamal al-Din al-Farisi, who was himself a brilliant scientific thinker.

When Ibn al-Haytham's Book of Optics was translated into Latin, it had great influence and was widely studied/read. It was published as a print edition in 1572 so that it could be made more easily available. The Polish astronomer Johannes Hevelius chose to honor Ibn al-Haytham, alongside Galileo, in his most famous work on the Moon, Selenographia, published in 1647.

Some questions Ibn al-Haytham raised remained unsolved for a thousand years. One such was called 'Alhazen's problem' for which he offered a geometrical solution: "Given a light source and a spherical mirror, find the point on the mirror where the light will be reflected to the eye of an observer." Ibn al-Haytham solved this problem geometrically but it remained unsolved using algebraic methods until it was finally solved in 1997 by the Oxford mathematician Peter M Neumann.

And yet, some mysteries remain. Ibn al-Haytham affirmed that an optical illusion was the reason for the Moon appearing so big when it's low in the sky close to the horizon in comparison to its size when at the zenith- and still no one knows why this happens. This, and other questions in science, has yet to be solved – leaving a legacy of intrigue for us to tackle today.

The camera we use to capture life's finest moments would not have existed had it not been for Ibn Haytham's revolutionary research. Prior to Ibn Haytham, many great thinkers wrote extensively and elaborated on the visual theories that were present but no real ground breaking progress was made.

In short, Ibn Haytham was the first to explain that vision occurs when light reflects and bounces off an object and then passes to one's eyes. So the next time you use your smartphone to take a selfie, a breath-taking scene or a photo at a family reunion, just remember that Ibn Haytham, a Muslim scientist, made it all possible.

FOUR ADVICE FROM THE QURAN

✓ Take care of your souls (5:105)

✓ Do good to your parents (17:23)

✓ Verily, Allah (SWT) forgives all sins (39:53)

✓ If you are grateful, I will give you more. (14:7)

They are the losers, those who make the religion hard and tough. They imperil themselves who enforce tough practices of Islam. They destroy themselves, those who are extremes. (Sahih Muslim)

Make things easy and convenient and don't make them harsh and difficult. Give cheer and glad tidings and do not create hatred. (Riyadh us-Saleheen, Volume 1:637)

"And never say of anything, "Indeed, I will do that tomorrow," Except [when adding], "If Allah wills."" (18:23)

"Once prayer becomes a habit, success becomes a lifestyle." Anonymous

A thought-provoking questions you should ask yourself every day

What am I most thankful for?

Practical Ways to Improve Yourself

<u>Take a break</u>

Have you been working too hard? Self-improvement is also about recognizing our need to take a break to walk the longer mile ahead. You can't be driving a car if it has no petrol.

Scheduling down time for yourself is important. Take some time off for yourself every week. Relax, rejuvenate and charge yourself up for what's up ahead.

<u>Explore your talents</u>

Are you aware of a skill or talent that you excel at? If you are, put some effort on enhancing it. Do you think that you don't have one? Well, everybody has something they're good at. If you think that you're not good at something in particular, you just haven't found it yet. Explore your talents. Try to look for activities that you might be interested in and turn out being very skillful at. When you do find your talents, be sure to enrich and practice them. You might even earn a living by them.

PRACTICAL TIPS FOR DEVELOPING THE GOOD MUSLIM MINDSETCHEATSHEET

5 TIPS FOR DEVELOPING THE POSITIVE MINDSET

1. Make realistic and down-to-earth positive affirmations everyday.

2. Daily self talk: Replace your negative self talk with positive self talk.

3. Find humor in bad situations.

4. Smile to a pathological level. Your body, mind and others around you will thank you.

5. Find positive company in your mentors, friends and family members. Stay close to people who radiate positive vibes.

4 TIPS FOR DEVELOPING A GRATEFUL MINDSET

1. Keep a gratitude journal.

2. Write gratitude letters to Allah.

3. Say you are thankful over small things to your family members (stop taking things for granted).

4. Contemplate, read current news about Muslims suffering in other places of the world to feel grateful.

AL-KHWARIZMI

Al-Khwarizmi was one of the greatest mathematicians ever lived. He was the founder of several branches and basic concepts of mathematics. He is also famous as an astronomer and geographer. Al-Khwarizmi influenced mathematical thought to a greater extent than any other medieval writer.

He is recognized as the founder of Algebra, as he not only initiated the subject in a systematic form but also developed it to the extent of giving analytical solutions of linear and quadratic equations.

He developed in detail trigonometric tables containing the sine functions, which were later extrapolated to tangent functions. Al-Khwarizmi also developed the calculus of two errors, which led him to the concept of differentiation. He also refined the geometric representation of conic sections.

He adopted the use of zero, a numeral of fundamental importance, leading up to the so-called arithmetic of positions and the decimal system. His pioneering work on the system of numerals is well known as "Algorithm," or "Algorizm."

Muḥammad Khwarizmi (c. 780 – c. 850), Arabized as al-Khwarizmi with al- and formerly Latinized as Algorithmi, was a Persian scholar who produced works in mathematics, astronomy, and geography. Around 820 CE he was appointed as the astronomer and head of the library of the House of Wisdom in Baghdad.

Few details of al-Khwarizmi's life are known with certainty. He was born into a Persian family and Ibn al-Nadim gives his birthplace as Khwarezm in Greater Khorasan (modern Khiva, Xorazm Region, Uzbekistan).

Al-Khwarizmi developed the concept of the algorithm in mathematics (which is a reason for his being called the grandfather of computer science by some people).

Al-Khwarizmi's algebra is regarded as the foundation and cornerstone of the sciences. To al-Khwarizmi we owe the world "algebra," from the title of his greatest mathematical work, Hisab al-Jabr wa-al-Muqabala. The book, which was twice translated into Latin, by both Gerard of Cremona and Robert of Chester in the 12th century, works out several hundred simple quadratic equations by analysis as well as by geometrical example. It also has substantial sections on methods of dividing up inheritances and surveying plots of land. It is largely concerned with methods for solving practical computational problems rather than algebra as the term is now understood.

Al-Khwarizmi confined his discussion to equations of the first and second degrees. He also wrote an important work on astronomy, covering calendars, calculating true positions of the sun, moon and planets, tables of sines and tangents, spherical astronomy, astrological tables, parallax and eclipse calculations, and visibility of the moon. His astronomical work, Zij al-sindhind, is also based on the work of other scientists. As with the Algebra, its chief interest is as the earliest Arab work still in existence in Arabic.

His most recognized work as mentioned above and one that is so named after him is the mathematical concept Algorithm. The modern meaning of the word relates to a specific practice for solving a particular problem. Today, people use algorithms to do addition and long division, principles that are found in Al-Khwarizmi's text written about 1200 years ago. Al-Khwarizmi was also responsible for introducing the Arabic numbers to the West, setting in motion a process that led to the use of the nine Arabic numerals, together with the zero sign.

Of great importance also was al-Khwarizmi's contribution to medieval geography. He systematized and corrected Ptolemy's research in geography, using his own original findings that are entitled as Surat al-Ard (The Shape of the Earth). The text exists in a manuscript; the maps have unfortunately not been preserved, although modern scholars have been able to reconstruct them from al-Khwarizmi's descriptions. He supervised the work of 70 geographers to create a map of the then "known world." When his work became known in Europe through Latin translations, his influence made a permanent mark on the development of science in the West.

Al-Khwarizmi made several important improvements to the theory and construction of sundials, which he inherited from his Indian and Hellenistic predecessors. He made tables for these instruments which considerably shortened the time needed to make specific calculations. His sundial was universal and could be observed from anywhere on the Earth. From then on, sundials were frequently placed on mosques to determine the time of prayer. The shadow square, an instrument used to determine the linear height of an object, in conjunction with the alidade for angular observations, was also invented by al-Khwarizmi in ninth-century Baghdad.

While his major contributions were the result of original research, he also did much to synthesize the existing knowledge in these fields from Greek, Indian, and other sources. A number of minor works were written by al-Khwarizmi on topics such as the astrolabe, on which he wrote on the Jewish calendar. He also wrote a political history containing horoscopes of prominent persons.

Muhammad ibn Musa al-Khwarizmi died in c. 850 being remembered as one of the most seminal scientific minds of early Islamic culture.

Six advice from The Quran

✓ Be nice to people who work under your care (4:36)

✓ Correct yourself and your families first [before trying to correct others] (66:6)

✓ Call people to the Way of your Lord with wisdom and beautiful exhortation. Reason with them most decently (16:125)

✓ Leave to themselves those who DO NOT give any importance to the Divine code and have adopted and consider it as mere play and amusement (6:70)

✓ And Allah (SWT) will not punish them, while they seek forgiveness (8:33)

✓ Our Lord! Forgive me and my parents, and (all) the believers on the Day when the reckoning will be established (14:41)

Ibn Abbas reported: The Messenger of Allah, peace and blessings be upon him, said, "Whoever increases his prayers for forgiveness, Allah will grant him relief from every worry, a way out from every hardship, and provide for him in ways he does not expect." (Musnad Ahamad, 2234)

"Give love in secret by praying for one another." Anonymous

A thought-provoking questions you should ask yourself every day

What do I want to learn today?

Practical Ways to Improve Yourself

<u>Stop watching TV</u>

I've not been watching TV for pretty much 4 years and it's been a very liberating experience. I realized most of the programs and advertisements on mainstream TV are usually of a lower consciousness and not very empowering. In return, the time I've freed up from not watching TV is now constructively used for other purposes, such as connecting with close friends, doing work I enjoy, exercising, etc.

<u>Be helpful</u>

Helping others is one of the best ways to make you a better person. When you help someone in need you will feel self-content and satisfied by your achievement. You will realize that what you do is worth something to other people and that you are bringing about good deeds with your help in'sha'Allah.

PRACTICAL TIPS FOR DEVELOPING THE GOOD MUSLIM MINDSETCHEATSHEET

4 TIPS FOR DEVELOPING A PRODUCTIVE MINDSET:

1. Have a system of monthly, weekly and daily planning in place.

2. Be aware of your brain tricks as it may fool you into over-planning. It'll convince you to put more on your plate than you can realistically complete which will create overwhelm.

3. Say no to many things and yes only to some. Keep no more than 2-3 priority tasks on your list. Ask yourself, "what can you take off your planner/ to-do list today?"

4. Review, track and record your productivity. It will motivate you to do better the next day and give you a sense of achievement at the end of each day.

5 TIPS FOR DEVELOPING EMOTIONAL RESILIENCE:

1. Don't keep cooking your emotions inside yourself. Express your emotions in a polite manner.

2. Create an emotional or a physical space to breathe.

3. When you feel spiteful towards someone who has hurt you, focus on a good quality of that person. Forgive & Forget.

4. Redirect piled up negative energy into an activity you love.

5. Let go of situations you can't control and problems you can't solve.

SALAHUDDIN AL-AYYUBI

Salahuddin was born in the Fort of Tikrit and his mother mentioned that when I was pregnant with Salahuddin; I saw a dream that in my stomach, I have a sword from the swords of Allah (SWT). Great men create other great men. And this was the environment in which Salahuddin was brought up. It was a military environment. There was never a day when the expulsion of the crusaders was not mentioned. But it was not only a military environment, it was a very religious-spiritual environment. And Salahuddin from a very early age became a 'Hafiz' of the Quran, he was a Shafee in Fiqh. And his greatest aspiration in life was to become a scholar, he loved the scholars.

He had the honor of being tutored by Nuruddin Zangi. Ibn Aatheer says, "The Muslims never had a man who was as upright and caring and compassionate as Nuuruddin Zangi." Salahuddin would say that Nuruddin is my master. He modeled himself on Nuruddin and also Nuruddin realized the potential in Salahuddin and this is why; when in Damascus, crime became rife, he made Salahuddin at a very tender age in charge of the entire police of Damascus. After a while; the crusaders attacked Egypt. And what Adid, the Khalifa in Egypt, did is that he cut the hair of his wife, and he sent it to Nuruddin. And this meant that we can no longer look after our women; assist us! And Nuruddin didn't want to assist them. Because Al Adid and the Egyptians were Fatimites but Shirkuh Ad-Din; the uncle of Salahuddin convinced him. Salahuddin says, "When my uncle came to me; to take me to Egypt; I didn't want to go." One because his aspiration was to become a scholar. But second, he mentions, "I thought I was going to die." You know it is a possibility that you will dislike something but there is good in it for you and by Allah SWT, Salahuddin going there was good for the 'Ummah'.

Shirkuh rid Egypt of the crusaders, and shortly after this; Adid remained the Khalifa but Shirkuh became second in charge. After a while, Shirkuh passed away and the 'Ulama' (scholars) and the 'Fuqaha' (jurisprudence) chose Salahuddin as in the place of Shirkuh and therefore Salahuddin became the second most powerful man in Egypt; he was only 32 at the time. Salahuddin showed what a real leader should be. The people loved Salahuddin, he won their hearts, he was a true leader, he showed love and compassion to people.

Now after Nuruddin passed away, Syria just fragmented and they began to side with the crusaders. And many of them were giving annual tributes. They were actually giving annual tributes to the crusaders and the people of Syria were disgusted because they were used to a man like Nuruddin, a powerful, charismatic man. The people of Syria turned to Salahuddin. This was the time that Salahuddin started his expeditions. Salahuddin spent longer fighting Muslims than he did non-Muslims. He fought with Muslims for over 10 years. Because he understood that if you are divided, you are weak. Many of them sided with the crusaders.

They released a man who was the greatest arch-enemy of Islam; a man called Reginald De Chatillon. For 15 years, this man had been in prison; Nuruddin had left him in the dungeons. And what did this man do? Soon as he mustered up an army; he marched on Mecca. And Nauzubillah, he was saying, "When I reach Mecca, I will bring the Khabah to the ground. I will go to Madinah, I will tale the camel herder from his grave" (speaking about the Prophet SAW) "And I will bring him back to my palace in Kerak and I well charge the Muslims to view his body." The narrations mention that when Salahuddin heard this; he took out his sword and he lifted it to the skies and he said, "By

Allah, I will kill Reginald with my own hands." Because he had a deep love for the Prophet (peace be upon him). And he dispatched an army under Husam Ad-Din Lu Lu. Husam Ad-din took a navy, he annihilated the army of Reginald. And then he captured his men, he took them to Madinah and he executed them in Madinah. And four years after this, again when the Muslims and the Christian had a truce; Reginald attacked a Muslim caravan traveling from Egypt to Syria.

When Salahuddin heard this; he again took an oath that he would kill this man with his own hands. And it was upon this occasion that Salahuddin bought forth an army and this is the famous battle; the Battle of Hattin. The crusaders bought forth an army. When Salahuddin consulted his men, he said, "What shall we do? Shall we carry on attacking their forts and their castles or shall we have a head-on confrontation?" They said, "Carry on attacking their forts." Salahuddin said, "No, we will take them head-on because none of us knows how long he is going to live." and then he said, "O my men, fight to please your Lord; do not fight to please me." They marched on to the army of the crusaders, the crusader army was considerably larger than the Muslim army. The crusader army was deeply trenched. And they had barricaded themselves, so Salahuddin didn't rush. He showed what a military genius he was. What he did, he went to a nearby fort and this fort had the women and the children of the soldiers there and he laid siege to it and then he put his back against the sea. The Christian charges were very strong, the Muslims had problems dealing with Christian charges. But tactically the Muslims were far superior. So what the Christians thought was one charge and Salahuddin will end up in the sea. And this is exactly what Salahuddin wanted them to think.

The next morning they marched. It was mid-summer; with them they had the true cross. The true cross was the most sacred relic in Christendom. It was believed that a part of this cross, upon it Isa Jesus (PBUH) was crucified. And they believed that as long as they have this, they could never lose a battle. They'd actually believed that they had won the previous 20 battles because of the Barakah of this cross.

Salahuddin had put archers on the way and what he did, he poisoned all the wells. So when they began to march, these archers began to shower arrows, so many arrows that the movements became snail pace. Thousands of them had perished and they thought the night would bring them relief but historians mention that Salahuddin's men had encircled them in a manner that not even an ant could go through. So, from the Muslim camp, there were the cries of 'Takbir': 'Allahu Akbar'! And from the Christian camp there were the cries of the dying and the wounded.

The next morning Salahuddin noticed that the brushwood was dry and the wind was blowing in the direction of the crusaders. So, its mid-summer, no water and they lit the brushwood. Now they began to choke on the smoke as well and it was here that the Muslims attacked and they were reciting the verse, "And indeed it is a right upon us that we assist the believers." Salahuddin wanted to afflict the final psychological blow; and that was to capture the true cross. Salahuddin sent an entire regiment to capture it. When the regiment captured it this totally demoralized the Christians. They fell by the wayside and only 150 of them remained standing. Around the king, 150 knights and the Muslims attacked and Salahuddin was watching this and his brother was standing next to him and he said, "Alhamdulillah we have defeated them." Salahuddin said, "Not yet" and then he attacked again and the Christians went back. His brother said again, "Alhamdulillah we have defeated them." Salahuddin said, "Wait not yet. When that tent falls, the tent of the king, then we have defeated them." When Salahuddin was saying this, the tent fell and what did Salahuddin do? What did he do? Did he jump up and down? He descended from his mount and he went into Sajdah. Because he understood that victory and defeat is from Allah SWT.

Salahuddin didn't ease up here; 2 days later he was in Acre North then they took Turan, Haifa, Arsuf, Beirut, Nablus and a number of other places. The reason he took all the ports so the crusaders could not get anymore reinforcements in. And then Salahuddin marched on the greatest aim in life and that was liberation of the holy places and somebody asked him, "You're the king of Egypt, Syria, Yemen, Lebanon, you smile very rarely? Salahuddin said, "How can I smile? How can food and water taste good to me? When the Baitul Muqaddas is in the hands of the crusaders?" One Astrologer had told Salahuddin, "O Salahuddin we have seen the stars; that if you try to take Jerusalem, you will lose an eye." Salahuddin said, " You're talking about me losing an eye, I swear by Allah, I will take the holy lands even if it means I walk into Jerusalem blind.

For 5 days Salahuddin went around Jerusalem until on the 20th of Rajab they found an ideal place to lay siege. And for 6 days they pounded the city. And on the 26th; Ballion came out to ask for terms. Salahuddin said, "I offered you terms initially; you didn't take them. Now the city is mine" and then Balian said, "If you do not offer us terms then we will kill the 5,000 Muslims in the city and we will destroy the 'Masjid.'" And really this is a testimony to the greatness of Salahuddin. He could have easily said, do it! And when we take it you will see what we will do to your men, women and children. He knew that these Muslims have been at the front for 88 years. And he didn't want them to go through any more suffering. He realized this and Salahuddin gave Balian terms. And Salahuddin entered when? He entered Jerusalem on the very night that the Prophet SAW entered Jerusalem. Salahuddin entered Jerusalem on the 27th of Rajab. And can you imagine how the Muslim must have felt when they entered? Can you imagine 88 years of persecution? When they entered the Masjid, they must have remembered the stories of how 70,000 Muslims were killed in the masjid one day; until the blood was running up to their knees of those who were doing the butchering. All these memories must have come back to the Muslims. But Salahuddin had a greater memory in the back of his mind. Which override all these memories and that was when the Prophet SAW re-entered Mecca, they must have seen the place where Billal was dragged until his skin would peel from his body. They must have seen that place where 2 young girls, Lubayna and Unaisa were killed for what? Because they believed in 'La Ilaha Illalah'. They must have seen the place where Ammar, Yasir, Sumayyah, the entire family would be persecuted. In the heat of the moment a Sahabi shouted out, "Today is the day of bloodshed, today is the day of retribution, today is payback time." The Prophet SAW heard this and he said, "O Saad come here. Change that cry into; today is the day of mercy, today is the day of forgiveness."

After the siege of Jerusalem in 1099, the Crusaders army took control of the city and indiscriminately slaughtered the Jews and Muslims they came across. Gesta Francorum Said,

"The slaughter was so great that [Crusader] men waded in blood up to their ankles…"

When Salahuddin took control of the city, the scene was a complete reversal of the bloody massacre of July 1099. The crusaders were allowed to leave. Noble families and commoners did so in a peaceful convoy without being harassed by the Muslims.

Salahuddin forbade any massacres or plundering of Christians, Frankish or oriental. He even strengthened the guards at their churches and gave them permission to return for their pilgrimages.

He granted them forty days to safely leave the city, along with their property and belongings. Part of the conditions of surrender was to pay ransom for their freedom. Salahuddin set the ransom at a low price so everyone could pay, and for those who couldn't, Salahuddin paid for their ransom from his own wealth.

Salahuddin imposed a symbolic exit tax to signal the surrender. The wealthy crusader princes refused to pay the fee on behalf of the poor. They only paid for themselves. Patriach Heraclius of Jerusalem gatheres all the money in the church coffers and carried it with him out of the city on several mules. He didn't pay a penny to free the prisoners inside the city.

When the patriarch of the city took chariots full of gold, carpets, and precious goods from the city, Salah al-Din's advisors were outraged.

"I said to the Sultan: 'This patriarch is carrying off riches worth at least two hundred thousand dinars. We gave them permission to take their personal property with them, but not the treasures of the churches and convents.' But Salahuddin answered: 'We must apply the letter of the accords we have signed so that no one will be able to accuse the believers of having violated their treaties. On the contrary, Christians everywhere will remember the kindness we have bestowed upon them.'

Here the chivalry of Salahuddin is clearly shown. From his own money, he paid the dues of those who wished to leave Jerusalem. This stands his eternal credit. Even his enemies recorded it.

This amazing example is a testament to the character of Salahuddin, as well as his God-consciousness and forward thinking.

It's his generosity and justice that earned him the respect of his later opponent, King Richard the Lionheart during the 3rd crusades. He and Richard (the Lionheart) grew to respect one another as military leaders. When Salahuddin Ayyubi heard that Richard had fallen ill in Ascalon, he sent peaches and pears to help restore him to health. He also sent packs of snow from Mount Hermann to cool the King's fever. At Arsuf, when Richard lost his horse, Salahuddin sent him two replacements. The Jewish philosopher Maimonides was one of Salahuddin Ayyubi's personal physicians. When Jerusalem was recaptured, Salahuddin invited the Jews, who had been excluded by the Crusaders to come back, in particular the Jews of Ashkelon responded to his request.

As author Amin Maalouf described it:

"Saladin had conquered Jerusalem not to amass gold, and still less to seek vengeance. His prime objective, as he himself explained, was to do his duty before God and his faith."

It's important to look at how victors behaved. Historically, many commanders have been too blinded by their victory. So, they kill and murder. But this man was different. Salahuddin is famous throughout history for his generosity, his justice and his ability to inspire his people. This has earned him respect on Christian side and Muslim side as well. As many stories to illustrate this. There is one story, when a Frankish women has a baby taken and kidnaped and it has taken to Muslim market and sold. She was obviously devastated by this. Some of her friends said, "Go to see Salahuddin. I am sure he will help you." Accounts from both East and West say, he took her hand and looked for the child everywhere east, west, north and south. He didn't rest until he finally found him. The mother knelt at his feet and said, "Oh Sultan, you are great. If only our Kings in the West could be as noble."

And similarly, Stanley Lane Paul mentions in his classic; that the Muslim king showed the Christians the meaning of compassion.

Saladin used to perform the five obligatory prayers on time, along with the supererogatory prayers. He never prayed except in congregation, and he never delayed a prayer. He used to always have an imam with him, but if the imam was not present, he would pray behind any pious scholar who might be sitting with him. He never quit a prayer except when he slipped into a coma for three days before his death.

He would spend most of his money on sadaqah (optional charity), and he never possessed enough wealth that would have required him to pay Zakah (obligatory alms). Although he always wanted to perform Hajj, he was occupied in jihad, so he did not have enough money to perform Hajj, and he died without performing it.

To be a great Sultan, one should be courageous, strict, and strong-willed, yet merciful, fair, and kind. On Mondays and Thursdays, Saladin used to sit and listen to his people's petitions in a general assembly attended by jurisprudents, judges, and scholars. He would then spend an hour during the day or the night writing his comments and opinions concerning every petition. He never let down anyone who called on him for help.

He never spoke badly about anyone and never allowed anyone to do so in his presence. He never uttered a rude word and never used his pen to humiliate a Muslim.

When Europe had heard that the Holy Lands had been taken from them; Europe went ablaze. Pope Urban the 2nd died out of grief, and then the subsequent pope wrote a letter to all the kings that they should send every able person to fight. Just from Germany; Frederick the King bought a million fighters, Alhamdullilah he frowned on the way and the army dispersed. Richard (England), Philip (France); they bought 600,000 men. Salahuddin was amazed at the zeal of Christendom. He wrote letters to all the Muslim leaders, nobody obliged. He would mention in the letters that they are more, Christians at Acre then there are waves in the sea. He says, "Every time we kill one; they send another thousand." And 600,000 crusaders camped at Acre. What they did is that they made trenches around them and barricaded themselves in. So, Salahuddin couldn't attack them from behind. And for 2 years, Salahuddin remained in the field. He would cry at the apathy of the Muslim leaders.

There were 3 Khalifas in the time of Salahuddin. Does anybody know the name of any one of them? Because they didn't care, so history forgot them. But history remembers Salahuddin because he cared. When they lived in their palaces, where did Salahuddin live? He lived in a tent. When they slept on comfortable beds, when others had big meals in the palaces, for 3 days Salahuddin ate nothing. When others lived with their family in their palaces; Salahuddin was on the battlefield dodging arrows. Ibn Shaddad mentions that one day the news came that Salahuddin's brother had passed away, then his nephew had passed away and he began to cry. And now we didn't know why he was crying but we began to cry with him. He says, "Salahuddin went on the battlefield and it was as though nothing had happened; he was the same Salahuddin". And this is why history remembers Salahuddin.

Finally, after 2 years, the Muslims in Acre asked for terms. Richard gave them 2 terms. And then after that he butchered every man, woman and child in Acre. Ibn Shaddad mentions that, the day I was sitting next to Salahuddin and he prayed 2 rakats and then he began to cry. He was making dua he said, "O Allah, all my own resources I had exhausted in assisting Your deen. And the only thing I have left is that I turn to You. And I hold on to Your rope and I ask You for Your fadi and Your grace." And Ibn Shaddad said, "I saw Salahuddin cry until his beard became drenched and then the mat in front of him became wet. And the next morning the news came; that the crusaders had lifted their siege, and Richard had said his famous statement, "As long as a man like Salahuddin is protecting Jerusalem you will never take it." And then it was Richard who asked for a truce. Salahuddin never asked for a truce, Salahuddin didn't want a truce, he would say, "I fear that when I die the Muslim armies will disperse and the Europeans will become strong, so the best that we can do is fight them."

After the truce, Salahuddin went back to Damascus, and the narration mentioned that one day he went to visit the Hajjis, when he came back it was cold, it's wet; he became ill and everyday his condition got worse. Al-Imad mentions, "I was with Salahuddin when he was ill, the weaker his body got the stronger his trust in Allah became." On the 9th day Salahuddin became unconscious and sheikh Jafar mentions, "I was reciting the Quran by his bed and when I reached the verse; "He it is Allah and no lord besides Him, the knower of the unseen; Salahuddin had been unconscious for a while and I heard a faint voice saying "Saheeh."" Then he mentions, "For 3 days I recited the Quran by the bed of Salahuddin" and he said, "On the final day when he passed away I reached the verse; "There is no God but Allah and upon him I trust and I saw Salahuddin face become radiant and he recited the "Shahadah."" And he left this dunya.

Ibn Shaddad mentions that this was the greatest calamity to befall the Muslims, since the demise of the 'Khulafa Rashideen'. He passed away at the time of Fajr. After Zuhur, they bought his body out. And the narrations mention that people screamed and cried as though the whole 'Dunya' had just become one place and many people when they saw his dead body; they couldn't believe it, they became unconscious.

The liberator of the Holy Lands and what did this king leave behind him? King of Egypt, King of Syria, Lebanon, Yemen;

what did he leave behind him? He left 1 dinar and 47 Dirhams, some armor and a horse. This is all he left behind him. But I'll tell you what he left behind him; he left a legacy. And on his tomb, they wrote; "O Allah as his Final Victory, open for him the gates of Jannah."

QUOTES BY SALAHUDDIN

"Victory is changing the hearts of your opponents by gentleness and kindness."

"If you want to destroy any nation without war, make adultery or nudity common in the young generation."

"I warn you against shedding blood, indulging in it, or making a habit of it. For blood never sleeps."

"Save your tears from others, they won't understand, never show them your emotions, they only reprimand."

FIRST CRUSADE

In the middle Ages, Europe and the Middle East were divided between Christian states, or Christendom, and Muslim states. They were uneasy neighbours, and frequently at war. On the frontline: the Eastern Roman or Byzantine Empire, the major Christian power in the eastern Mediterranean. But in the 11th century, a powerful new force emerged that threatened its very survival. The Seljuk Turks, originally from Central Asia, migrated south, converted to Sunni Islam, and carved out a great empire for themselves.

In 1071, at the Battle of Manzikert, the Seljuk Turks inflicted a crushing defeat on the Byzantine Empire. They went on to conquer most of Anatolia. Cities such as Nicaea and Antioch, rich in Christian history, fell to the Seljuk Turks. In 1092, the

Great Seljuk Sultan Malik Shah died, and his empire began to fragment.

The Byzantine Empire came under renewed attack, as local warlords sought territory and plunder. In 1095, Byzantine Emperor Alexius I Comnenus wrote to Pope Urban II, making a desperate appeal for military aid from his fellow Christians in the west. It wasn't the first such appeal by the Emperor, but this time, the results would be unlike anything ever seen before.

Pope Urban saw the Emperor's appeal as a golden opportunity...... a chance to heal the rift that had emerged between Western and Eastern churches in the Great Schism...... to assert his own, papal authority over the unruly barons and bishops of western Christendom... And to drive back 'the infidel', and reclaim Christianity's most holy sites – most of all, Jerusalem, lost to Muslim rule 400 years before.

"Around the time of the Crusades, Europe experienced several droughts which made people lose faith in everything," says Antoine Domit, history professor at the Lebanese University.

A struggle between church and state was taking place in Europe: Who would rule over the people of Europe, the pope or the king?

"For Europeans, the east is 'A Thousand and One Nights'. It represents wealth, beautiful clothing, young concubines, thriving public life, songs and culture," says Elias al-Kattar, history professor at the Lebanese University.

While the Muslim east lived in prosperity, Europe had slipped into relative poverty and conflict.

"Medieval western society was a feudal society, which meant that you had the aristocracy in charge of a large amount of people that had no land possessions," says Jan Vandeburie, of the School of History, University of Kent.

Ishaaq Abaid, history professor at Ain Shams University, explains that "only one percent of people who had the titles of 'count', 'duke' or 'baron', owned all the agricultural lands. Ninety-nine percent of the European population were called serfs and worked on these lands."

Most Europeans in the 11th century lived in poverty and were struggling to survive, while war and conflict among knights were part of everyday life.

At Clermont in France, Pope Urban preached a sermon to a gathering of clergy and nobles. He called on Christian knights and foot-soldiers to go east, to aid their brother Christians, and free Jerusalem from Muslim rule. And he offered a unique spiritual incentive:

"Whoever for devotion alone, not to gain honour or money, goes to Jerusalem to liberate the Church of God can substitute this journey for all penance."

He was offering Europe's knights, who lived in fear of damnation because of the violent lives they led, the chance to atone for their sins through holy war.

What's more, their objective - Jerusalem – was a city that captivated the medieval imagination like no other - the most holy place on earth. The Pope's offer exhilarated his audience – his words were met with cries of 'Deus vult! Deus vult...God wills it! God wills it!'

The Pope's appeal was preached across Europe, sparking a wave of religious fervour. Thousands of lords, knights and ordinary people vowed to travel to the Holy Land and fight for Christ. They identified themselves by wearing a cross, later becoming known as 'crucesignatus' - crusaders.

A few of these men saw opportunity in the east for fame and

fortune. But overwhelmingly, they went in search of spiritual salvation – willing to undertake a long, expensive and perilous journey to save their souls from the fires of hell.

Pope Urban had intended the crusade to be led by nobles, and made up of knights and experienced soldiers. But the viral success of his appeal led thousands of ordinary townsfolk and peasants to take the cross. Pope Urban II drew up a schedule for the first campaign which should set out in the summer of 1096. But some ignored the holy command and found a leader who would immediately guide them to the east: an old monk called Peter the Hermit.

In the Rhineland, some of these crusaders, fired up by old prejudices and talk of holy war, attacked local Jewish communities, slaughtering around 5,000 men, women and children, and extorting money from those they spared. These massacres were condemned by the church, but too little effect.

In the summer of 1096, the People's Crusade, 20 to 40,000 strong, made its way east. The main contingent, led by Peter the Hermit, travelled along the River Danube. But they were ill-disciplined and poorly-prepared. When they ran out of food in Hungary, they attacked and looted Christian settlements. They continued to pillage the land of their upposed ally, the Byzantine Empire.

When they reached Constantinople, the Emperor quickly ferried them to Anatolia, to be rid of them.

In enemy territory, lacking discipline or leadership, their main force was soon ambushed and slaughtered by the Turks.

Meanwhile, some of Europe's most powerful feudal lords were departing for the Holy Land at the head of their own contingents. They were much better armed and organised than the disastrous People's Crusade. They included, from Lorraine,

Godfrey of Bouillon, with his brothers Eustace and Baldwin of Boulogne. Hugh of Vermandois, younger brother of the French King. Count Robert of Flanders, and Duke Robert of Normandy, son of William the Conqueror. The wealthy Stephen of Blois. From Provence, Count Raymond of Toulouse, accompanied by the Crusade's spiritual leader, papal legate Adhémar of Le Puy. And from southern Italy, Norman lords Bohemond of Taranto, and his nephew Tancred. The various contingents converged for their agreed rendezvous at Constantinople. Together, they formed a huge army, perhaps 60,000 strong - probably the largest seen in Europe since the fall of the Western Roman Empire.

The Byzantine Emperor, Alexius, had expected to welcome a small force of Western mercenaries, who'd serve under Byzantine command. But the giant Crusader force that began arriving in December 1096 made him nervous and distrustful – particularly the presence of Bohemond of Taranto, who'd spent much of his life attacking the Byzantine Empire.

Alexius gave the Crusaders money, supplies and guides, but only after their leaders swore oaths of fealty, and promised to return all Byzantine territory to the emperor - not keep it for themselves. Only then were they ferried across the Bosphorus, into Anatolia.

The Crusaders were a mighty military force, particularly the armoured knights, who made up about a sixth of their strength. But they'd have to adapt rapidly to the heat, terrain, and hit-and-run tactics of their Turkish enemy.

In their favour – the Islamic world, and the Great Seljuk Empire itself, was badly divided – its Turkish governors, or atabegs, were busy fighting each other, as well as the Shia Fatimids of Egypt. None of them was prepared for the First Crusade, or had any real understanding of its strength or aims.

The Crusaders' first success came at Nicaea, which fell after a six week siege. But the city surrendered to the Byzantine forces, cheating the Crusaders, as they saw it, of their rightful plunder. It was a further strain on the delicate relations between Crusaders and Byzantines.

They began marching inland, through intense summer heat, in two columns - a vanguard under Bohemond of Taranto, and rearguard under Godfrey of Bouillon. Then near Dorylaeum, Bohemond's vanguard was ambushed by the main Turkish army. Based on Crusader chronicles, this is our best understanding of how the confused fighting unfolded...

Bohemond, seeing he was about to be attacked by a large force of enemy cavalry, sent an urgent message to the rearguard, asking for assistance. Then he formed up his knights, and ordered his infantry into a defensive formation behind them, protecting the camp followers.

The Crusaders came under attack from all sides – facing a hail of arrows from Turkish horse archers, as well as javelins, and hit-and-run strikes from their faster light cavalry. The knights were driven back onto their own infantry. Over several hours, losses mounted, but the Crusader line held. Meanwhile, Godfrey was racing up with the rearguard to join the battle. Troops were fed into the fighting as soon as they arrived. On the Turks' left flank, the Crusader advance was hidden by the terrain, so that they appeared suddenly, threatening the Turks with encirclement. When the Christian knights all charged together, the Turks panicked, turned and fled. It was a major victory for the Crusaders, and allowed them to continue their advance across Anatolia without serious opposition.

At Heraclea, they defeated a small Turkish force, then split up. The main force struggled through the mountains of Cappadocia, losing many of their baggage animals, and running dangerously low on supplies.

Meanwhile Baldwin of Boulogne and Tancred, probably out to seize land and plunder for themselves, travelled south into Cilicia, capturing the city of Tarsus and other settlements. Tancred later rejoined the main army, but Baldwin was invited by local Armenian Christians to travel to Edessa, where he was soon installed as Count Baldwin of Edessa – ruler of the first 'Crusader state'.

In October 1097, the rest of the Crusaders reached Antioch, the next stepping-stone on the road to Jerusalem. But outside its walls, the First Crusade would come to the brink of disaster, decimated by disease and starvation, and encircled by their enemies. It would take a miracle to save them from annihilation.

October 1097, Two years had passed since Pope Urban II preached a crusade to help the Byzantine Empire in its war against the Seljuk Turks.

Now the First Crusade had reached the great city of Antioch. It was the last major Turkish stronghold standing between the Crusade and its goal, the holy city of Jerusalem. But Antioch was virtually impregnable – with its citadel atop a 1000 foot mountain – and too large to encircle. The giant Crusader army could only camp outside its walls, and pray for a miracle.

But that winter, they ran out of food. Horses, men and camp followers began to starve. A trickle of supplies continued to arrive by sea, mostly from the Byzantine-controlled island of Cyprus. And they defeated an attempt by Radwan of Aleppo to break the siege at the Battle of Lake Antioch. But the Crusaders' situation seemed hopeless. Morale fell, as deaths and desertions rose steadily. In March a Crusader fleet arrived with much-needed reinforcements and supplies.

Finally, one night, Bohemond of Taranto and 60 of his men

scaled a tower on the southern wall, whose commander had been bribed. As dawn broke, Bohemond's men opened the city gates, and the Crusader army poured in. They massacred soldiers and civilians alike, while desperate Muslim survivors fled to the citadel, which continued to resist all attacks. Antioch had fallen.

But now a giant Turkish army was assembled under the command of Kür Bugha, governor of Mosul. First he attacked Baldwin in Edessa, but abandoned his siege after three weeks, and marched on Antioch.

The Crusader army was exhausted, starving, and now trapped. They could expect no help from the Byzantines – Emperor Alexius, busy securing his own territory in Anatolia, had received false reports that the Crusade had already been destroyed. Fearing a Turkish counter-attack, he withdrew to Constantinople.

Then, inside Antioch, a relic was miraculously discovered, supposedly the 'Holy Lance', thrust into Christ's side at his crucifixion – and the Crusaders' faith in their holy mission was renewed.

Although heavily outnumbered, the Crusaders decided to meet the Muslim army outside the city walls. With the zeal of religious fanatics, seeing visions of saints and angels, they charged the Muslim army... which turned, and fled. Kür Bugha, accusing his commanders of treachery – possibly correctly - set fire to his camp and withdrew. The Muslim defenders in the citadel, witnessing this stunning victory, quickly surrendered.

In summer 1098, Fatimid forces from Egypt captured Jerusalem from the Artukid Turks. Al Afdal, Grand Vizier (or chief minister) of Egypt, saw the Seljuk Turks as his greatest enemy, and even tried to make an alliance with the Crusaders against them. But the Crusaders were not interested. Instead, they spent five months around Antioch, foraging supplies and arguing among themselves. Stephen of Blois and Hugh of Vermandois had already given up and returned home. Now Bohemond of Taranto claimed the former Byzantine city of Antioch for himself, breaking his oath to Emperor Alexius to return such territories to him. Bohemond argued that the Emperor had broken the oath first, by failing to help the Crusaders during the siege. Divisions deepened after Bishop Adhemar of Le Puy died from illness – he'd been the Crusade's spiritual leader, and a unifying presence on their council.

Meanwhile, Crusaders carried out a brutal massacre of civilians at Ma'arat al Nu'man. Pressure from the mass of ordinary Crusaders forced their leaders to put aside their differences, and march south towards Jerusalem – except for Bohemond, who remained in Antioch, where he declared himself prince.

As the Crusaders entered Fatimid territory, many local rulers offered up money and supplies to avoid violence. Other villages had been abandoned. As the Crusaders neared Jerusalem, they found wells poisoned, trees cut down, and animals driven away. Anything that could help the Crusaders had been destroyed.

On 7th June 1099, the Crusaders got their first sight of Jerusalem – many fell to their knees, and wept with joy. But they faced a serious challenge. They were now reduced to about 12,000 fighting men, not enough to encircle the city, and they were running out of food and water.

Jerusalem would have to be taken by storm. The barren landscape meant the Crusaders had no timber to build siege engines. And on 13th June, their first assault with a single scaling ladder was easily repulsed. Four days later, six Genoese galleys arrived at Jaffa, where they were soon blockaded by the powerful Fatimid fleet. So the sailors took apart their ships, and carried the timber to the siege at Jerusalem. The Crusaders foraged more wood from the surrounding land – enough to build two siege towers: These mobile wooden structures would be wheeled up to the outer wall, and allow the Crusaders to directly assault the enemy battlements. One tower was stationed with Raymond of Toulouse's forces in the southwest, the other was with Godfrey of Bouillon's troops to the north.

On 8th July, seeking God's aid in the impending assault, the entire Crusade walked in procession around the city, finishing with a religious service on the Mount of Olives. On the night before the attack, Godfrey suddenly moved his siege tower to a less well-defended section of the city walls.

The final assault began on 15 July 1099. In the north, Godfrey of Bouillon's troops managed to fight their way across from their tower onto the city walls, establishing a bridgehead.

There followed a mass slaughter of all the Muslims and Jews of Jerusalem, the latter being seen as accomplices. Figures of 10,000 (William of Tyre), 65,000 (Mathew of Edessa) or 75,000 (Ibn al-Athir) killed are all very likely an exaggeration as a contemporary Muslim source (Ibn al-Arabi), which had no motive for minimising the carnage, puts the figure at 3,000 of the city's probable 30,000 residents. Still, the barbarism of the Crusaders shocked even Christians, and the episode would never be entirely forgotten or forgiven by the Muslim states.

William of Tyre's description of the carnage, written in the 12th century CE, became one of the standard reports of the slaughter (despite the chronicler being born 30 years after the event):

"It was impossible to look on the vast numbers of the slain without horror; everywhere lay fragments of human bodies, and the very ground was covered with the blood of the slain. Still more dreadful was it to gaze upon the victors themselves, dripping with blood from head to foot." (Phillips, 33)

According to Antoine Domit, they started "with an infamous massacre. They killed people in the streets, in their houses and in alleyways."

Venderburie explains that it was very difficult for the crusaders to distinguish between local Christian, Muslim, and Jewish population because they all looked the same to them, they all "looked like Arabs."

The city was systematically ransacked and looted for its precious objects, and when the dead piled up to such an extent that they threatened to spread disease, Muslim prisoners were forced to burn the bodies of their fellows outside the city in huge pyres before themselves being massacred in cold blood.

The First Crusade had secured its goal in the face of overwhelming odds. And just four weeks later, at the Battle of Ascalon, the Crusaders smashed a Fatimid relief army, sent to recapture Jerusalem. Most Crusaders, their vows fulfilled, soon returned home to Europe. Only around 300 knights remained to defend Jerusalem, under Godfrey of Bouillon, now named Defender of the Holy Sepulchre.

The man who'd set these great events in motion, Pope Urban II, did not live to hear the news that Jerusalem had been taken – he died just two weeks after the city's fall. The new Crusader states that emerged – the Kingdom of Jerusalem, the County of Tripoli, the Principality of Antioch, the County of Edessa – lived on precariously, surrounded by enemies.

"The success of the First Crusade in conquering Jerusalem is important not only because it realised a European dream, but also because it punished the Muslims and Arabs for their divisions and infighting," says Abdu Qassem.

And the Muslim world would not remain so catastrophically divided for long. Soon it would unleash its own holy war against the Crusader states, turning the Holy Land into a battleground for almost two centuries.

In response, more crusades would be launched from Europe – but none would ever match the bloody, spectacular success of the First Crusade.

BATTLE OF HATTIN

During the second half of the 12th century, a dramatic Muslim revival reaches its' zenith under the command of Salah ad-Din Yusuf ibn Ayyub, a courageous and brilliant leader, known to contemporary Muslims as 'al-Nasir' (The Victorious), and to Europeans as 'Saladin'

He seeks nothing less than to unite all Muslims between the Euphrates and the Nile against a common enemy. In late 11th century the Fatimid Caliphate is in decline and the Seljuk Empire is crumbling. In this period of Muslim weakness the First Crusade strikes the Levant.

Christian lords and knights impose institutions of Western Europe upon the social and political structures of the conquered lands. Their rule is relatively stable largely thanks to Muslim disunity.

But as 12th century rolls on, less than five decades since European Crusaders arrived in the region, the Zengid dynasty rises to prominence in northern Levant.

Under competent leadership of Imad ad-Din Zengi they defeat the Crusaders and retake the city of Edessa in 1144 - thus in effect provoking the Pope to call for the Second Crusade.

Although Imad is assassinated two years later, in 1146, his son Nur ad-Din successfully continues the fight against the Crusaders, until the Second Crusade eventually fizzles out, and he expands his father's realm over the years, bringing much needed stability and prosperity to his people. It is during Nur ad-Din's reign that Saladin begins his rise to prominence.

Born in 1137, in Tikrit (in modern day Iraq), Saladin spends his formative years in Damascus. From a young age he is educated in Greek philosophy, mathematics, poetry, astronomy, law, and above all he becomes an ardent student of the Quran and theology. His upbringing is helped by members of his family who served as skillful diplomats and administrators first in the Seljuk Empire and later for the Zengid Dynasty.

Growing up, Saladin's uncle Shirkuh and Nur ad-Din became his biggest role models. They instilled in him the principles of chivalry, piety, nobility, justice, humility, generosity, brotherhood, mercy and fogiveness, all of which would come to define Saladin's life and legacy.

He joins the military at the age of 14 and is ably trained by his uncle Shirkuh, a military commander in the Zengid army. A quick learner, Saladin soon impresses his mentor. His performance in early battles enables him to take on leading responsibilities in military campaigns, and over the years he distinguishes himself through his bravery, military leadership, sharp intellect and loyalty to his leaders.

Saladin's star truly begins to rise during the 1160's when Nur ad-Din decides to intervene in the affairs of the weakening Fatimid Caliphate, aiming to forestall Amalric's quest to expand the Kingdom of Jerusalem into Egypt. Recognized as a competent, trustworthy and ambitious leader, in 1164 Saladin is sent to Egypt as part of the command-structure of a Zengid army commanded by his uncle Shirkuh.

He becomes an integral part of several campaigns over the years, and his uncle's second-in-command. By early 1169, the army of Amalric I, King of Jerusalem, is finally expelled from Egypt. Saladin's uncle Shirkuh is named vizier of the Fatimid Caliph, al-Adid, which gives Nur ad-Din de-facto control over Egypt. But just one month later, in March 1169, Shirkuh suddenly dies after a short illness. Without his right-hand man, Nur ad-Din's influence in Egypt is threatened. And al-Adid senses an opportunity to strengthen his own position and quickly appoints Saladin without waiting for a decision from Damascus, thinking that a young vizier with no political power in Egypt will be easy to control.

However, the 31-year-old Saladin proves to be more than what al-Adid has bargained for. The young vizier takes advantage of the Fatimid political system and through clever tactics he gradually installs his close family members in key government and military positions, which enables him to consolidate his power enough to overthrow and dissolve the Fatimid Shia Caliphate just two years later in 1171, thus founding the Ayyubid dynasty. Saladin can now concentrate on strengthening Egypt as a bastion of Sunni Muslim power with himself as governor in the name of Nur ad-Din. He revitalises the economy, establishes civic institutions, and greatly improves education by building a law college in Alexandria and a vast number of schools all over Egypt, giving school administrators and teachers good salaries, which attracts many scholars from across Asia and Europe, turning Egypt into an intellectual powerhouse of the 12th century.

He abolishes tolls for Muslim pilgrims who cross the Red Sea, and pays compensation to Mecca for any loss of income - a shrewd move that makes him popular among the people and also makes him a patron of Mecca.

Saladin transforms Egypt into a salient against the Crusaders by creating an entirely new army, loyal only to him and starts rebuilding the navy to protect Egypt's coasts. Military forays soon follow to secure and expand the borders, first against Nubia where hostile remnants of the Fatimid establishment still persist, then into Lybia where Ayybid armies push west to Tripoli and expel the Norman occupiers, although Saladin never manages to consolidate his authority west of the province of Barqa.

Most importantly, Saladin turns his attention towards tightening his grip over Hejaz and captures Yemen, thus gaining control over the Red Sea and its' vast maritime trading potential, which immensly increases Egypt's commercial wealth.

By all accounts Saladin is actively building an empire which creates friction with Nur ad-Din, his master in Syria. Tensions rise and almost result in conflict, but then Nur ad-Din dies suddenly in 1174, probably of a heart attack.

In the ensuing power vacuum his 11-year-old son As-Salih cannot fill the void left by his father's death. But Saladin can. And he now sees before him a grand vision. He can unite Egypt and Syria for a holy war against the Christian invaders. He proclaims the need for unity and jihad as reasons to intervene in Syria.And his claims are not without merit.

By controlling the Red Sea and by reconquering the area south of the Shawbak castle, Saladin is already recognized as the 'liberator of the Hajj Road'. Securing pilgrimage routes from Sudan and Egypt to the holy cities of Mecca and Medina earns him a lot of credibility and as a result his arrival into Syria is much welcomed by ordinary people, but not so much by some members of the Zengid dynasty.

Nevertheless Saladin brings most of the Zengid territory under his control either through diplomacy or military intervention, becoming the Sultan of Egypt and Syria.

Meanwhile, across the border King Amalric I of Jerusalem plans to exploit the political instability in Syria and expand his territory, but he dies of dysentery in July 1174.

In Saladin's view, Amalric's death is a sign of God's favor. With the throne passing on to Baldwin IV, a mere boy suffering from leprosy, and the Frankish nobles angling for positions in the kingdom, the threat of a major Christian invasion subsides.

But Saladin knows that the time is not yet right to fight the Crusaders, as he must consolidate his position against Nur ad-Din's relatives who still pose a threat from their bases in Aleppo and Mosul.

But as Baldwin IV matures, the kingdom adopts a proactive foreign policy. The Crusaders then try to take Hama and Harim, but fail in the attempt.

In 1177 Saladin responds by leading a large invasion force into the Kingdom of Jerusalem, to counter the Frankish aggression.

Baldwin, now 16 years old, despite being vastly outnumbered proves he is a capable leader, able to unite his nobles against the Muslim threat. And with the help of Raynald of Chatillon, his second-in-command, he manages to catch Saladin by surprise at Montgisard due to a rare tactical error by the Sultan. Saladin suffers a crushing defeat, narrowly escaping with his own life, with many in his army killed or taken prisoner. But Baldwin lacks the resources to follow up on the victory and the Sultan manages to regroup.

In April 1179 Saladin strikes back and decisively defeats Baldwin in the Golan region, nearly capturing the king. Another Christian army is defeated in June of the same year, and just two months later an important Templar fortress situated on the pilgrimage route is destroyed. Finally in 1180, Saladin and Baldwin agree a two-year truce.

But even before the ink is dry, it is clear that the mighty fortress of Kerak will become the next flash point. Virtually impenetrable atop a steep hill, with its' 80 meter entrance-tunnel and walls thick enough to withstand the battering of siege weapons, Kerak is the home of Raynald of Chatillon. His fortress sits on the key road between Damascus and Mecca and from there the baron is able to tax, raid and rob the passing camel-caravans of traders and pilgrims. Truce or no truce Raynald thinks that Muslims should not be allowed to pass freely. In the summer of 1181 he rides deep into Arabia and intercepts a major Muslim caravan, strips the traveleres of their posessions and takes many prisoners.

Saladin demands compensation from Baldwin, but the king cannot force Raynald to recompense. Saladin holds a group of Christian pilgrims hostage in Damietta as leverage, but Raynald still refuses to free the Muslim pilgrims. In response, Christian pilgrims are sold into slavery.

Then in 1182 Raynald puts more strain on the already delicate truce. The rogue Crusader sends troops via Red Sea, declaring that he will destroy the Kaaba and exhume the Prophet's tomb in Hejaz.

But thanks to Saladin's naval reforms, Egypt is well prepared. Al-Adil, Saladin's brother and governor of Egypt, dispatches the Ayyubid fleet. Most of the Christian raiders are captured

and executed on the order from the Sultan. Eulogies of Saladin abound in the Muslim community as he is yet again seen as the protector of Islamic holy places and pilgrimage routes. And then the tide turns in favor of the Muslims.

In 1183 Aleppo finally surrenders to Saladin, who now becomes the mightiest ruler of the Muslim world, and the leader of a unified Muslim front against the Latin Crusaders. Excercising uncontested authority over Egypt and Syria, he is supported by the Sunni Caliph in Baghdad and is recognised as the lord of Arabia and patron of the Holy Cities of Mecca and Medina. But most importantly, ordinary Muslims that Saladin sought to bring together are jubilant that Islam is again united.

The news of Saladin's conquest of Aleppo shocks the Crusader states. Saladin can now direct his vast resources to put pressure on the Kingdom of Jerusalem almost along its' entire border. A devastating raid into Christian lands is followed by several probing attacks on the fortress of Kerak, testing the resolve of the Franks and putting strain on their resources. To make matters worse for the Crusaders, the tragic life of Baldwin IV is over.

The king's final act was to try and secure peace by sending Raymond of Tripoli to negotiate a four-year truce, which Saladin readily agrees to, because he has problems of his own with the Zengid ruler in Mosul, who is forming a coalition against him. But the lepper King's successor Baldwin V is a sickly child, and he dies just a year later, triggering a succession crisis.

After a period of political turmoil, the throne passes on to Baldwin IV's sister, who in turn crowns her husband Guy of Lusignan as Kin of Jerusalem. But the new king is not able to control his vassal nobles. Then come troubling news from the south. In December 1186, Raynald of Chatillon once again violates the truce. He overruns another rich caravan, slaughters and imprisons many Muslims.

Saladin immediately dispatches an envoy, demanding the return of hostages and treasure, threatening the truce-breaker with vengeance. But Raynald, resting on his laurels behind the walls of Kerak, refuses to even receive the envoy. Upon hearing of this, Saladin finally loses his patience and swears that he will take the life of Raynald with his own hand, his anger beyond words... beyond bounds.

In early 1187, Saladin gathers his generals in Damascus to draw up plans for a major invasion. Messengers gallop to all corners of the state, urging action, vengeance, a war of liberation and annihilation. The words "Jihad" and "Jerusalem" are on the lips of all Muslims who answer Saladin's call. Saladin leaves garrisons along the border to protect the northern flank and begins raiding Christian lands.

During one of the raids, a chance encounter between a Muslim cavalry advanced guard and a Christian contingent of 130 knights, 400 turcopoles and infantry, at the Springs of Cresson, ends in disaster for the Templars and Hospitallers. Heads of knights on lances, and prisoners chained to horses are paraded in front of Tiberias.

The calamity at the Springs of Cresson is a wake up call for the Christians, who quickly mend old rivalries and unite in the face of the conflict that is coming...

On June 26th 1187, Saladin regroups his troops, and marches towards the river Jordan. His army numbers around 30.000, and is divided into three wings, with Taqi al-Din commanding the right, Gökböri commanding the left, and Saladin himself in the centre.

On June 27th the army reaches the river Jordan and makes camp in a marshy area near Lake Tiberias. Raiding parties are sent into Christian territory to ravage the area and set the stage for the invasion. Some 25 km west, a Christian army, some 20.000 strong encamps near Saffuriya, a highly strategic location because of its' rich water resources.

On June 30th, Saladin sends a contingent nort to block Tiberias and then challenges the Crusaders by moving his main camp closer to Saffuriya, some 10km west of Lake Tiberias. But as neither side takes action, Saladin decides to make the first move.

On July 1st he sends scouts to monitor an alternative road on his northern flank that connects Saffuriya and Tiberias. Later in the day reports confirm that the Crusaders are not advancing on either route, and on July 2nd Saladin takes the initiative.

He marches east towards Tiberias with most of his infantry, a cavalry contingent, siege engineers, and their equipment. By late morning they reach Tiberias, where Raymond's wife is staying, and they besiege the town. Not long after, Muslim troops breach the walls and the town is seized by nightfall. Raymond's wife barricades herself inside the citadel with her guards and sends messengers, urging King Guy to send help.

Back west, plumes of smoke can be seen in the sky above Tiberias and when news of the siege reaches the Crusader camp, King Guy holds a war council to debate what should be done.

At first, Raymond of Tripoli makes a persuasive argument against marching to raise the siege, insisting that the Christian army has a strong defensive position at Saffuriya and should stay put. But the count's cautiousness is met with accusations of cowardice and treachery, mainly from the Templar master Gerard de Ridefort and Raynald of Chatillon, who push for a more aggressive stance and put pressure on King Guy with strong political, military and diplomatic arguments. Persuaded, the king sends a herald through the camp to sound the call that the army will march to the rescue of Tiberias at dawn.

And on July 3rd the Crusader army makes way. They set out with Raymond of Tripoli commanding the vanguard. King Guy leads the center where the bishop of Acre carries Christendom's greatest relic, the True Cross, on which Christ is believed to have been crucified.

Balian of Ibelin commands the rearguard where the Templars and Hospitallers are stationed. King Guy orders the men to march with haste, planning to reach the besieged town by the end of the day. But as noon approaches and the sun rises across the clear, cloudless sky, it becomes apparent that the day will be extremely hot.

There is no breeze and the scorching heat slows down the coloumn. By midday the army reaches the next watering point at the village of Tur'an, only one third of the way. But as they press on, there is no escaping the sun and the thick dust raised by the marching troops. It becomes clear to King Guy and his officers that they will not reach Tiberias in a single day.

As the column moves away from Tur'an, detachments of Saladin's fast moving horse archers appear from nearby hills and begin harassing the Christians, cutting off their line of retreat. The Crusader infantry closes rank to protect the cavalry against hit and run attacks, but the number of casualties in men and animals begins to rise.

The day wears on, and the constant harassment, and sporadic clashes slow the Crusader rearguard down to a crawl, and they become separated from the rest of the army. Fearing the loss of his elite shock cavalry, King Guy orders the center to stop to allow the rearguard to catch up.

He relays the message to Raymond, ordering him to halt the vanguard. But as the entire Crusader column gradually gets encircled by the ever increasing number of Saladin's horse archers, it becomes clear that they have fallen into a trap.

After quickly taking Tiberias, Saladin had time to return, leaving only a small garrison to block the citadel, and with his main contingent he is now blocking the road. With nightfall fast approaching, the exhausted Christian fighters, slowed by thirst and hemmed-in by Muslim forces, cannot fight their way past Saladin's fresh troops.

King Guy has no choice but to order his men to make camp where they stand. Not far from the king's tent, the main Muslim contingent also encamps for the night. But the night ahead will be a difficult one for the Crusaders.

Their column stretches some 2km and it's not protected by any natural terrain features. Muslim horse archers continue to pepper the camp throughout the night. Skirmishers clash with the Crusaders and set tents on fire along the camp perimeter. Unable to rest and with their water supplies dwindling, the smoke and the heat from the fire drains the energy from the Christians.

Come morning, things quiet down. Saladin waits for the heat to rise and to see what the Christians will do. Crusaders, now without any water and tormented by thirst, have only one aim - the village of Hattin, where there is a water source.

They make way across the valley, keeping the same formation of three squares, with infantry shielding the cavalry. Saladin's troops set fire to the nearby brushwood, sending choking clouds of smoke on a westerly breeze towards the Crusaders. And with the sun beating down from the clear sky, the Christians push on towards Hattin, desperate to reach the water well.

To prevent this, Saladin sends Taqi al-Din's wing galloping to block the valley, determined to fully encircle the enemy and not allow them to quench their thirst. He especially wants to wear down the knights and their heavy cavalry, aware of just how dangerous their frontal charge is. Taqi's skirmishers ride in close, then hit and run to test the flanks of the Christians. Horse archers then unleash volley, after volley onto the Crusader column - reportedly hundreds

Exhausted, thirsty and disheartened, the Crusader infantry starts to break away from the mounted knights. They disperse and flee, with a large group heading east towards a hill called the Horns of Hattin and another group fleeing north towards the village of Nimrin. Seeing the fleeing troops, Muslim riders open gaps their line to draw out the enemy infantry.

King Guy and his officers realize that they are doomed unless they can break through.

But the Muslims charge the rear of the column, and the Templars and Hospitallers become heavily engaged, forcing Guy to halt for a second time to prevent the cavalry formations from breaking up. But in the front, Raymond of Tripoli is already edging away from King Guy's cavalry formation.

As he advances the Muslim riders begin opening another gap in their line. Raymond, decides not to sit and wait. He gathers his knights and charges Taqi al-Din's cavalry. The Muslim riders let the the galloping Christians pass through, showering Raymond and his men with arrows as they retreat from the battlefield.

Back in the smoke-filled valley, the Christian knights are dying. Guy orders the cavalry to move towards the Horns of Hattin through a gap already created by the retreating infantry. He knows that there are shallow pools of water at the top of the hill and hopes they are not dry.

Meanwhile on the hill, Saladin's troops close in and begin engage the Christian infantry. Exhausted, the enemy infantry barely put up a fight and they are quickly overwhelmed. The Muslims then turn towards the King of Jerusalem himself.

Throughout the incessant close quarter fighting, Christian knights gather around to protect the True Cross as they retreat towards the hill. But at the top they find no relief and no water. King Guy rallies the knights and raises his red tent to provide a focal point. But to no avail. Muslim troops push up the slope and engage the Christians. In the melee the True Cross falls into Muslim hands.

Seeing this, the surviving Christian knights rally and charge downhill to retrieve it, pushing the Muslim line back. But they have no fight left in them and they soon begin to take heavy casualties.

Finally, King Guy orders them to surrender. The knights dismount and collapse on the ground. King Guy is also found on the ground at his tent, utterly exhausted, barely having enough strength left to hand over his sword.

 Saladin's army has won a great victory.

King Guy is captured along with many nobles and knights, among them, Rayland of Chatillon. Saladin orders that ice cold water be brought and offered to the King. Then, according to Imad Al-din: "The King, having drunk some of it, handed the cup to Raynald of Chatillon. Whereupon the Sultan said to an interpreter: Say to the king: "It is you who give him to drink. But I give him neither to drink. Nor to eat." By these words, Saladin wishes that it be understood that honor forbade him to harm any man who had tasted his hospitality. And with that he swings his sword and strikes Raynald on the neck, thus fullfilling his oath to kill the truce-breaker.

But more importantly, the large Crusader army that is destroyed at Hattin cannot be replaced. Without it, Christian castles, towns and cities are now defenseless.

It is worth noting that we mainly focused on Saladin's military achievements. There is much more to the man who was admired by his European enemies. And loved by his fellow Muslims. Saladin was a courageous Muslim leader who's firm foundation in the religion and its' prime values lead to his commitment to the Islamic cause.

In just twelve years he united Mesopotamia, Syria, Egypt, eastern Lybia, western Arabia and Yemen, using his skills in diplomacy and administration to piece together this divided region. His scope of vision was that he gave each situation its due attention and weight, and he never broke a bridge of diplomacy or peace initiative with his opponents. The power or wealth he acquired never spoiled him.

He was a man of restless energy geared to serve his goal in driving the invaders out of Muslim lands.

THREE ADVICE FROM THE QURAN

✓ In your collective life, make rooms for others (58:11)

✓ "Be steadfast in prayer, practice regular charity, and bow down your heads with those who bow down (in worship)" (2:43).

✓ Be generous to the needy wayfarer, the homeless son of the street, and the one who reaches you in a destitute condition (4:36)

✓ "The charity of those who expend their wealth in the Way of Allah may be likened to a grain of corn, which produces seven ears and each ear yields a hundred grains. Likewise Allah develops manifold the charity of anyone He pleases, for He is All-Embracing, All-Wise." (2:261)

A man asked the Prophet (saws), "O Allah's Messenger (saws)!

What kind of charity is the best?" He (saws) replied. "To give in charity when you are healthy and greedy hoping to be wealthy and afraid of becoming poor. Don't delay giving in charity till the time when you are on the death bed when you say, 'Give so much to so-and-so and so much to so-and so,' as at that time the property is not yours but it belongs to so-and-so (i.e. your inheritors)." (Sahih Al-Bukhari Hadith 4.11)

Allah's Messenger (saws) said, "Envy is not permissible except of two men. A man whom Allah has given the knowledge of the Book and he recites it during the hours of the night, and a man whom Allah has given wealth, and he spends it in charity during the night and the hours of the day." (Sahih Al-Bukhari Hadith 6.543)

"Spend (in the Cause of Allah) from the provisions that We have given you before death should come to any of you and then he should say, "O my Lord, why did You not reprieve me awhile that I should have given in charity and become of the righteous." But Allah does not at all reprieve a person when his term comes to an end, and Allah is well aware of what you all do." (Quran 63:10)

I heard the Messenger of Allah (saws) saying, "Save yourself from the (Hell) Fire even with half a date (to be given in charity); and if you do not find a half date, then with a good pleasant word." (Sahih Al-Bukhari Hadith 4.793)

"Allah still loves and shows mercy to those who disobey Him, so imagine how much He loves those who obey Him." [The Wondering].

A thought-provoking questions you should ask yourself every day

Where will we go after we die and what's going to happen to us?

Practical Ways to Improve Yourself

<u>Show kindness to people around you</u>

You can never be too kind to someone. In fact, most of us don't show enough kindness to people around us. Being kind helps us to cultivate other qualities such as compassion, patience, and love.

PRACTICAL TIPS FOR DEVELOPING THE GOOD MUSLIM MINDSETCHEATSHEET

5 TIPS FOR DEVELOPING THE GIVER MINDSET:

1. Give quality time and attention to your family.

2. Make it a daily practice of giving something to the creation of Allah. (Give food, money, time, smile, water etc)

3. When someone exclusively asks you for help with something difficult for them, say YES. Don't deny help to others.

4. Give yourself a treat and some personal time to avoid burnout.

5. Find a generosity partner that will motivate you to give.

5 TIPS FOR DEVELOPING THE CONFIDENT MINDSET:

1. Take your morning bitter self-acceptance pill (accept one insecurity by being brutally honest with yourself).

2. Present the best version of yourself (Dress up modestly).

3. Believe in self and belief in Allah's plan for you.

4. Make a list of your strengths and weaknesses. Focus and work on your strengths.

5. Make this du'a- [Qur'an: Chapter 20, Verses 25-28]

Fudayl ibn Iyad

There was a highway robber, a thief very famous at his time. He was in love with one girl and he had the habit of sneaking to her house some way and observing her for some time.

At night, he would go and attack caravans, Hajj caravans, travellers. He would strip them of their property and the wealth and their belongings. He was notorious to the extent that a lot of the caravans most of the time would change route to avoid that area.

One night he climbs up the wall of the house of that girl that he loves. As he was making his way into the house someone was praying. Someone was praying standing before Allah (SWT). Reciting the words of Allah (SWT),

أَلَمْ يَأْنِ لِلَّذِينَ آمَنُوا أَنْ تَخْشَعَ قُلُوبُهُمْ لِذِكْرِ اللَّهِ

"Has not the time come for the hearts of those who believe to be affected by Allah's Reminder?" [Qur'an al-Hadeed: 16]

The words shook him! And grabbed his heart and he was moved deep inside. He started to think about these words. He forgot the main reason why he came to this house. The only response that was on his tongue; his spontaneous response was, "Indeed my lord the time has come." And that moment he changed.

So, he went out of this house. Roaming aimlessly, contemplating his life, contemplating his past, his behaviour, his reputation, his future and his relationship with Allah (SWT). He ended up with a group of people or gathered together. They lit a fire and there were travellers, strangers. He asked their permission to join them. He sat with them and they were disputing whether to spend the night there or to carry on their journey. One of them said, "We should stay here. Because there's that famous thief;

that famous robber's area. If we carry on traveling, he might jump on us and you know, we all will be in trouble. So let's spend the night here then we will set off in the morning."

The name they mentioned, the name of that thief was this very person. It made him think to himself, "What did I do that people; fear me that much. What kind of curse I have become to humans that people don't even feel safe about their lives and their property because of me." All of this made him question his life. And then he made the decision that I will change. Because it's my responsibility. It's not someone else's responsibility to change me and set me on the right course. It's my own initiative and if I don't take it; it might never happen. I will face the consequences on the day of judgement. And that's exactly what he did. He became one of the famous scholars in the history of al Islam. That is al-Fudayl ibn Iyad.

Ar-Rashid, a first century ruler, once said to al-Fudayl bin Iyaad, "Admonish me."

"O Leader of the believers!" said al-Fudayl. "Indeed your grandfather, al-Abbas, the uncle of the Prophet, once went to the Prophet and said, 'O Messenger of Allah, appoint me to be a leader.' The Messenger of Allah said, 'My uncle, indeed, being a leader leads to sorrow, and regret on the Day of Resurrection. If you are able to go without ever being a leader, then do so!'"

Moved to tears, ar-Rashid said, "Give me more."

al-Fudayl looked at ar-Rashid and said, "O one who has a handsome face, if you are able to protect that face from the Hell-fire then do so. And beware of ever cheating or betraying your people."

Being much moved by al-Fudayl's words, ar-Rashid wanted to reward him.

"Do you have any debts?" he asked.

"To my Lord, yes, and He will hold me accountable for them," said al-Fudayl.

"I am of course referring to debts to other human beings," said ar-Rashid.

After al-Fudayl answered in the negative, ar-Rashid said to one of his assistants, "Give him 1000 dinars, which he can use to help his family."

Al-Fudayl was greatly offended by these words and said, "How perfect Allah is! I am guiding you to safety and you want to reward me with this paltry, worldly sum!" He then left, refusing to take anything.

Ibraheem ibn al-Ash'ath also said, "I've never seen a person that would glorify Allah with his heart like Fudayl. If he mentioned Allah, if Allah was mentioned in his presence, or if he heard the Quran, you would see the fear on his face, tears would flow from his eyes and he would cry until those that were present would show him mercy. He was always sad and he did a lot of thinking. I haven't seen a man who would seek Allah's reward with his knowledge, his actions and even when he would give and receive things. He would seek Allah's reward by loving and hating for the pleasure of Allah, and he was like this in all of the actions he performed."

Quotes by Al-Fudayl ibn Iyad

"Whoever desires to be mentioned by the people, will never be mentioned, and whoever dislikes to be mentioned by the people will be mentioned."

"A person's fear of Allah depends on his knowledge of Allah, and a person's abstaining from the dunyah (i.e. this worldly life), depends on his desire for the akhirah (i.e. the next life)…"

"Nothing beatifies a person more than truthfulness and seeking those things that are permissible…"

"The most untruthful person is the one who denies his sins, the most ignorant person is the arrogant one who points out the good deeds he has performed, and the most knowledgeable person of Allah is the one who fears Him the most. The servant of Allah will never be complete until his deen (religion) has an effect on his desires, and he will never be destroyed until his desires have an effect on his deen."

"Whoever fears Allah, no one will be able to harm him, and whoever fears other than Allah, no one will be able to benefit him."

Fudayl ibn Iyad was asked, "What is abstaining from the dunya (i.e. worldly life)?" He said, "It is to be content." So it was said, "And what is piety?" He said, "Avoiding those things that Allah has prohibited." Then he was asked, "And what is worship?" He said, "To perform that which Allah has made obligatory upon you." It was asked, "And what is humility?" He responded, "To submit to the truth." Then Fudayl added, "The most severe form of piety is with the tongue."

"Your hearts are prevented from tasting the sweetness of imaan until you abstain from the dunya (i.e. worldly life)."

Al-Fudayl ibn Iyād once said (addressing himself): "O you meagre individual! You do evil yet think you are a doer of good! You are ignorant but think you have knowledge! You are stingy yet think you are generous! You are foolish yet think you are intelligent! Your life is short but your hopes are long!"

"Whosoever is saddened by loneliness and feels tranquil around the people, is not safe from Rīyā'.

"If you mix with people, mix with those who have good character; it only invites to good. Do not mix with those who have bad character, for it only invites to evil."

"Five things are associated with difficulty in life: the heart is hard, the eyes don't shed tears, to have limited hayya, to desire the material world, and to have lengthy hopes/desires in your life."

"As long as people are doing fine, their true nature is concealed, but when calamity strikes, their true natures are revealed, so the believer resorts to his faith and the hypocrite resorts to his hypocrisy."

"A believer in this life is worried and sad. His worry is the objective of preparing himself. So whoever's condition in this life is such, then he has no concern other than taking provisions from what will benefit him during the return to his homeland. So he does not compete with the people of the land, among whom he is merely a stranger, in what they consider honorable. And he does not become worried if he seems insignificant among them."

"The believer speaks little and does a lot, whereas the hypocrite speaks a lot and does little. When the believer speaks, it is with wisdom, when he is silent, it is in deep thought, when he sees, he takes lessons, and when he acts, it is a cure. If this is the way you are, then you are in the constant worship [of your Lord.]"

We ask Allah, The Most High, to aid us in striving to be like those righteous imams of Islaam who came before us, and may prayers and peace be upon our prophet Muhammad, his family and all of his companions.

FIVE ADVICE FROM THE QURAN:

✓ Keep yourself clean, pure (9:108, 4:43, 5:6)

✓ Fulfill your promises and commitments (17:34)

✓ The life of this world is merely enjoyment of delusion. (3:185)

✓ Therefore remember Me, I will remember you, and be thankful to Me, and do not be ungrateful to Me. (2:152)

✓ Indeed Allah is with those who fear him and those who are doers of Good. (16:128)

The Prophet (peace be upon him) said, "Lose no time to do good deeds before you are caught up by one of seven calamities awaiting you: a starvation which may impair your wisdom; a prosperity which may mislead you; an ailment which may damage your health; an old age which may harm your senses; a sudden death; the Dajjal (Antichrist); or Doomsday, which is indeed the hardest and most bitter." (At-Tirmidhi)

"Indeed, those who have believed and done righteous deeds will have gardens beneath which rivers flow that is a great attainment." (Surah al-Buruj 85:11)

"If you are grateful, I will surely increase you [in favor]." (Surah Ibrahim 14:7)

"Forbidden love stories end at marriage, while true halal love stories begin at marriage and end with both entering paradise." [Abdulbary Yaha Bari]

A thought-provoking questions you should ask yourself every day

What is one thing I could start doing today to improve the quality of my life?

Practical Ways to Improve Yourself

<u>**Quit a bad habit**</u>

Are there any bad habits you can lose? Oversleeping? Being lazy? Being late? Slouching? Nail biting? Smoking?

<u>**Listen**</u>

It's very important to listen to people. Sometimes when you listen carefully, you'll learn things that you wouldn't have known if you haven't given an ear to it. Although people these days are always busy and in a rush, try to make some time to listen to others because it will definitely affect your life positively in'sha'Allah.

PRACTICAL TIPS FOR DEVELOPING THE GOOD MUSLIM MINDSETCHEATSHEET

5 TIPS FOR DEVELOPING THE PURPOSEFUL MINDSET:

1. Understand the purpose of life of a Muslim mentioned in the Quran.

2. Redefine the purpose of your life as a Muslim.

Ask yourself these questions:

A) What am I really good at? What are the skills that I've been blessed with?

B) What are the talents/ skills you possess that you are proud of and enjoy doing? There's a difference between being good at something and enjoying it too.

3. Make sure what you pursue in life falls within the "halal" boundaries.

4. SUMMARY: Choose a purpose that encompasses the necessary skills you possess, things you enjoy doing and that are halal, with the intention of earning your Akhirah from it.

5. Whatever you decide to do, do it with PASSION. DON'T drag yourself

THE PIOUS MAN AND FIRE

There's a story mentioned by Ibn Jawziyyah ®,

He says there was a man who used to fast throughout the day and he used to pray (qiyam al layl) throughout the night. He never used to involve himself in anything that was haram (forbidden). He knew that the people that were around him in his land were corrupt. So, he didn't sit in their gatherings because all they used to do is backbite and slander. So he would just stay in his house and never leave his house. When he ran out of food, he would leave his house and he would store and buy enough food to last him as long as it can. He would remain in his house just worshipping Allah (SWT).

The people of the land gathered together and they said, "Look at this man, does he think that he is better than us? He doesn't come and sit in our gatherings; he doesn't walk around or talk to us. We just see him and he looks down on the floor and he goes to the shop and he goes back to his house. Never did this man look right or left or even in front of him; he would just look down and walk." So the people became jealous of this man and this is how they were. Shaytaan doesn't just attack you by himself. Shaytaan has people that he has inspired his haram into them and he commands them to attack the believers.

So, this is what they did; so what they did was they looked around the land until they found the most beautiful woman in that land. And she was a young woman and she was a chaste woman and they approached her and they said: "We want you to seduce that man and we want you to commit zina with that man." She said, "How can I do such a thing?" She was amongst the poorest women in that land and she found it very difficult to live. So they said to her, "If you can do this then we will give you the equivalent to your weight in gold and even more than this and all of this poverty that you are facing today; it will end. All you have to do is commit zina with that man." So, the woman, she went home and she began to think until she looked at her situation and she thought, "SubhanAllah (what she thought to herself) there is nothing left for me, I am going to die of poverty and I have nothing left." so she accepted the task that they had given her and she said, "I will go and I will commit Zina with this man."

So one cold night she went and she knocked on the door of the house of this man. He opened the door and he saw a woman. He closed the door. She raised her voice and she said, "Please allow me to come into your house. I was traveling and I thought that I would reach my destination before night but now the night has come and I am in the middle of nowhere. And I do not know where I am, I do not know anyone in this land. And if you do not accept me into your house then I fear that something will happen to me outside." He said, "We have many neighbors around please go and knock on the house of these neighbors and if Allah wills, they will help you." The woman she left, a little while later she knocked on his door again. And she said, "I went to the houses of the neighbors but no one is home. It is really cold outside and I fear I may die if you do not accept me and do not allow me into your house." He said, "Just go further down the hills and you will find there are a few more houses over there. In Shaa Allah, they will allow you to live with them." He said, "There is no one in my house so it is not permissible for you to be with me." So the woman she left. A little while later she came back again and she knocked on his door so he opened the door and he saw the woman. She said, "Wallahi! If you do not allow me to come into your house and if any man puts his finger on me; and he rapes me. And he takes away my chastity then, Wallahi! On Judgement Day I will stand in front of Allah and say you were the one that was the cause of this. It is because of you he raped me and it is because of you this happened. And I will blame it on you!" When he heard the name of Allah (SWT); he became really scared, why? Because when the believers, when the name of Allah (SWT) is mentioned, their hearts tremble. So, this man he became really scared and said he has two rooms in his house; so he said to her, "Come and sit in this room and do not knock on my door and do not say anything to me. As soon as the time of fajr approaches leave my house and continue with your journey." So the man, he left this woman in this room and he went into the second room that he had and he locked the door and he continued with his recitation of the Quran.

Now, the people of the land (they know that she has entered his house) they have gathered around the house. Waiting to catch the two of them committing zina (and this is a pious man) and he has never faced anything like this in his life. So he is in his house now and he is reciting the book of Allah (SWT) and this woman is ready to commit zina with this man. And the people of the land have gathering around the house, waiting to enter and catch them committing zina. The man now (he's reciting the Quran) and the woman she begins to scream, she screams and she screams and she screams. So, the man he opens his door and he walks into the room where the woman is (he has an oil lamp with him). Only to find that she is lying on the floor without her clothes on and she is calling him towards her. This man now for the first time in his life, he is seeing something that he has never seen before because his gaze has always been lowered. He is feeling something in his heart now that he has never felt before. His mind is telling him things that it has never told him before. He has the most beautiful woman of their land in front of him calling him for zina. What does he do? What would a person in this situation do? He has never seen anything like this in his life. The people now know they heard the first scream from the woman. So, they know that very soon they will catch them committing zina. They came closer to the door of the house of the man. The woman now all of a sudden begins to scream and she screams and continues to scream and scream and scream.

The people of the land they break down the door of this mans house and they enter to find that the woman is on the floor and the man is also on the floor but the woman is in one side of the room and the man is on the other side of the room. And the woman continues to scream and she continues to scream. They look at the man and he is crying in the corner of the room and his hand is in the fire of the lamp that he has and he is crying and he is crying. And the woman is screaming so, they take the woman out of the house. And she says, "Take me away from this man because Wallahi the Imaan of this man is killing me. I see something in front of me that I cannot describe and this has done something to my heart and my mind. The Imaan of this man is killing me so take me away." The man is crying in the corner because every single time the man took a step towards the woman, he put his hand in the fire. And he said, "Remember the Fire of Jahanam. Hell is hotter than this fire of this world." Until he would fall to the floor and then when he was able to stand up again; he would stand up again and take a step towards the woman, and when he took a step towards the woman again; he would put his hand back in the fire and say "Remember the fire of Jahannam. Hell is more severe than this fire of this world." And he kept on doing this until his hand was left inside the fire. And the woman began to scream and she was taken away; then this man he turned to Allah (SWT). He said, "Oh Allah forgive me for the sin that I have committed." What sin has the man committed? What did he do? He stayed away from zina, he stayed away from the most beautiful woman of the land. What sin did he commit? He said, "Oh Allah forgive me for the footsteps I took towards that woman."

Look at the Imaan Imaan of the righteous people; nothing will tempt them, nothing will take them away from Allah (SWT).

THREE ADVICE FROM THE QURAN

✓ Did he not realise that Allah is watching? | Al-Alaq-14

✓ So whoever does an atom's weight of good will see it | Al Quran Al Zalzalah Verse 7

✓ Then as to him who is given his book in his right hand. He shall be reckoned with by an easy reckoning. And he shall go back to his people joyful. And as to him who is given his book behind his back. He shall call for perdition. And enter into burning fire. (84:7-12)

Narrated Aisha: Allah's Messenger (ﷺ) said," (On the Day of Resurrection) any one whose account will be taken will be ruined (i.e. go to Hell)." I said, "O Allah's Messenger (ﷺ)! May Allah make me be sacrificed for you. Doesn't Allah say: "Then as for him who will be given his record in his right hand, he surely will receive an easy reckoning?" (84.7-8) He replied, "That is only the presentation of the accounts; but he whose record is questioned, will be ruined." (Al-Bukhari, 4939)

A thought-provoking questions you should ask yourself every day

What is my purpose and mission?

Practical Ways to Improve Yourself

<u>Truthfulness</u>

Being true is one of the core habits that every civilized society appreciates in its members. When people adopt truthfulness, it actually means that they have laid the most important foundation stone upon which they are going to construct a building of great character.

🍽 SUNNAH DIET- DAILY CHECKLIST 🍽

	Sunnah foods	Mon	Tue	Wed	Thu	Fri	Sat	Sun
On empty Stomach	Apple cider vinegar/ Lemon juice + Water + Honey	√						
Pre-Breakfast	Water + Water							
With Breakfast	A bowl of oats or barley + milk +black cumin/ + kalongi							
	Seasonal fruit (Make a fruit bowl/ however you like)							
Pre-Lunch	Water +Water							
With Lunch	Salad Cucumbers & any other veges + Olive oil + Lemon juice/ Vinegar							
	A small bowl/ 1-2 spoonfuls of Yogurt (organic-preferably home-made)							
Pre-Dinner	Water +Water							
With Dinner	Salad with olive oil & lemon juice/ vinegar							
	Green Tea (Optional)							
Before Bedtime	Dates (3-5) with Almonds & other nuts +Milk							

REMINDER: This checklist is designed to serve as a reminder for Muslims to consume the food items that are essential for our daily health. There are plenty of other foods mentioned in sunnah, but the foods mentioned above are most beneficial if consumed everyday.

HEALING REMEDIES FROM THE SUNNAH

Narrated `Abdullah bin Ja`far bin Abi Talib: I saw Allah's Messenger (ﷺ) eating fresh dates with snake cucumber. (Bukhari, 5440)

Narrated `Aisha: that whenever one of her relatives died, the women assembled and then dispersed (returned to their houses) except her relatives and close friends. She would order that a pot of Talbina be cooked. Then Tharid (a dish prepared from meat and bread) would be prepared and the Talbina would be poured on it. `Aisha would say (to the women),"Eat of it, for I heard Allah's Messenger (ﷺ) saying, 'The Talbina soothes the heart of the patient and relieves him from some of his sadness.'" (Bukhari, 5417)

Narrated Sa`id bin Zaid: I heard the Prophet (ﷺ) saying, "Truffles are like Manna (i.e. they grow naturally without man's care) and their water heals eye diseases." (Bukhari, 5708)

Narrated Saud: I heard Allah's Messenger (ﷺ) saying, "If Somebody takes seven 'Ajwa dates in the morning, neither magic nor poison will hurt him that day." (Bukhari, 5769)

Narrated Ibn `Abbas: (The Prophet (ﷺ) said), "Healing is in three things: A gulp of honey, cupping, and branding with fire (cauterizing)." But I forbid my followers to use (cauterization) branding with fire." (Bukhari, 5680)

Narrated Um Qais: I went to Allah's Messenger (ﷺ) along with a son of mine whose palate and tonsils I had pressed with my finger as a treatment for a (throat and tonsil) disease. The Prophet (ﷺ) said, "Why do you pain your children by pressing their throats! Use Ud Al-Hindi (certain Indian incense- such as chandan/sandalwood) for it cures seven diseases, one of which is pleurisy. It is used as a snuff for treating throat and tonsil disease and it is inserted into one side of the mouth of one suffering from pleurisy." (Bukhari, 5713)

Narrated Khalid bin Sa`d: We went out and Ghalib bin Abjar was accompanying us. He fell ill on the way and when we arrived at Medina he was still sick. Ibn Abi 'Atiq came to visit him and said to us, "Treat him with black cumin. Take five or seven seeds and crush them (mix the powder with oil) and drop the resulting mixture into both nostrils, for `Aisha has narrated to me that she heard the Prophet (ﷺ) saying, 'This black cumin is healing for all diseases except As-Sam.' Aisha said, 'What is As-Sam?' He said, 'Death." (Bukhari, 5687)

13 FOODS RECOMMENDED BY THE PROPHET (S)

1. Dates

Dates are free from cholesterol and contain very low fat. They are rich in vitamins and minerals and are a good source of dietary fibre, tannins, vitamin-A, iron, Potassium, calcium, manganese, copper and pyridoxine (vitamin B-6)

2. Meat

Prophet Muhammad (PBUH) called Meat the king of foods. It is rich in protein, iron, zinc, selenium. Meat is good for bones, teeth, strengthening the immune system, body tissues and many more. The prophet (pbuh) was particularly fond of lamb, and it is now known that mutton it is much healthier compared to beef.

3. Figs

Figs are low in calories and good for bones. They are also known as one of the fruits of Jannah and offer various health benefits, nutrients and anti-oxidants.

4. Grapes

The Prophet (PBUH) was very fond of grapes. They are useful in purifying the blood, provide vigour and health, strengthen the kidneys and clear the bowels due to their high fiber content.

5. Milk

It strengthens the back, renews vision and improves memory apart from providing calcium for teeth and bones.

6. Honey

Prophet Muhammad (PBUH) said. "Honey is the cure of every stomach disease." He use to drink honey + water in the morning. In fact honey is considered the best remedy for diarrhea when mixed in hot water. It is the food of foods, drink of drinks and drug of drugs. It is used for improving appetite, strengthening the stomach, eliminating phlegm; as a meat preservative, hair conditioner, eye soother and mouthwash.

7. Olive & Olive Oil

This food is mentioned in Quran. Prophet Muhammad (PBUH) said: "Eat the olive oil and apply it (locally), since there is cure for seventy diseases in it, one of them is Leprosy". Olives are said to be the food of Prophets. Olive oil is excellent treatment for skin and hair, delays old age, and treats inflammation of the stomach, not to mention its low calorie cooking benefits.

8. Water

The Prophet (PBUH) said: "fever is (like) vapour of hell. So cool it with cold water". And "the best drink in this world is water, when you are thirsty drink it by sips and not gulps".

9. Melon

The Prophet (PBUH) said: "None of your women who are

pregnant and eat of water melon will fail to produce off spring that is good in countenance". Melons also have very high water content and are great for hot summers.

10. Squash or Pumpkin

It was Prophet Muhammad (PBUH)'s favourite vegetable. It is good for the Lungs and protects against birth defects. It is also good in asthma, colon cancer, pain, blood pressure and heart disease to name a few.

11. Vinegar

Prophet Muhammad (PBUH) called Vinegar the best curry. It is healthy and makes for great salad dressings. As a matter of fact, vinegar also helps fatigued muscles recover after strenuous physical activity.

12. Barley

Barley is recommended for curing fever and should be taken like a soup for the best results.

13. Black Caraway

Last, but definitely not the least, is Black Caraway, which according to the prophet (pbuh), is a cure for all diseases except death. Black Caraway includes natural antibiotics along with essential nutrients and vitamins likes Vitamin A, phosphates and iron apart from other compounds.

These super foods are no doubt good for your health and should be part of your grocery list next. If you try any of these on a regular basis.

THIRTEEN SUNNAHS OF EATING

Say Bismillah. Eat with your right. Eat that nearest to you.

The above three Sunan of eating are all taken from the Hadith of Umar Ibn Abi Salamah: "I was a boy under the care of Allah's Messenger ﷺ and my hand used to go around the dish while I was eating. So Allah's Messenger ﷺ said to me:

'Oh boy! Mention the Name of Allah and eat with your right hand, and eat of the dish what is nearer to you." Since then I have applied those instructions when eating." Sahih Al-Bukhari and Muslim

Eat on the floor: It is narrated that the Prophet ﷺ said: "I eat just as the slave eats, and I sit just as the slave sits". Abu Ya'la (Sahih)

Eat with three fingers: Ka'b Ibn Malik states: "The Prophet ﷺ used to eat with three fingers and lick his hand before he wiped it." Sahih Muslim

Eat together: Abdullah Ibn Umar Narrated: "I heard my father say: 'I heard 'Umar bin Khattab say: "The Messenger of Allah (ﷺ) said: 'Eat together and do not eat separately, for the blessing is in being together.'" Sunan Ibn Majah (Hassan)

Don't overeat: The Messenger of Allah ﷺ said: 'The human does not fill any container that is worse than his stomach. It is sufficient for the son of Adam to eat what will support his back. If this is not possible, then a third for food, a third for drink, and third for his breath." Al-Tirmidhi (Sahih)

Don't criticise food: Abu Huraira narrates that: "The Prophet ﷺ did not criticise any food ever. If he desired the food, he would eat it and if he disliked it, he would leave it." Sahih Al-Bukhari.

Compliment tasty food: Jabir reported:

The Prophet ﷺ asked for sauce and was told that there was nothing except vinegar. He asked for it and began to eat from it saying, "How excellent is vinegar when eaten as a condiment! How excellent is vinegar when eaten as a condiment! Sahih Muslim

Don't discard any food: From the Hadith of Jabir:

I heard Allah's Apostle ﷺ as saying: The Satan is present with any one of you in everything he does; he is present even when he eats food; so if any one of you drops a mouthful he should remove away anything filthy on it and eat it and not leave for the devil; and when he finishes (food) he should lick his fingers, for he does not know in what portion of his food the blessing lies. Sahih Muslim

Lick your fingers: Jabir Bin Abdullah narrates that the Prophet ﷺ said:

"He should not wipe his hand with a tissue until he licks his fingers, for he does not know in which part of his food is the blessing". Sahih Muslim

Wipe the dish: Anas Ibn Malik narrates:

"(The Prophet) commanded us to wipe our plates". Sahih Muslim

Praise Allah after eating: Anas Bin Malik narrates that the Prophet ﷺ said:

"Allah is pleased with a servant if he eats his food, he praises Allah for it; or if he drinks his drink he praises Allah for it". Sahih Muslim

She Died On Her Wedding Night

True story told by Shaykh Abdul Mohsen al Ahmad. It happened in Abha; the capital of Asir province in Saudi Arabia. After performing Salat Al Maghrib, she put her make-up, wore her beautiful white dress preparing herself for her wedding party, Then she heard the Adhan of 'Ishaa and she realized that she broke her Wudu she told her mother, "Mother, I have to go to make wudu and pray 'Isha.

Her mother was shocked: "Are you crazy? Guests are waiting for you, to see you! What about your make -up? It will be all washed away by water!" Then she added, "I am your mother and I order you not to perform salah now. Wallahi! If you make wudu now, I will be angry at you." Her daughter replied, "Wallahi! I won't go out from here till I perform my salah. Mother you must know that there is no obedience to any creature in disobedience to the Creator."

Her mother said, "What would our guests say about you when you'll show up in your wedding party without make-up? You won't be beautiful in their eyes and They will make fun of you." The daughter asked with a smile, "Are you worried because I won't be beautiful in the eyes of creations? What about my Creator? I am worried because, if I miss my salah, I won't be beautiful in His eyes."

She started to make wudu, and all her make-up was washed away, but she didn't care. Then she began her salah and at the moment she bowed down to make sujud, she didn't realize that it will be her last one! Yes! She died while in sujud!

FOURS ADVICE FROM THE QURAN

✓ "For such the reward is forgiveness from their Lord, and Gardens with rivers flowing underneath—an eternal dwelling. How excellent a recompense for those who work (and strive)!" (3:136).

✓ "But give glad tidings to those who believe and work righteousness, that their portion is gardens, beneath which rivers flow" (2:25).

✓ "Be quick in the race for forgiveness from your Lord, and for a garden whose width is that (of the whole) of the heavens and of the earth, prepared for the righteous" (3:133)

✓ "Allah has promised to Believers, men and women, gardens under which rivers flow, to dwell therein, and beautiful mansions in gardens of everlasting bliss. But the greatest bliss is the good pleasure of Allah: that is the supreme felicity" (9:72).

And a place in Paradise equal to an arrow bow of one of you, is better than (the whole earth) on which the sun rises and sets." (Al-Bukhari, 3253)

Narrated Abu Huraira: Allah's Messenger (ﷺ) said, "Allah said, "I have prepared for My Pious slaves things which have never been seen by an eye, or heard by an ear, or imagined by a human being." If you wish, you can recite this Verse from the Holy Qur'an:--"No soul knows what is kept hidden for them, of joy as a reward for what they used to do." (32.17) (Al-Bukhari, 3244)

"Everyone who is taken by death asks for more time, while everyone who still has time makes excuses for procrastination." Ali Ibn Abi Talib (R.A)

A thought-provoking questions you should ask yourself every day

"What is the most important thing I can do today to get me closer to my goal?"

Practical Ways to Improve Yourself

Consistency

Consistency is another key attribute that results in a person achieving success. When one is consistent, then he or she sticks with things and takes them to completion. This consistency gives birth to steadfastness which then finds its roots in trust in Allah Almighty. Therefore, in every undertaking a Muslim must be as consistent as possible. Hazrat Ayesha (RA) narrates:

"The most beloved action to Allah's Apostle was that which is done continuously and regularly." (Bukhari)

Be thankful and appreciative

Thank Allah for the countless blessings that He showers upon you each and every day, and appreciate what you have instead of obsessing over what you wish you had. Also thank people for whatever good they do to you and appreciate their thought and effort.

Conclusion:

In a nutshell, every Muslim must try making the aforementioned attributes as habits. Once a Muslim makes these attributes as habits, the ultimate result is he or she achieving success with balance in this life and in the life hereafter as well In Sha Allah.

/ /   ☐MON ☐TUES ☐ WED ☐ THUR ☐ FRI ☐ SAT ☐ SUN

Ayah / hadith / quote of the day: ....

....

Most important tasks of the day :

ISLAM	FAM ILY /SOCIAL
WORK/STUDY	PERSONAL (ME-TIME)

Using the Pomodoro Technique: circle

(mainly for Work / Study)   Target   of pomodoros   Achieved

Task#1:............................. ... ☐   ☐☐☐☐☐   ☐

Task#2:............................. ... ☐   ☐☐☐☐☐   ☐

Task#3:............................. ... ☐   ☐☐☐☐☐   ☐

Task#4:............................. ... ☐   ☐☐☐☐☐   ☐

My productivity score

1   2   3   4   5   6   7   8   9   10

Not Bad   **Good Job**   **Awesome**

Pending Tasks (Do first thing tomorrow):	Bread Crumbs (Minor TO-DO List):
Note to Self:	

For More Info visit: https://www.themuslimyouthprogramme.com

HOW TO USE THE PLANNER

Ayah/ hadith/ quote of the day: Write an ayah that touches your heart while reading Quran, or an inspiring hadith or quote you come across somewhere (eg. social media). Not only will you will learn it this way, you can repeat it in your head every - time you feel low!

Date & day: Write the date and tick the day to begin your Planning for the day!

Most important tasks of the day: Learn to prioritize your tasks. Do the most important tasks first and the tasks of secondary importance at the end.

Pomodoro technique: 1. Decide on a task to do 2. Set the timer to 25 mins 3. Work or study until the timer rings 4. Take a 5-min break 5. Repeat the process 4 times 6. Then take a 15-20 min break 7. Repeat cycle.

Task: 1. Write the most important task of the day in front of TASK #1. 2. Write in the box "Target," the target number of pomodoros (time) in which you plan on completing the task. 3. Each circle is a pomodoro & it comprises of 25 mins. After complet - ing a pomodoro for a given task, put a tick in a circle. 4. Finally, in the box "Achieved" count and write the number of pomodoros in which you managed to achieve the task. * This way you will know your speed of working or studying and will set a goal accordingly.

Productivity score: Tick the number of pomodoros you achieved all day (while working or studying). Why is it important? 1. You will feel a sense of achievement. 2. It will also motivate you to do better next time. 3. It will show you how productive you have been all day.

Pending tasks: Any task you have failed to start or complete, jot it here. This will make sure you remember to do that task the next day.

Note to self: Any great idea that decides to pop in your head? Anything you want to remind yourself of? Maybe a habit you are working on? Scribble it in this little box.

Bread crumbs: This is your minor to-do list. If you have to do laundr y, or wash the dishes, or go pick someone from the airport etc you get it. This little baby covers anything that doesn't grab a spot on the most important tasks list!